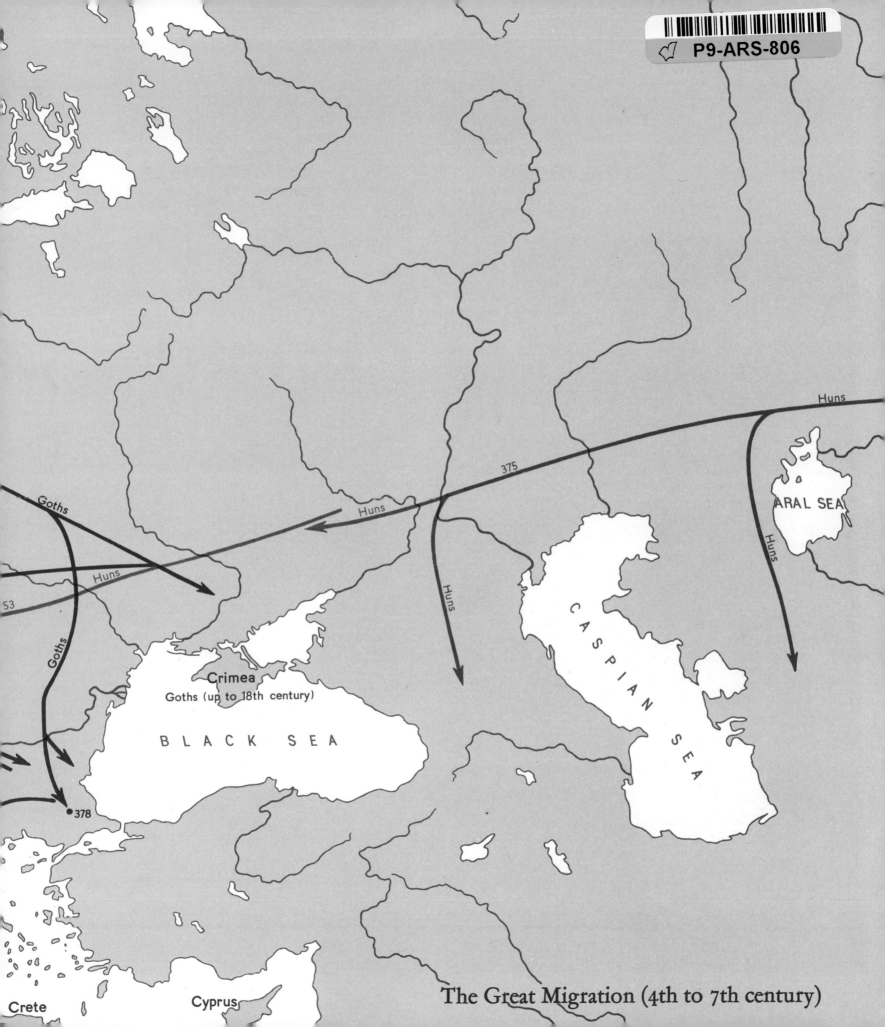

Goths

Huns

375

Huns

ARAL SEA

Huns

53

Huns

Goths

C A S P I A N   S E A

Goths

Crimea
Goths (up to 18th century)

●378

B L A C K   S E A

Crete

Cyprus

The Great Migration (4th to 7th century)

Diesner · The Great Migration

HANS-JOACHIM DIESNER

The
Great
Migration

HIPPOCRENE
BOOKS, INC.

Translated from the German
by C. S.V. Salt, B. A. Hons.

Designed by Volker Küster
Line drawings by Lutz-Erich Müller
© 1978 by Edition Leipzig
First American edition 1982
by Hippocrene Books, Inc.
ISBN 0-88254-641-4
Produced by Druckerei Fortschritt Erfurt
Manufactured in the German Democratic Republic

Contents

Foreword

IN THE PAST, A HISTORY OF CIVILIZATION usually offered the reader a choice of two possibilities: a mostly very thorough but one-sided review, oriented towards the history of human thought and to this extent idealistic in concept, or a history of morals and culture which, for many readers, involved associations which had little in common with civilization in the sense of a creative activity of general interest. The latter type of book of the 19th century does indeed have a certain significance and merit. From the viewpoint of the history of knowledge alone, these works have a firm place in the general development of historical research and description since they have helped to shed light on the history books of the Age of Enlightenment and from this point back into the Renaissance period, the Middle Ages and ultimately Antiquity itself. Indeed, it cannot be denied that the motivation, content and, in some respects, even the method of history of civilization date back to Antiquity in fact. At least, Dicaearchus of Messene in the 4th century B.C. laid down the aims for a history of civilization (which had already been largely anticipated by Herodotus, 5th century B.C.) which exercised an influence throughout the whole of Antiquity and up to the end of the Great Migration. In many respects, Tacitus's short history of the Germans is a politico-cultural opus since he devotes equal attention to both material and intellectual achievements. The authors of the period concerned here also judged events from the viewpoint of the history of civilization although to some extent this was done indirectly and by including other subjects. Some of them, such as Cassiodorus, Boethius and Isidore of Seville, clearly attached greater importance to cultural history than to political history.

The study of the culture of the period of the Barbarian invasions thus follows an old tradition. A great deal of information is available since the profusion of literature from this time is supplemented by a vast number of inscriptions, coins, and, above all, prehistoric archaeological finds, a representative selection of which is mentioned in this book. All this material enables a fairly clear conclusion to be drawn in many cases. Nevertheless, there is much which is difficult to interpret and there are even contradictions between the archaeological and the literary material. These complications are both difficult and fascinating for the historian but they cannot be ignored if a clear and balanced picture of a remote epoch is to emerge.

Since the present subject is of a complex nature and should not be forced into a narrow historical, chronological or geographical frame, it is important that the reader should receive an idea in word and picture of the important and representative elements. The intention is to throw more light on the reciprocal relations between the Mediterranean area dominated by the Romans and the peoples descending from the North and East on this specific zone of civilization with its Greek, Hellenistic and Roman character. The time from the beginning of the 4th century to the 7th or 8th centuries is the epoch to which most attention will be paid here. For obvious reasons, however, occasional ventures to the periods before and after this epoch are made in order to give greater clarity to the picture which emerges. To begin with, it has been found expedient to start with the conditions in the late Roman Empire since for a variety of different reasons the advancing tribes and peoples had to wage protracted struggles against the Roman armies before they could take possession of the lands which, in many cases, subsequently became early feudal states. From the end of the 4th century at the latest, however, it was only the recruitment of mercenaries from these same tribes and peoples which enabled the defence of the Empire to be maintained since it was constantly being shaken by increasing internal contradictions and class struggles and was also gradually disintegrating in the cultural sense, too. Thus even in the early stages of the Great Migration there was a mingling of Roman and "Barbarian" interests and ambitions. There is a certain fascination in tracing these developments since this was how new mixed civilizations began to evolve. As an illustration of this process, two of the major resistance movements in the Roman Empire—the Circumcellions and the Bagaudae—have been examined in more detail. Movements such as these acted not merely as a negative stimulus but also as a positive one for the people living in the areas freed from Roman rule. Even though this may not have been so clearly apparent in the Western Mediterranean area as in Egypt, for example, where Coptic art and culture developed independently, this aspect should not be disregarded today.

Some parts of the description are presented in a compressed form whilst in others a looser approach is followed. A choice also had to be made in respect of the invading "migratory peoples" and smaller groups—such as the Suebi and the Bavarians who were largely on the edge of the main events—have had to be left out. Even as regards peoples such as the Huns, Goths or Vandals who occupied the centre of the historical stage, attention has had to be concentrated on certain major aspects so that many phenomena and relations could not be considered here. For the sake of completeness, the last section deals with those groups and peoples who were directly or indirectly involved in the final phase of the process known as the Barbarian Invasions or the Great Migration since Arabs, Berbers, Avars and above all Slavs and Normans played a considerable part in the emergent feudal society of large areas within and around Europe and certainly mark the ultimate chronological and regional limit, the final chord, of the Great Migration in Europe.

The summary of events in Chapter 4 and the chronological table provided at the end of the book represent some sort of compensation for all that which could not be included in the main part of the book.

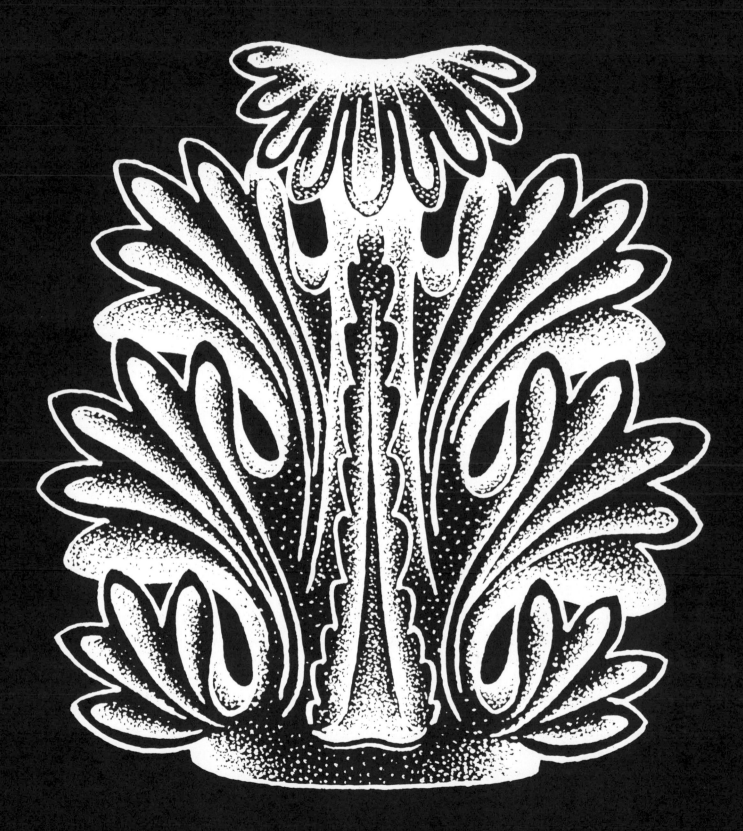

Ideology and Society
in the Late Roman Period

MUCH ATTENTION HAS RECENTLY BEEN devoted in Soviet and other international research to the subject of this chapter. Its purpose here is to introduce the reader to the subject of the book in general and, with account being taken of some important aspects, this can be done in a fairly concise form.

Over the last few years, the view has increasingly gained ground that from the end of the 2nd century A.D. or thereabouts Late Roman society was shaken by a permanent crisis. First noticeable as a crisis of the forms of ownership and of a mode of production based on slavery, this decline was nevertheless soon felt in all spheres of life and can even be traced in all fields of cultural and intellectual development. We are far from regarding the developments of Late Antiquity, the emergence of the Catholic State Church or the achievements of Late Roman activity in the arts as being primarily or only the result of this crisis, but close relations between the increasing socio-economic misery and the simultaneous fluctuations in culture are unmistakable. Indeed, they can often be identified in detail.

In the 2nd century A.D. at the latest, it had become clear that further socio-economic development was being obstructed by the restrictions on land ownership imposed by the city or state and by a mode of production based on slave labour. Although a variety of attempts was made to increase the production of the private or publicly owned villas and latifundia by efficient organization of the system of exploitation, by intensified checks on the larger estates which even led to a kind of estate police being set up and, on the other hand, by improvements in agricultural technology (plough with mould-board and wheeled front part; harrow; reaping machine; wine and olive presses), the scene was marked by ever greater stagnation. The crisis manifested itself in the most diverse ways. Falls in revenue, a shortage of money which was coupled with barter tendencies, hunger riots in the cities and a movement away from the countryside were only some of the more obvious signs marking the beginning of this crisis. The ruling circles naturally made numerous attempts to keep a grip on the political and economic situation. By specialization among the slaves, by a division of labour, by various forms of co-operation and also by the alloca-

tion of limited holdings (*peculium*) to slaves, they endeavoured to halt this retrogressive development or to put a progressive stamp on it. Disobedient or lazy slaves continued to be harshly punished as in the past but any who worked with a will could reckon with a peculium and subsequently with his freedom. The slave-owner had to assert his influence over his slaves by utilizing the persuasive arguments of a highly developed demagogic expertise. By ensuring the economic security of those slaves who were valuable to him and who carried out specialized work, by even giving them authority over others and appearing to guarantee the prospect of freedom sometime in the future, he gave them about the same status as those who were poor but free. It was often the case that educated slaves, especially when they were owned by the emperor, were much better off than the poor plebs or proletarians who had more legal rights, it is true, but were in a much worse economic situation and enjoyed far less social security. The outward similarity in the status of the slaves and the poor free-born citizens assumed the most diverse forms and frequently led to apparently insuperable contradictions between the two groups, although their objective interests lay largely in the same direction. On the other hand, under the influence of Stoicism, the cult of Mithras and early Christianity, there was often common ideological ground as well between slaves and the impoverished free citizenry which led not only to close co-operation in religious communities but also to joint participation in the "collegia" of the ordinary people.

It is almost self-evident that also the more prosperous artisans, the owners of municipal land and other members of the middle strata saw a serious deterioration in their position take place in the course of a protracted period of crisis interrupted only by the occasional quieter phase of development, as is well-documented by the legislation that was passed and the inscriptions that have survived. Few of these people retained their socio-economic position, most of them falling back in the social scale and becoming economically and even juristically dependent on rich lords. The only chance by which these strata could improve their position was via a military or official career and—somewhat later—by joining the ranks of the clergy with its

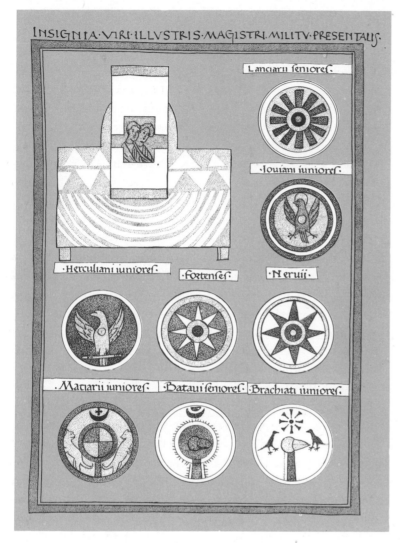

INSIGNIA·VIRI·ILLVSTRIS·MAGISTRI·MILITV·PRESENTALIS·

Lanciarii seniores·

·Iouiani iuniores·

·Herculiani iuniores· ·Fortenses· ·Neruii·

·Matiarii iuniores· ·Bataui seniores· ·Brachiati iuniores·

Insignia of a Roman general and coats of arms of military units

increasing range of privileges. A man such as Augustine, the son of a minor official, was able to become a professor of rhetoric and then a bishop. Some generals even began their career as ordinary soldiers or warriors from Barbarian tribes but this upward trend was exceptional, the exact opposite being far more likely to be the case. From the 3rd century onwards, free peasants and municipal land-proprietors increasingly joined the ranks of the agrarian coloni and similar dependent strata whose situation still requires to be analyzed more precisely in this connection.

The colonate developed at the latest after the insurrection headed by Spartacus, first in Italy and then in the provinces under Roman supremacy. To begin with, the coloni were largely free tenant-farmers, often disposing of a considerable area of land which they in their turn rented to others, and owning slaves and agricultural equipment. This system of colonate, which competed for centuries with that based on slavery, possessed many advantages over the latter and developed economic forms which, to some considerable extent at least, anticipated the later feudal system. Since the coloni at the beginning only had to hand over a fixed amount or a certain percentage of what they had produced to the landowner—whether this was the State or a private person—and were obliged to perform only limited compulsory services, their economic situation was tolerable and often even good. Due to the limitation of their contribution under the payment-in-kind system, they had a much greater interest than the slaves in raising production and they also took greater care of their livestock and implements than the latter. After all, one of the most notorious acts committed by slaves was to damage or destroy the implements they had to use since they regarded them not as aids but primarily as the property of the slave-owner.

In the course of time and with considerable variation from region to region, two great groupings in particular of coloni emerged. These were the free tenants, who farmed leased property and their own land, and the *originarii*, who worked only tenanted land and were tied to the soil. While the former, who sometimes may have conveyed the impression of small latifundistas, often disposed of large areas of land, their own coloni and slaves and, of course, adequate numbers of livestock and implements, the decline in the position of the originarii increasingly reduced them to about the same level as slaves, from whom they could scarcely be distinguished in the socio-economic sense. As tenants who were considered to be bound to the land, they received their instruments of labour from their patroni. The fact that far and wide the masters acquired the right to chastise and punish their tenants illustrates the low level of the legal status of the dependent coloni. Paradoxical as it may sound, however, they were more valuable to the State than the slaves, since tenant-farmers, bound to their land, were still subject to military service. Recruited via the tax system as determined by the patroni, they were nevertheless not eligible for the higher military ranks. For these reasons, there are only a few aspects of this kind of land-settlement with farmers bound to the soil which may be said to point towards the early feudal mode of production. On the other hand, the free coloni of the Late Roman period and other kinds of tenant-farmers (e.g., *precarist*) are much closer to feudalism. This is also true of certain high categories of retainers in the service of influential generals and senators. As bodyguards (*buccellarii*) or in similar functions, they received not only payment in money and kind but generally also had a claim to the use of an estate which they farmed in feudal manner with the aid of tenants and semi-servile labourers but without having full rights of ownership. The granting of plots of land as fees, in association with a graduated system of rights and obligations, thus begins at a relatively early date. We will return to this problem in connection with the fully-developed world of the nations which took part in the great migrations.

Parallel with the decline in the fortunes of most of the coloni, a crisis occurred in the urban populations to which reference has already been made. This must be re-examined since many aspects of this so far inadequately investigated special sphere are still open. If a simple definition is wanted, it could be said that the mode of production based on slavery and land ownership had to find itself in a critical situation as soon as slavery itself was no longer able to perform the function assigned to it.

Colonate was indeed a general substitute for agrarian slavery but it also meant that at a subsequent date it would no longer be able to send such a large part of the surplus product to the cities as was usual during the heyday of slavery. The urban way of life, once the ideal of all rich and educated persons and, of course, of their dependents and imitators, became less and less attractive. The urban patroni became impoverished or concentrated their financial resources in rural estates, which were now efficiently guarded and farmed more intensively. The large numbers of the ruling class moving to the countryside were also followed by the artisans and craftsmen who depended on them. The many rural residences of Late Antiquity with their profusion of carvings and mosaic decorations bear testimony to their skill, as do the numerous commodities which were also made on the big estates, such as weapons, ceramic articles and agricultural implements. Only some cities with a highly specialized production—for instance jewelry, precious arms and valuable textiles—could retain their economic position. With only slight exaggeration, it can be said that only those cities remained centres of production in which the State maintained mints, arms manufactories or clothes-making facilities, the workers here being slaves or forced labourers. Once production and trade had been thrown off balance by the endeavours of the big landowners to achieve independence on the one hand and by the coercive measures taken by the State on the other, it was difficult to find a compromise—and then this was mostly in a limited area and only for a short time. The outward picture, too, of the Late Antique city, which was gradually compelled to withdraw to a more restricted area behind mighty fortifications for protection from the increasing raids of the Barbarians, is usually lacking the glorious architectural points of interest which had been created all over the empire since the time of Augustus. Imperial forums, triumphal arches, theatres and gymnasiums of great size and magnificent design had marked the golden age of the imperium but new buildings were rare in the period that followed and even then were usually much more modest and built mainly for specific purposes—such as defence. Only church buildings of the basilica type sprang up and saw their heyday. It was naturally charac-

teristic and even typical that religious structures were now given a clear priority over secular buildings. Such a change in architectural thinking, which everywhere ceased to be concerned with the immediate needs of this life, would have been unthinkable without profound changes within society. Apart from the decline in the power of Rome in general, these buildings—which were still mostly concentrated in the centres of the towns—reflected a certain change in influence, which was closely linked with a redistribution of wealth and property.

In the course of this crisis, the ancient cults and religions had likewise declined and were ultimately eclipsed by Christianity. Various reasons can be quoted for this protracted process. There had already been major changes in the early Imperial period in the old Roman pantheon—Jupiter, Juno, Minerva, Mars and so on. Since the Romans and the Italic peoples no longer made up the majority of the population of the world empire, an ideological redeployment was inevitable as a first stage. The Greeks and the Oriental nations received, to a certain extent, ideological compensation for their political losses: deities such as Isis and Sarapis of Egypt, the Dea Syria or Adonis, the hero linked with plants, appeared at Rome and not long afterwards cults such as that of the Persian Mithras or the various sun-god cults began to exert an influence on the classical religion and even to absorb it. While the mystery cults, which were not associated with or even disapproved of the existing class hierarchy, made more of an impact on the poorer and deprived sections of the population, the members of the upper class tended to keep to the old State religion which, since Augustus, was associated with the veneration of the emperor, also after his death and deification. Many of the more enquiring minds turned towards the Hellenistic philosophy of religion of Late Antiquity, the numerous fresh interpretations of which were embodied in Stoicism, Neo-Platonism and the various Gnostic systems. As always, speculation about God and the Cosmos, Nature and Man, played a major role in these philosophies. It was scarcely possible to progress beyond the tenets of Greek-Hellenistic philosophy. However, under the influence of the social crisis, more and more consideration began to be paid to ethical problems. Epictetus,

the Stoic philosopher, and Marcus Aurelius, the Stoic philosopher on the Imperial throne, are outstanding examples of this and established or consolidated many philosophical standpoints, which also benefited the ideology of the oppressed. Admittedly, most of the Stoics were preoccupied with moral pathos and they somehow lost touch with reality. Their essential demand for a life in harmony with Nature, in the service of one's fellow-men, and for constant practice of the so-called cardinal virtues (justice, leniency, piousness, courage) was often unrealistic since the society of the time scarcely allowed the implementation of these ideas. They liked to expound on the equality of all men but it was impossible to realize this which is why Marcus Aurelius, in place of it, preferred to advocate a somewhat vague but seriously held cosmopolitanism. In his "Meditations", he reminded himself of this time and again so that he would not forget his duties towards his subjects and even the slaves. Ethical strictness, as exemplified by Stoicism, was of course proclaimed by primitive Christianity in an even more direct manner. The virtues demanded by Christ himself — humility, charity and purity as the precondition and the result of service to God — ensured that this religion, which originated in Palestine and gradually spread throughout the empire, rapidly won the sympathy of the poor and the persecuted, the slaves and the deprived. To them, the simple doctrine of the founder of the new religion, often disseminated in the form of parables in the course of his travels as a miracle-worker, was more easily understandable than philosophical ideas which were inaccessible to all but the educated. Another factor was that the early Church also advocated a form of primitive communism which—more or less—was already known from earlier socio-utopian doctrines of the Hellenistic period and encouraged many to emulate it. The persecution of the early Christians by the emperors served to keep alive the distrustful and even hostile attitude of the Christian community towards the State (as with Tertullian) and this was another aspect which naturally attracted the lower classes and strata in particular. It is quite clear that Christianity, even during the time when it was persecuted by the State, underwent a significant process of transformation which was not only intimately associated with its internal problems, especially the safeguarding of the pure teaching of Christ against heretic errors, but also with its changed outward attitude. In the 3rd century, the place of the post-apostolic community order, which was characterized by certain democratic features, was taken by the monarchistic episcopate. The office of the bishop increasingly assumed a pre-eminent position, becoming a dominant feature of the ecclesiastical hierarchy which now bore a marked resemblance to the pyramidic structures of the temporal ranks and classes. The bishops assumed most of the rights of the previously autonomous communities and—especially in their joint appearances at synods and councils—were henceforth regarded as the sole guarantors of the apostolic tradition and as "infallible" teachers. Outside the Church their authority was reinforced by their ever greater judiciary power within the religious community. This process, which was further advanced by the increasing numbers of educated and powerful men entering the Church, attained a first climax in the 4th century. After the recognition of the Christian Church by Constantine the Great and especially following the establishment of a Catholic State Church in the time of Theodosius the Great, the change from the small religious community of voluntary members to a comprehensive church community in which membership was obligatory was practically complete. The State promoted this process in every way possible during the period which is often called the time of Constantine. In the course of this process, as is self-evident, the social aims of Christianity were largely forgotten. The Church not only took over the standard of values of the temporal hierarchy but also most of its interests. The frequently close personal links between temporal and spiritual leaders naturally led to slaves and other dependents now being kept out of ecclesiastical positions and only still being tolerated in the mass of the congregation. However, better account was taken of social matters by the ascetic communities and monastic orders which were now emerging. Following the early Christian tradition, they—and many schismatic and heretic groups, too—paid serious attention to the care of the poor and, in the case of the Donatists, this was almost a programme.

Despite the continuing intensification of the crisis and the diverse influences of the philosophical systems, the mystery religions and Christianity, too, the whole sphere of official learning and culture remained largely untouched by change. Higher education, enjoyed only by a relatively small and privileged group, was based on the canon of Graeco-Hellenistic pedagogics which, however, had been modified by the Romans, most of whom were practical and pragmatic in their thinking. Instruction in Greek and Latin grammar and literature was often followed by rhetoric and philosophy studies at the higher schools of learning as the usual training for the highest positions in public life. Almost all the intellectual talents of Late Antiquity still developed within this frame of education in preparation for their later role in society. The mathematical disciplines were overshadowed by legal studies and it is characteristic that the most prominent theologists of the time not only had a philosophical training but also extensive knowledge of jurisprudence. Almost all other subjects received less than their fair share of attention, physical education being mainly concentrated on practical training in riding, swordsmanship and swimming. Seen as a whole, intellectual and cultural development from the 3rd century onwards still has to be regarded as retrograde. Apart from the crisis of the system as a whole, certain individual factors such as the anti-pagan and—since all education up till now had been based on pagan principles—often anti-educational attitude of Christianity contributed to stagnation in this sphere. The Barbarian invasions with their secondary effects also did their share since they often not only led to the destruction of schools, theatres and other cultural centres in many frontier zones of the empire but also contributed to its "barbarization" in general. Since general education had remained mostly at a very low level, especially in the outlying provinces, it was from such areas that illiteracy, vulgarization of the language and other phenomena increasingly spread elsewhere, as documented by numerous inscriptions from this time. Latin not only absorbed many elements from the Germanic, Slavic and Semitic languages and dialects but also lost more and more of its grammatical precision. Even important authors of the late period displayed not only a dwindling knowledge of Greek but

also serious shortcomings in their mastery of Latin. This was the start of a process which ultimately led to the emergence of the Romance languages from Vulgar Latin.

For the poor, prosperity and luxury, education and culture remained far beyond their reach and, time and again, a substitute had to be found for all that of which they had been deprived. There was little that could be done although the plebeians of the larger towns did receive a certain compensation from time to time. Following the principle of "bread and games", the authorities and private patrons normally guaranteed them enough food to live and distracted them from their everyday misery by animal shows, gladiatorial combats and other blood-thirsty spectacles. However, as mentioned before, the mystery religions and early Christianity also promised much to the poor and oppressed who joined them: equal participation in the life of the religious community, compassion for the poor and the sick and the "guarantee" of a better life after death. The consequence was that for many centuries large numbers of slaves, freed men and other oppressed persons flocked to these communities. When the Church changed to a hierarchical order and ultimately, seen as a whole, became a State Church, the majority of these groups joined the schisms and heresies which still practised the early Christian notions of equality. Naturally, these people who were excluded from the blessings of education frequently brought very primitive and even atavistic beliefs into the heretic movements. Thus they linked old deities such as Priapus, Saturn or Hercules, from whom they had always expected help in return for their modest sacrifices, with their new faith in God and Christ, although Christian dogma naturally remained alien to them. Even elements of the ancient family and tribal cults of the slaves and "ordinary people", often including features of black art, fetishism and totemism, were adapted to Christianity in this manner. Many festivals, holidays and even specific religious and liturgical phenomena (Mariolatry) date back to the ancient beliefs of the deprived sections of the population who took a more or less active part in the life of the religious community. It can be assumed that this participation was normally on a modest scale and did not really reveal the true motivation of the oppressed. Nevertheless, there were exceptions. Commodian, a Christian poet from Syria who may have lived in the 3rd century although the exact dates of his life are disputed, used Vulgar Latin as the vehicle for the very lively expression of the wishes and demands of the persecuted Christians. In two works, the *Instructiones* and *Carmen Apologeticum*, he made an ideological and political protest in verse form against Rome and the persecutions of the Christians linked with the name of Nero. In his strongly chiliastic description, Commodian quotes fearful details of the empire's persecution of adherents of this religion. But he links his criticism of the Imperium with violent disapproval of the rich Christians. He sees them as prepared to compromise, seeking personal peace instead of supporting other members of their faith and putting their wealth at the disposal of the cause. The harshness and hatred in Commodian's words sometimes make one doubt whether he really was a Christian. At least, he represents a particularly militant group of early Christians having something in common with the special African developments which will be examined later under the names of Donatism and Circumcellionism. What is striking and impressive is the range and scope of Commodian's critique. He links the social questions with the political and ideological problems and, in his remarkable prophecies, he announces the destruction of Rome by the Barbarians, the enslavement of generals and high officials and even the sacking of the colonies and other settlements. Only then does he see the way clear for a just order, a Golden Age, which he obviously regards as guaranteed by the alliance of the Christians with the Barbarians. Commodian's visions, which derive from ancient social utopias and apocalypses of the Hellenistic and Jewish past, may be regarded, as testimony of contemporary criticism and of the ideology of the oppressed, as being just as interesting as the documentation of the first advances of the tribes taking part in the great migration—especially the Goths—which also falls within the 3rd century.

The theoretical demands of Commodian and some other authors are particularly significant since practical conclusions were drawn from them, at least in some parts of the empire. These events have to be traced in greater detail, especially in Africa and Gaul.

In North Africa, one of the richest possessions of Rome and the source of wheat, oil, wine, animals and precious stones, the socio-economic contradictions in the 4th and 5th centuries led to various revolts and military dictatorships, mostly on the part of the Circumcellion resistance movement. This was a specifically African affair, marked by the peculiar ethnic and social structure which had emerged in Southern Numidia where it also had its centres in towns such as Bagai. This movement spread over large areas of the whole of Roman Africa and in some places even became identified with the opposition of the tribes hostile to Rome. Strikingly enough, the Circumcellions were not a slave movement. It was rather the case that they consisted largely of free farmworkers, day-labourers and probably poor smallholders who were little Romanized and were characteristic of the lowest class of the free population. Characterized by the African schism of Donatism in their ideology, the Circumcellions went beyond their own interests by concerning themselves with the miseries of the slaves and the coloni as well who willingly fled under their "patrocinium". A vivid although not entirely apt description of the Circumcellions between A.D. 330 and 350 was given by one of their adversaries, the Catholic Bishop Optatus of Mileve (*Contra Parmenianum Donatistam*, III, 4). He summarized the events of the year 347 in Southern Numidia as follows: "There came Paulus and Macarius to talk unto the poor everywhere and separately and to urge every individual one to unity. And when they drew nigh to the town of Bagai, the other Donatus, as told already, the (Donatist) bishop of the town, so as to put obstacles in the way of unity, sent messengers into the surrounding villages and to all the markets, calling on the quarrelsome Circumcellions (*circumcelliones agonisticos*) to gather in this town. And so a gathering of precisely those men was caused whose unreason had shortly before been provoked by the bishops themselves in blasphemous manner. For when these fanatical men against unity wandered through the land and called Axido and Fasir the "leaders of the faithful" (*sanctorum duces*), none could trust to the safety of his possessions. Pledges lost their worth, no creditor could collect his debts, and all were terrorized by the letters of those who

boasted of being the 'leaders of the faithful'. And if any hesitated to obey their orders, there came straightaway a wild band, preceded by fear, so that those who really should have been begged for respite were driven, through fear of death, to make humiliating entreaties. Each hastened to forget even the largest debts and even considered he was fortunate to have escaped their violence. Not even the roads were safe since they took pleasure in taking the masters from their chariots and making them run in front in the manner of their slaves, who took their masters' place. On the judgement and command of these, masters and slaves exchanged places. From this cause there arose at that time the enmity with the bishops who are said to have written to the Comes Taurinus, saying that such men could not be improved in their church and that they must be brought to order by the said Comes. As a reply to this letter, the Comes despatched soldiers to those markets where the wild Circumcellions were accustomed to carrying on their mischief. In the village of Octavia, very many were beaten to death and many executed, the bodies of whom may still be counted between the white-washed altars or tables of sacrifice. When they began to bury some of them in basilicas, the priest Clarus of Subbula was compelled by his bishop to exhume them again ... The numbers (of the Circumcellions) later increased. So it was that Donatus of Bagai found enough to bring together a wild horde against Macarius, persons of the kind who, desirous of a false martyrdom, provoked persecutors to their own detriment. They likewise include those who gave up their base souls by casting themselves down from the peaks of high mounts. Thus were the men from whom the other Bishop Donatus had formed his columns. Fearful by this, they (Paulus and Macarius), who had money with them to be distributed to the poor, resolved to demand troops from the Comes Silvester—not to use force against anyone but rather to prevent the acts of violence which would be committed by the aforesaid Bishop Donatus. And so it came to pass that armed soldiers appeared. What came to pass, you can see yourself to whom it must be attributed. They had gathered together there (in Bagai) an exceedingly great multitude and had also taken care to provide sufficient victuals. They had made almost a public granary out

1 Monumental bronze statue of Barletta (near Bari). It was previously believed that this "Colossus of Barletta" depicted Valentinian I but more recent investigations indicate that it represents an emperor of Eastern Rome, in all likelihood Marcianus, and was brought here from the Orient by the Venetians in the 13th century, being abandoned in Barletta due to shipwreck. The statue, produced by the cire perdu method, shows the ruler with two tunics, armour, ornamental belt, chlamys and diadem crowning straight hair. In 1491, arms and legs were added to the statue and it was erected near the Church of San Sepolcro in Barletta. One of the most important works of sculpture of the Great Migration epoch, the colossus is characterized by linear forms with expressionistic exaggeration.

2 Castel Sant' Angelo (Moles Hadriani) in Rome. This structure, which follows the Oriental and Antique tradition of monumental tombs, was erected by the Emperor Hadrian (117–138) for himself and other members of his dynasty which he founded by adoption. Up to the 3rd century, Imperial burials took place in this monumental building which is in the form of a cylinder of 64 m diameter on a square base measuring 90 m along each side. The history of this structure is particularly eventful. Incorporated by Aurelian in the mighty city-wall of Rome and besieged by Goths and Byzantines, it served as an important bulwark of the Vatican, especially from the time of Gregory the Great, who had a statue of the Archangel Michael placed on it. In the course of the centuries, numerous structural changes were made. Thus, in the Renaissance period, the Great Door of Antonio di Sangallo was added while Bramante built a loggia on the side facing the Tiber for Julius II. The Castel Sant' Angelo, which was almost destroyed in 1378 and now serves as a museum, was used for a long time as a prison and place of execution, reason enough for it to figure in art and literature, too, as a place where notable events took place (Stendhal; Puccini).

3 Equestrian statue of Marcus Aurelius—situated from the 12th century onwards in front of the Basilica of St. John Lateran and then erected by Michelangelo on the square in front of the Capitol. The only bronze equestrian statue of Antiquity, it owes its survival to the fact that the philosopher emperor (161–180)—better known for his "meditations" than for his political and military achievements—was thought, for a long time, to be the Christian Emperor Constantine the Great. The dignified posture of the emperor and his air of mildness may have contributed to this confusion of identity. As regards his steed, Jacob Burckhardt in *Cicerone* remarks that it is "well carved and with a lifelike movement but otherwise is the accurate representation of a loathsome animal, perhaps one of the emperor's war-horses".

4 Tetrarchic group—southwest corner of St. Mark's, Venice. This well-known porphyry group was carved in the 4th century in Constantinople and depicts the unity of the tetrarchy (rule by four emperors) introduced by Diocletian, this being stressed in particular by the pose of embrace.

5 Baths of Caracalla. The brick masonry still remaining from the mighty thermal baths of Rome (area about 120,000 sq.m.) conveys an impression of the vastness of this establishment which was built in the early 3rd century as a kind of "recreation centre" for the people of this densely populated district of the city. Apart from the swimming and bathing facilities, these late Antique baths also included lobbies, sports areas and even reading rooms.

6 Roman travelling-wagon from Maria Saal near Klagenfurt (Austria). Illustrations such as this of a well-equipped, covered travelling-wagon from the "Roman Stone" of Virunum from the 1st or 2nd century reflect the level of both public and private traffic on the Roman Imperial roads.

7 Roman milestone at Wengen, Kempten district (Allgäu). This milestone, the inscription of which indicates that it was placed eleven Roman miles (approx. 16 km) from Kempten, dates from Imperator Caesar Septimius Severus Pertinax Augustus.

8   Roman aqueduct at Arles. The remnants of the arches show the course of the aqueduct which supplied the important Roman administrative centre of Arles (Arelate) in the South of France.

9   Pont du Gard, aqueduct in South France. This famous link in the Roman water system from Uzès to Nîmes (Nemausus), dating from the first half of the 1st century, crosses the valley of the River Gard at a height of 49 m and measures 270 m in length. The two storeys of large arches support a third series of small arches with the actual water-course.

10 Gate in the town wall of Hissar(ja), dating from the end of the 4th or the beginning of the 5th century. In Antiquity, the town of Augustae was probably situated on the site of the present-day spa of Hissarja, also known as Hissar. The fortifications still visible today were built over a structure which, as recent excavations indicate, was destroyed by the Goths (376–378). For the walls and gates still standing, this gives a *terminus post quem*; the masonry technique also points to the 4th century or the beginning of the 5th.

11 View of the great thermal baths at Varna. Unlike the Late Antique baths at the port, this massive complex was begun already at the end of the 2nd century and was in use up till the 4th century. Almost the whole of the marble facings was then removed and used for other buildings. In the 5th century, much of this magnificent complex of buildings was destroyed in an earthquake.

12/13 Imperial baths of Trier. In size (230 by 140 m), these baths dating from about A.D. 300 are comparable with the Caracalla and Diocletian baths in Rome and are modelled on the layout, harmony and masonry technique of the latter. Only the walls of the caldarium (hot bath) survive.

of the basilica and now awaited those upon whom they might vent their anger ...When, as is usual before troops move in, some of their members were dispatched in front to find billets, these were not received in accordance with the teaching of the Apostle who says (Romans 13, 7): '... tribute to whom tribute is due; custom to whom custom; ... honour to whom honour. ... Owe no man any thing ...' The soldiers who had been sent ... were mishandled together with their horses ... The grievously beaten soldiers returned to their units and what had happened to two or three aroused the anger of all. They were all incensed and their commanders were unable to hold back the furious soldiers. Thus happened, as you will recall, that which made unity the target of criticism."

Optatus then refers to a terrible bloodbath which took place among the Circumcellions. Struggle against the rich landowners and support for slaves and others who were oppressed—this is the programme which clearly emerges from Optatus's description of the "Circumcellion horror". The Catholic bishop also throws light on the basic religious and ideological doctrine of this resistance movement. He shows that they were poor Donatists who regarded themselves as the "faithful" or the "holy ones", were headed by leaders whose Berber names are significant, and anticipated the later participation of the Berbers in the Great Migration. With their poverty and fanatical belief in a Church of the poor and the just, they possessed a militancy enabling them to challenge even superior forces and even to commit suicide when faced with overwhelming odds. Religious and secular factors both played a part in this and, obviously, could not always be distinguished. The Circumcellions sought the martyrdom of Christ in atonement for the sins of their fellowmen. At the same time, they were sure of the world to come and of honour as martyrs on Earth. Contemporary sources, especially the often somewhat obscure *vitae* of the saints, are filled with descriptions of the life and death of martyrs from the ranks of the Donatists and Circumcellions. They refused to accept that the Church and Christianity were no longer persecuted in this world. They extended and perpetuated the old strife between Church and State since they felt themselves as outcasts of society and were not prepared to make a compromise with the ruling class. This led to the confrontations mentioned already which were noteworthy in magnitude and intensity and provoked the corresponding reaction of their opponents. On the other hand, these actions had much that was scurrilous and atavistic about them, which can be associated with the original African background of the entire movement. Thus the suicides recall the human sacrifices of the Punic period made at Tophet to Molchomor (the old and incorrect name of Moloch is nevertheless still in common use). Other aspects are a reminder of the ancient belief of the common people in the deities Baal-Hammon and Juno Caelestis or of features of the ancestor cult. From a modern standpoint, it is much easier to understand how the Circumcellions were able to find the strength to fight against a superior order, with a far better technical and organizational base to that which they themselves possessed or were about to establish. Defeats and setbacks were nothing to them. Accustomed to hardship and want, they always continued the ideological struggle and the politico-military confrontation at every opportunity which presented itself. Even the losses resulting from self-sacrifice and suicide were nothing to them since for each of the deeply revered and duly celebrated martyrs there were several new candidates eager for such honour and ready to take their place.

For all that, there were also quieter intermediate phases in the course of these struggles of the mid-4th century. Conditions in Africa stabilized to a certain extent and even the landowners had learned something from the danger they had barely escaped. From now on, they made more efforts to divide their slaves and coloni by the different ways in which they treated them and also restrained them with the aid of private police. It is only towards the end of the 4th century that tales of horror of the kind already mentioned again appear. A fact of particular interest is that they mainly originated from the pen of Augustine who, as Bishop of Hippo Regius and advisor to the Carthaginian Metropolitan, had to face numerous confrontations with Donatists and Circumcellions.

There is clear evidence that the Circumcellions took part in the insurrections led by the native rebels Firmus (370–375) and

Gildo (397–398), although not in a prominent manner. The uprising headed by Gildo in particular was aimed at the complete independence of Africa. He rejected the authority of the Western Emperor, placed himself at the disposal of the Eastern Emperor and steadily consolidated his personal position on the basis of the supreme command over Roman troops in North Africa which had been assigned to him in 386. He gained the support of numerous African tribes or tribal groups, put the civil administration under his command and maintained close contacts with the Donatistic Church—obviously realizing that by supporting the Africans and the anti-Roman Donatistic Church he would have a firm ideological bulwark in the expected struggle with the central government. It is likewise considered that he was preparing a property and land reform although it could not in fact be implemented. Despite all this, the government of Western Rome succeeded in destroying Gildo and his army in the summer of the year 398 by a single action. With the stamping out of the insurrection, fighting again flared up in many parts of North Africa, including not only tribal revolts and Barbarian rebellions but also insurrections by many Circumcellions. The big landowners were again the target and the columns of the Circumcellions also proceeded against the Catholic clergy who, under the leadership of Augustine himself, proved to be their real religious and ideological adversary. Priests were beaten and slain and their houses laid waste. Slaves and coloni became increasingly restive and called the avenging bands of the Circumcellions to the estates of those masters who were considered especially harsh. Retaliation followed and the masters were not only forced to free their slaves and destroy debt records but also compelled to work as slaves themselves or turn millstones like beasts of burden. Such direct retaliation is quite typical of insurrections in Antiquity and characterizes not only the consciousness but also the limitations of the revolutionary instinct. One can scarcely speak of real revolutionary aims in this connection. Apart from this, the capacity of the Circumcellions to unite with all the other enemies of Rome in North Africa was also limited. Linguistic, ethnic, ideological and doubtlessly various other reasons prevented co-operation on any real scale. This is shown,

among other things, by a decree recognizing the Circumcellions as an *ordo*, a group within the State. This recognition would have been unthinkable if large numbers of Circumcellions had not been prepared to compromise to a certain extent with the ruling order which, for its part, urgently needed them as agricultural labourers. It is therefore probably correct to speak of a split in the ranks of the Circumcellions in the last phase of their development. A progressive wing, which consistently fought against the existing order and the Catholic Church as being essentially identified with this order, was counterbalanced by a moderate group which only intervened when the situation became serious. The moderate wing consisted solely of those Circumcellions who were recognized as free agricultural labourers and, under their leaders, worked on the big estates, especially during the harvests. The elements in the radical wing tended to become increasingly diverse since it included not only the younger and more active Circumcellions but also escaped slaves, coloni and other unfortunates who flocked to it in steady numbers.

The persecution by the State, as instanced by several decrees from 412–414 aiming at the liquidation of the entire Donatistic movement, was directed primarily at the Circumcellions as far as the practical measures taken were concerned. Threatened by severe retribution, most of the followers of this remarkable resistance movement lost their lives in the struggles which ensued. Those that ultimately yielded, as a condition of the *Codex Theodosianus* (XVI, 5, 54) would appear to indicate, were forced to settle as labourers on the big estates. Only a few isolated groups succeeded in surviving to the period of the Vandal invasions, which devastated North Africa from 429 onwards. It is readily apparent that the militancy of the Circumcellions and similar groups hostile to Rome caused great harm to the interests of the ruling class of Roman North Africa and, directly and indirectly, helped to prepare the way for the invasion by the Vandals since the area was not at all ready to defend itself in 429.

In many ways quite different but no less serious was the Bagaudae movement, which was concentrated in Gaul but was felt as far afield as Spain. The name is of Celtic origin, meaning

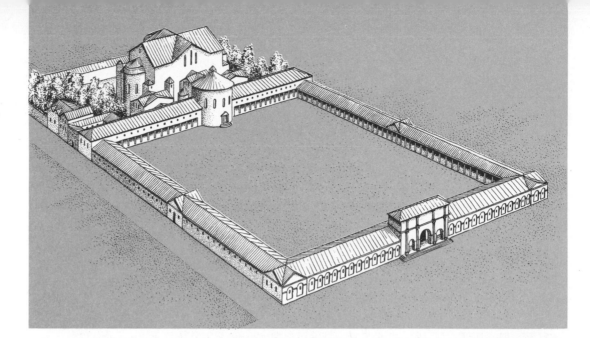

Reconstruction models of the Imperial baths at Trier

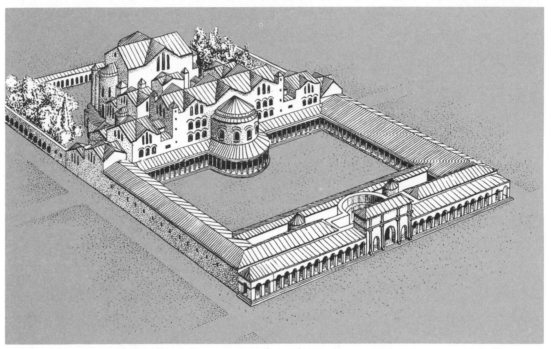

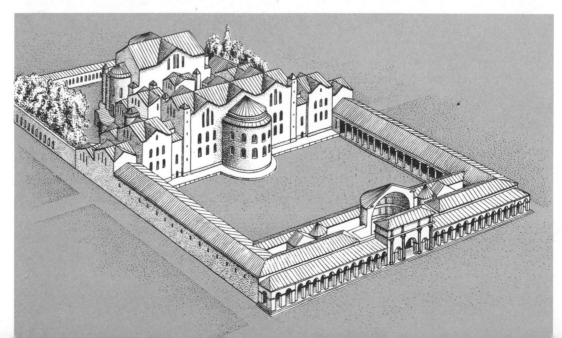

originally "fighters". The general Roman designation for these resistance fighters was *latrones* (robbers), which was often applied to the Circumcellions as well and is to be understood as an example of psychological warfare. This movement first made its appearance around 280. Due to the struggle for the throne before the succession of Diocletian, conditions in Gaul became chaotic with one Barbarian invasion following another and with the regional authorities paying more attention to the intensified exploitation of the rural population than to repulsing the enemy. The result was that groups of embittered peasants, herdsmen and slaves banded together to secure their rights. Unlike the Circumcellions, the Bagaudae immediately organized themselves in a more military manner. Taking the example of the Roman troops and the Germanic invaders, they practised the use of weapons and even set up separate cavalry and infantry units. Fortifications were built at various points and use made of existing strongholds which had fallen into their hands. The leaders, named in the records of the time (Eutrop. IX, 20, 3; Orosius, *Historia adversum paganos*, VII, 25, 2) as Aelianus and Amandus, must have pursued more ambitious aims in their plans than the Circumcellions. They probably struck their own coins, indicating that they had something like full state sovereignty and complete independence from Rome in mind. Unfortunately, nothing is known about the ideological basis of the Bagaudae movement, neither about any links with early Christian ideas nor of any association with the so-called Gallic empire defeated by Aurelian in about 274.

After Diocletian had assumed power, it was very soon decided that the Bagaudae represented a serious threat and the emperor even appointed the general Maximianus as co-regent specifically for the pacification of Gaul. After several encounters and sieges, in which the Bagaudae are said to have suffered severe losses, Maximianus succeeded in re-establishing the *Pax Romana* in 285/286. In this connection, popular tradition speaks of the protracted siege of a *castrum Bagaudarum* near the mouth of the Marne.

The sources for the Bagaudae movement are even more sketchy than those referring to the Circumcellions, which is why practically nothing is known about the extent and subsequent

Fortress vignette of Argentorate (Strasbourg)

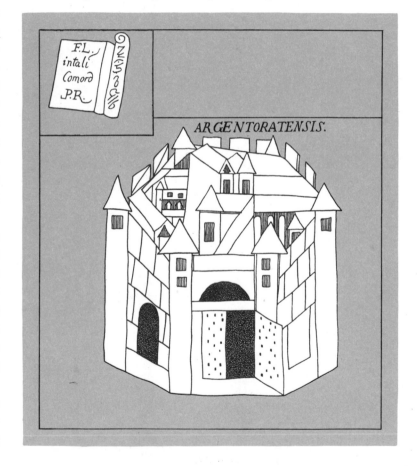

existence of anti-Roman groups in 4th-century Gaul. For the 5th century, however, a plentiful stream of information is again available. The raids by the Vandals, Alans, Suebi and other tribal groups and wandering bands of warriors provided the dissatisfied elements in the country with the opportunity to again make common cause against the Roman troops and officials. Peasants, herdsmen, slaves and also deserters and robbers organized themselves in armed bodies to fight against the Roman units where the local terrain gave them an advantage—especially in the Central Plateau and also in the Alps. At the beginning of 408, an army of the central government under the command of the Roman-Gothic general Sarus lost the whole of its campaign booty to the Bagaudae. The movement spread to more and more areas so that also large parts of the Loire district and Brittany in particular were practically lost to Roman rule. It is possible that here and there the political separatism of the upper stratum was linked with the socio-revolutionary endeavours of the Bagaudae but alliances of this kind were not of a lasting nature. Proof of this is the fact that the Bagaudae movement in Brittany began to decline from that time on when the prosperous Romans and Neo-Latins of Britain, in the face of Anglo-Saxon pressure, withdrew to Gaul and above all to Brittany. The interests of the richer strata as a whole were always identical with those of the central authority of Rome whereas the aims of the poor and the oppressed at this time were largely parallelled by those of the invading Barbarians. This view is strengthened by reports dating from the third decade of the 5th century which state that in 435 or so almost all the free smallholders and slaves (plus the coloni) of Gaul made common cause with the Bagaudae. They began to make fundamental changes in the social structure of many areas by expropriating or expelling the big landowners and driving away the tax officials and judges. Where they failed in this, they tried to enlist the aid of the Barbarians for their plans, or they put themselves directly under Barbarian rule, especially that of the Visigoths who at that time were beginning to consolidate their power in Southwest Gaul—even if this was initially still with formal recognition of Roman sovereignty. As evident from the vivid description by the Massilian priest Salvianus with his keen appreciation of social movements, Bagaudae and Barbarians often came to an understanding which may be attributed to the interests they had in common at that time and to the defence of aims which were primitive but more legitimate than rule by Rome. About 445, Aetius, one of the most renowned generals of Late Antiquity, conducted a successful campaign against the Bagaudae. In a panegyric, the poet Merobaudes reports that Aetius pacified Aremorica and forced the population to abandon their alliance with the Goths. It seems likely that Merobaudes himself also led troops in the action against the Bagaudae. A poem by Apollinaris Sidonius (Carm. V, 210–213) also refers to the Bagaudae movement of these years which, in the meantime, had long since spread to Spain. The situation there was similar to that in Gaul and Roman rule in many of the Spanish provinces had already been overthrown by the Vandals and then by the Suebi and Visigoths or at least reduced to an insignificant level. Rome likewise lost much of its influence in the Tarraconensis which was located in the Ebro Valley, this being obviously due to a joint action by the Suebi and Bagaudae. However, it was precisely this rich area which the government of Western Rome wanted to retain at all costs and several generals with powerful armies were dispatched to Spain. Violent battles took place in 441 and 443 while in 449—clearly as the outcome of an alliance between the Suebi and the Bagaudae—Ilerda (Lérida) was lost and the districts around Saragossa devastated. It seems likely that the Bagaudae were now also able to rely on the heretic movements of the Manichaeans and Priscillianists who exercised great influence in Spain and, by the nature of things, were hostile to Imperial rule.

The end of the Bagaudae movement came in 454. Through an alliance with the Visigoths, the Emperor Valentinian III again succeeded in establishing a firm foothold in Spain. Rechiar, the king of the Suebi, also agreed on a compromise with Ravenna at this time and left the Bagaudae to their fate. With monstrous cruelty, the Bagaudae of the Tarraconensis were annihilated by an army of the Visigoths.

It is illuminating that the movement collapsed at a time when the state of Western Rome as a whole was practically disintegrating and—even if this process was disguised by a variety of names—was having to relinquish large parts of its empire to the Barbarian powers. The Bagaudae had clearly performed their mission by the time the Barbarians were beginning to consolidate their states in Gaul and Spain and to establish a social structure which already contained the seeds of feudalism. Although a certain increase in population followed and many Teutons had to be settled on the third parts of Roman estates and latifundia made available to them, the level of exploitation declined appreciably. In the new state structures, there was at first absolutely no need at all to establish a system of administration and taxation. The reduction in taxes which thus automatically occurred benefited to a certain extent the lower strata as well, whose struggle against the outdated Roman order was thus confirmed and legitimized, at least indirectly.

Of course, this applies not only to the Bagaudae or Circumcellions but also to a whole series of other resistance movements which cannot be examined here. The southeastern Balkans, Asia Minor and Egypt in particular were likewise shaken by numerous struggles similar to those in the lands mentioned. Nevertheless, they were not so significant since neither the class struggles nor the Barbarian invasions contributed to the defeat of Roman rule here. The empire of Eastern Rome, whose economic structure was more compact than that of her western sister, was able to withstand the enemies from without and within, even though this was not without hardship. To a certain degree, it even diverted threats such as that of the Huns towards the West and then consolidated its position, unaffected by the battles which raged for generations on the other side of its somewhat restricted frontiers.

Preparations before
the Onslaught of the Barbarians

THE SUBJECT OF THIS CHAPTER MAY SEEM UNusual but the choice is deliberate. Of course, neither the Barbarians on their travels nor the Romans in their repulse of continuing raids and invasions had ever organized themselves with such a programme in mind. Nevertheless, at least as seen from a present-day standpoint, the Roman work of reform beginning in 284 with the accession of Diocletian appears as the preparation by the Roman Empire for its last trial of strength with its opponents at home and abroad, in which it was finally vanquished some two centuries later. The period set by history for overcoming the internal crisis and throwing back the enemies of the empire was not at all ungenerous and, indeed, the snail's pace at which events proceeded is something to astonish anyone familiar with more rapid phases of development, modern revolutions and processes of transformation resulting from technical change.

How was this time used by the Roman emperors, the actual representatives of the ruling class? Did they succeed, at least temporarily, in halting the decline and restoring the ancient glory of the name of Rome? The answer is a relatively positive one, which may cause some astonishment, after the remarks made in the first chapter. Processes taking place in accordance with natural laws often follow a different and often more irregular path in the course of historical development than that expected by the observer largely accustomed to a technical or scientific set of facts.

This is best illustrated by a sketch of the outward events which preceded or ran parallel with the Barbarian migrations. In 284, Diocletian, the son of an Illyrian freed slave and up till this time the commander of the Imperial bodyguard, was proclaimed emperor by the troops. He ended the period of the "soldier emperors" who, by and large, were synonymous with the odium of a permanent crisis in the internal and external affairs of the empire.

Partly under his personal command and partly with the aid of his commanders, some of whom soon attained imperial rank, successful defensive campaigns were waged by Diocletian against the Persians, invading Barbarian tribes and enemies within the empire such as the Gallic Bagaudae. From the early years of his reign onwards and after the first attempts to reform the army and the administration, a new system of government emerged which may be described as an absolute monarchy (*dominat*). For a time, with two senior emperors and two subordinate emperors, this was a tetrarchic system, revealing the necessity for a division of power based on territorial considerations. Diocletian himself ruled from Nicomedia, his colleague Maximian held power in Milan and the two subordinate emperors (*caesares*) had their seats in Sirmium and Trier. Under this new arrangement, Rome and its Senate lost their privileged position in many respects since Italy, too, was included in the decentralized administration which divided the entire empire into four prefectures with twelve dioceses and more than a hundred provinces, civil and military administration being strictly separate henceforth. Diocletian also finally divided the army into the frontier army (*limitanei*) and the mobile forces (*comitatenses*), new elements such as the armoured cavalry (*cataphractes*) which originated in the East being incorporated in the latter. With the aid of drastic reforms, he tried to improve or control the catastrophic socio-economic situation. In connection with a coinage and tax reform, which aimed at reversing the drop in state revenues by improving the coins minted and above all by a thoroughly devised basic capitation tax system (*capitatio iugatio*) which, however, put a heavy burden on the direct producers, the coloni were bound to the soil even more systematically from this time on and the artisans were forced to organize themselves in colleges. It is true that a high-grade gold coin, the aureus, was now put into circulation and, together with silver and nickel-silver coins, improved monetary exchange but the success of the reform was nevertheless very limited. This was because the exchange values of the metals in relation to each other had been set arbitrarily and because the lower classes scarcely received any money—apart from that which was immediately taken by the tax authorities. An edict on prices and wages, issued in 301 and setting maximum levels, did not really change this, even though its basic aim, correct enough as such, was to halt inflationary tendencies. Reconstructed from fragmentary inscriptions, this edict is the most important document of the economic history of Antiquity and is also interesting from

the viewpoint of the history of civilization. The first part, with rhetorical exuberance, sets out the reasons for the regulatory measures, criticizes the greed of the rich and laments the numerous "pictures of extreme poverty". However, a specific criticism appears in the following part: "Who is so indifferent and so bereft of human feelings that he could not know, nay, that he could not have long since noticed, that in respect of the goods which are distributed by wholesalers or sold in the daily business of the cities the arbitrariness of the price structure has become so great that the uncontrolled urge to make money is moderated neither by large stocks of goods nor by the harvest blessings of fruitful years; so that without doubt precisely those people who are engaged in these businesses are constantly endeavouring to read the lie of the land from the movement of the stars and, in their wickedness, cannot suffer it when the rich fields are watered by the rains streaming down from heaven, awakening the hope of future harvests, so that they regard it as a personal misfortune when favourable weather produces a surplus of wares. They are always thinking how they can make a profit even from the gifts of the gods, to hinder the progress of the public well-being and, in a year when a bad harvest occurs, to haggle over losses and debts. And although each one of them has an abundance of the greatest riches, enough to supply entire peoples, they still cast a greedy eye on smaller fortunes and demand ruinous interest-rates. To set limits to their covetousness is what we have to do when we think of humanity in general, you inhabitants of our provinces."

There is a noteworthy breath of criticism here although the background of the economic crisis was not fully covered—something which was impossible, considering the level of development of the time. Both a rationalist and a pragmatist, Diocletian obviously believed he could implement his maximum-price tariff by strict measures—including the death penalty—and by the further development of the administration and judicial system. This was soon to prove a mistake. Although wages were high in relation to food prices, they had to seem low when compared to the charges for services and craft products. In addition, this price-edict clearly applied only to the wages which the orderer paid the manufacturer so that the basic wages which the owners of the means of production actually paid their workers were not included. Unless workers were paid directly by the State, their real wages must have been considerably less than specified in the edict. This means that for the mass of the working population they were even less able to afford retail prices after the measures taken by Diocletian than before and, indeed, the edict remained in force only for a few years.

Diocletian's last years were overshadowed by the deficiencies of the economic reform, by renewed persecution of the Christians and by dissention within the tetrarchy itself. When he retired in 305 to the residence of his old age, the famous palace in Spalato (Split), disorders broke out which came close to civil war, from which Constantine the Great ultimately emerged as the new autocrat. Already in 306, after the death of his father Constantius Chlorus, he was proclaimed emperor by the troops at Eburacum (York) and, to begin with, revealed his mettle in defensive actions against the Franks and the Alemans. After the death of several rivals, he finally consolidated his position with a victory over Maxentius at the battle of the Milvian bridge near Rome (312). This memorable event was at the same time the guarantee of the end of the persecutions of the Christians and the beginning of the recognition of Christianity (Milan Tolerance Edict or Constitution of 313) since Constantine attributed his victory to the aid of the god of the Christians. The riddles concerning Constantine's attitude to religion and to Christianity in particular, which largely originate from contemporary writings (Lactantius, Eusebius of Caesarea), can only be touched on here to the extent that they are relevant. Without doubt, Constantine had a strongly religious bent which may seem astonishing in a man who began as an officer and "soldier-emperor". Like many warriors, he initially acknowledged the invincible Sun God (*sol invictus*), then changed over to a monotheism associated with the cult of Apollo and was finally converted to Christianity. He was baptized only shortly before his death (337) which raises the question, first formulated by Jacob Burckhardt, as to whether he was a Christian by expediency or by conviction. The answer appears to be a combination of both. Constantine furthered

Christianity in the Catholic form in which it slowly emerged both from inclination and for reasons of expediency since he recognized that the Church, with its episcopal hierarchy headed by a Roman bishop soon aspiring to a position of primacy, was in no way opposed to the temporal ruler. It was rather the case that the Church was in a position to give a religious consecration of a special kind to his monarchical power. Consequently, measures promoting the Church (privileges for the clergy, Sunday celebrations, the building of churches) were supplemented by intervention on a major scale in the still vague sphere of ecclesiastical law, as demonstrated by Constantine's participation in the Donatist conflict (from 312) and by his personal appearance at the Council of Nicaea (325). Such action seems to show the concern of the emperor for the emergent religious community and his claim to be some kind of Christian leader. Otherwise, the emperor treated the Christians and the pagan cults still recognized in the manner characteristic of an absolute ruler. He harshly suppressed deviations such as Donatism and Arianism, his jurists basing their arguments on old concepts of the right of coercion of the sovereign.

This juridical aspect is also of importance for the general domestic policy of Constantine and his successors. This is apparent both from the vigorous legislation affecting all spheres of life and from the increased number of jurists and government lawyers trained for the ever-growing bureaucracy. Careers in administration were developed and the staffs of the civil and military dignitaries often formed offices in which hundreds of senior and minor officials, watched by supervisory bodies and motivated by a certain system of promotion, checked the work of the common people and, with the aid of a constantly more sophisticated tax system, supplied the court, the army and the bureaucratic organization itself with everything which was required. The impression one has is of something like an octopus since this smoothly operating bureaucratic organization covered the whole territory of the empire, not forgetting the tiniest workshop nor the last frontier station. Disregarding the emperor, the immediate court entourage and his State Council (*consistorium*) which, in the last instance, had the right to decide all questions, this bureaucratic pyramid was headed by the Magister Officiorum, a kind of state and household minister, to whom all offices and especially the secret police (*agentes in rebus, curiosi*) were responsible. It is also an interesting fact that specialist ministeries were set up only for the fiscal and finance spheres. The rest of the central administration was in the hands of the Magister Officiorum or the Praetorian prefects who, in the Late Roman system, were former bodyguard commanders who had been promoted to the top of the supra-regional administration of the individual parts of the empire.

Of course, through his reforms, wars and not least the building of the new (second) capital of Constantinople, Constantine—like his predecessors—was obliged to manipulate the monetary and tax systems. The new gold standard, the solidus, at least helped to prevent a fairly rapid return to a barter economy. Success was also obtained, for a time, in imposing an effective tax on the rich senators who had to pay a special impost and in registering for tax purposes all those engaged in trade and commerce without exception. On the other hand, there was a rise in the expenditure for the army and armaments in general, offensive and defensive duties still probably being equally divided. The monumental fortifications around Constantinople, which were modelled on the Aurelian Wall at Rome, were reflected on a smaller scale throughout the empire, especially along the "limes" and the river frontiers where large fortified camps alternated with smaller citadels or watch-towers. This was the time when the word *burgus* was coined, a term of no small importance for the future. The fleets on the rivers and the units on the frontiers and within the empire had to be continually reinforced or built up again after hard-won wars, as against the Alemans (332) or the Persians (334). Since there was a lack of suitable recruits from within the empire, this was now done to an increased extent by enlisting Barbarian mercenaries and often by recruiting those groups of adversaries who had just been subjugated (Foederati, Laeti). This involved not only difficult financial questions but also problems which had a big impact on the social structure of the empire. This was because the Barbarians were often better soldiers than the Romans of Late Antiquity and, whether the

latter liked it or not, had to be assigned fairly frequently to elite formations and bodyguard units (*protectores domestici*), paid a high wage and given better prospects of promotion. The time was not far distant when men of Barbarian descent, such as Stilicho, Sarus or Aspar, could aspire to the highest military commands or become a maker of emperors. On the other hand, another problem was represented by those Barbarian formations which, stationed in the vicinity of the frontier, had caused serious socio-economic upheavals. They either formed an elite in relation to the provincial population or they allied themselves at critical moments with rebellious subjects of the empire and did the opposite of what they were supposed to do. Under Constantine's successors, his sons Constantine II, Constans and Constantius II († 361) and his nephew Julian Apostata († 363), who continued his dynasty, such shortcomings of the military apparatus were clearly apparent. On the other hand, they also succeeded at least provisionally in subjugating new Barbarian peoples and in winning frontier areas, such as Armenia, as client-states for the empire. Despite this, Constantius II, who became the sole ruler of the entire empire in the years after 350, already had difficulty in repelling the powerful onslaughts of the Persians who had found new strength under the Sassanid dynasty. Exactly as in the Rhine-Danube area, the Roman positions along the eastern frontier were gradually moved back, too. Admittedly, internal struggles were also partly responsible for this, such as those which took place between Constantine the Great's sons after his death and lastly between Constantius and various usurpers (Magnentius, Vetranio). In actual fact, the new dynasty proved to be rotten from the very beginning. Several vain attempts were made with various forms of government, including two and three emperors and a monarchy. Constantius tried to give a new Christian-theocratic basis to the latter instead of looking towards Catholicism with a touch of Arianism. In the course of this, he spared neither his supporters nor his ideological opponents and, with the ban on pagan sacrifices and the closing of numerous temples, began an energetic campaign against the pagan bastions.

On the occasion of his only visit to Rome (357), where he celebrated his victory over the Persians, he had the famous altar of Victory removed from the senatorial curia. This psychologically incomprehensible action and the severe taxation of the nobility at that time caused the most influential circles of this nobility to become abruptly hostile to Christianity and to practically withhold its support for the government in its conflicts with usurpers or enemies of the empire. From this time on, it became increasingly more apparent that two wings had formed which only occasionally worked together. On one side there was the emperor, the court, the army and the central bureaucracy while the other consisted of the senatorial landowners with their immense retinue of slaves, coloni, freed men, bodyguards and clients of various categories. Of course, there were links between the two wings and, if it was in their common interest, there was sometimes close collaboration between them. Nevertheless, the contradiction in their basic interests was unmistakable.

The withdrawal of the senatorial wing from the influential groups around the emperor would not have been a disaster for the government if, in place of it, the latter had been able to win the support of the mass of the people, who had increasingly turned to Christianity. But this was not possible since, as always, the popular masses were still opposed to the ruling stratum and their opposition was kept alive by the demands and extravagance of Constantius's government. At the same time, the hostility of the urban masses and many of the numerous ascetics and monks of the open countryside was aroused by the persecution of the frequently very popular Church leaders (Athanasius) by the emperor who, at the end of his reign, also had to deal with attacks by the Quadi, the Sarmatians and the Persians. Another threat which confronted him was the usurpation of his power by his cousin Julian (Apostata), who in 355 had been appointed Caesar for the Gallic part of the empire in order to relieve the pressure on Augustus reigning in Constantinople. Julian, who had been educated in the spirit of Late Hellenistic-Gnostic philosophy by Jamblichos and other teachers and was himself active in the literary sphere, in which he from the start revealed his anti-Christian tendency, devoted himself to his task with great élan. Surrounded by Constantius's spies and despite serious contradictions within his own camp, he succeeded in re-establishing the frontier along the Rhine which had been threatened by the Franks and the Alemans. He reconquered Cologne for the Imperium and, after repulsing an enemy attack on his winter quarters at Sens, fought a decisive battle near Strasbourg (357).

The fighting which took place in these years may be regarded as the prelude to the great migrations. Whereas previous Barbarian invasions had still been more in the nature of plundering expeditions rather than attempts to permanently occupy land, this situation changed very quickly. The Germanic tribes were no longer satisfied with the frontier along the Rhine and the Upper Danube which had been established in the 3rd century and began to systematically carry out the conquest of parts of Gaul and other areas close to Rome. At Strasbourg, however, Julian succeeded for a last time in energetically halting this plan, displaying strategic and tactical qualities of an exemplary order. After turning Tabernae (Saverne) into a fortified base and bringing up his army of some 15,000 men to face the enemy, who probably had twice this number, he wanted to await the attack of the Aleman prince Chnodomar in a newly fortified camp. In such a dangerous situation, it was tactically correct to allow the enemy to take the initiative and, at the same time, to apply the principle of attrition. However, the young general was urged by his soldiers and especially by the more senior commanders to join battle immediately. Consequently, taking advantage of the high morale of his troops, he launched an attack in a phalanx-type battle-order against the enemy, who was drawn up in a formation of closed wedges along the Rhine. Julian gained an advantage by drawing up his forces in three deep lines and by holding back, in a covered position, an elite unit and a cavalry formation as a strategic reserve. This order of battle followed a proven tradition (Hannibal, Caesar) while the Alemans likewise drew up their forces in the manner to which they were accustomed. In the course of the battle, it was soon evident that the numerically superior Aleman cavalry had an advantage and they threatened to roll up the right flank of the Roman army. However, the decisive role here was played by the reserve which had wisely been held back by Julian. It not only halted the Germanic attack but also captured Chnodomar and his numerous retinue. The isolat-

ed Barbarian groups sought safety on the other side of the Rhine while Julian exploited his success by likewise crossing the river and destroying Aleman settlements on the other bank. This victorious crossing of the Rhine by Julian was one of the last offensives on Barbarian territory in which, admittedly, there was no occupation of land but where the strategic initiative was clearly asserted or regained. In this situation, Julian appears as one of the last great generals of Antiquity and, indeed, this impression is confirmed by his subsequent successes against the Persians. Since his cousin Constantius suffered heavy losses in the fighting which was going on at the same time in the East and seemed to fear a strengthening of the position of the younger co-regent, he attempted to undermine Julian's position in the West in an indirect manner. The latter was instructed to make troops available for the Eastern army which was too weak. This demand, brought to him in Paris, was rejected by Julian's troops over his head. However, this was also a decision against Constantius himself and the Western army, steeled in constant fighting against the wandering tribes, proclaimed Julian as Augustus. Since Constantius was not prepared to recognize this new constellation, a conflict was inevitable. Fighting between the Eastern and Western armies of Rome seemed unavoidable but this was prevented by the sudden death of Constantius in Cilicia.

As the acknowledged monarch, Julian entered Constantinople in December 361 and immediately began to implement a great work of reform. Genuinely desiring a relaxation in the tension within the empire which, considering the still dangerous situation in foreign affairs, seemed to be urgently necessary, Julian reformed the judicial system, the administration, the court household and not least the policy concerning religion. However, almost as if he had known that there was little time left, he gave effect to his measures with too much haste and attempted to satisfy the needs of as many sections of the population as possible—apart from the Christians. He sought the favour of the rich by making the contribution of gold for the *aurum coronarium*, traditional at a change in government, a voluntary affair, and also improved the position of the curials and other strata by reducing the official burdens on them. On the

other hand, when Julian tried to restrain the notorious greed of the corn speculators of Antioch, it seemed as if he was returning to the policy proclaimed by Diocletian in the Price Edict. Numerous clauses in the *Codex Theodosianus* reveal the intensity of his legislation and of his almost exaggerated endeavours to achieve scrupulousness and justice. Even the writers of the period, such as Ammianus Marcellinus, Libanios or Themistios, who were fairly close to the emperor, make many references to his reform legislation and, sometimes with tongue firmly in cheek, describe the drastic changes made in the administration and Imperial Household. When one day the emperor called for a barber to come and cut his hair and a splendidly garbed person appeared before him, Ammianus (XXII, 4, 9) reports him as saying: "I ordered a barber, not the treasurer." From experiences such as this, Julian—who regarded himself as the successor of the philosopher-emperor Marcus Aurelius—made drastic economies in his own household. He restricted the notorious sinecure and eunuch system which had flourished since the time of his predecessor and was able to achieve a reduction in the burden of taxation. He relieved the fiscal pressure on the curials in particular so that the urban curiae—miniature editions of the Roman Senate—now regained their influence after being almost totally paralyzed. And it is certain that many of his more humble subjects felt relief when they realized the humanity and simplicity of Julian who, in contrast to Constantius, rejected the title of "Lord and God" and the pomp and circumstance of the solemn audiences and processions associated with it. Quite obviously, Julian was inspired by the old Stoic ideal of a ruler which he even updated by adding republican features since, even if he was the best ruler, he was constantly obliged to prove this in actual fact. Particularly impressive evidence of this is again provided by Ammianus who relates the following episode: "On the kalends of January (362), at the official installation in office of the consuls Mamertinus and Nevitta, the emperor was seen standing among people of high rank who were present at the ceremony. This attitude pleased some but was criticized by others since it seemed to them to be affected and excessively patronizing. After the state ceremony, Mamertinus had arranged for circus games to take place. When the slaves, who according to ancient custom were to receive their freedom on this occasion, were brought in by servants, Julian himself spoke the words setting them free. When it was pointed out to him that on this day it was the privilege of someone else to do what he had done, he immediately condemned himself for his mistake to a fine of ten pounds of gold." Nobleness of this order, which certainly seemed affected to many people, could naturally mean different things to different persons. Many, who regarded Julian's honest desire to make reforms and his personal achievements—not least his success in throwing back the Barbarians—as exemplary, would have approved it and even shown a certain enthusiasm for the re-birth of a Roman Empire with a new spirit. Many of the pagan senators were certainly impressed by the tolerance of the emperor and his endeavours to put through a reform in education which were parallelled by the attempt to establish a "pagan State Church" on the Christian model. Large numbers of the urban middle-class were involved in Julian's prosperity programme and he had the backing of the soldiers, even though he demanded a great deal from them. They began to become accustomed again to strict discipline and to proper service regulations. Apart from the "spartanic" example of the emperor, it was above all the regular attention paid to military equipment and to the appointment of the right men as commanders which contributed to the restoration of a fighting spirit which lasted until the disaster at Adrianopolis (378). This can be seen from the interest which Julian took in the corps of bodyguards known as *protectores domestici*. This formation was organized in four units of fifty men each and was both a guard regiment and an "officers' school" at the same time. The individual members were entrusted with a diversity of tasks to prepare them for gradual promotion and most of them subsequently attained positions of high rank. Many of those who later became famous generals of the Late Roman period passed through this school precisely during the time that Julian was in power and they included, not least, his successor Jovian.

Above all, it is the achievements and measures of the emperor in the philosophical, ideological and religious spheres

—aspects which have attracted much attention in modern research—which make it clear that there could never have been a serious possibility of the peace probably sought by Julian, following the example of Marcus Aurelius. He displayed insufficient patience to even achieve the aims which seemed to him attainable so that ultimately many groups felt that he was discriminating against them: the representatives of the Catholic Church since he gave preference to the heretics and pagans; the rich since he prevented profiteering; the poor and the uneducated since they, from their incompatible socio-economic standpoint, could not understand the emperor's humanism and his enthusiasm for education. At the same time, many of the poor, especially in the East, were already followers of Christianity. Spurred on by the clergy and the bishops, who had lost their privileges and felt themselves threatened by new sacrificial services and the reconstruction of temples, the popular masses in Antioch, Alexandria and other cities were talked into destroying places of pagan worship. Riots broke out, in the course of which even the graves of martyrs were desecrated, and both parties appealed to the emperor. Almost always, he decided against the Christians and banished men like the steadfast Athanasius, who had already been frequently in conflict with the State authorities. However, to prevent a hostile Christian front emerging, Julian favoured in a noticeable manner sects such as the Donatists (and also the Jews), the result being that new religious struggles flared up in North Africa. Finally, with his school law of 362, he delivered an almost overwhelming blow against the theological circles of the Church: henceforth Christians were no longer permitted to be rhetoricians or grammarians, i.e., they were excluded from the official sphere of education. The educated Christians felt doubly penalized. Many had been robbed of their ability to earn a living, others saw this as discrimination, if not worse. Furthermore, they were forced to choose between no education for their children or having them educated by pagan teachers. Julian's reason for this harsh edict was understandable to some extent. He used the sharp Christian criticism of much of that education which was often morally very free and based on the ancient religion as the excuse to bar access to that education "innerly rejected". By allowing the young people to decide whether they wanted to go to the pagan teachers or not, he naturally won sympathy for his own standpoint and drove a wedge between the older and younger generations of the Christian upper class. At the end of his short period of government, he attempted to completely crush Christian ideology by setting up a kind of pagan State religion in opposition to it. By reason of the old Pontifex Maximus office retained by all the emperors, Julian really considered himself as the Imperial High Priest and installed High Priests in the individual provinces who were in charge of the entire system of cults and of those running them. Where possible, Julian made use of Christian experience in the practical implementation of this new project which, admittedly, did not get further than the initial stages. He advocated the purity and dignity of the college of priests who had to be of sound education. Charitable activities were likewise given a position of central importance. Julian provided a good example in this respect by making corn and wine available for beggars and pilgrims who were to be cared for in state or municipal hostels in future. Other measures scarcely reached the stage of practical implementation, one of which was the promotion of Judaism, to which Julian was well-disposed on account of the Jewish-Christian antagonism and the impressively severe and undivided ritual. Even the rebuilding of the Temple in Jerusalem was begun with Imperial support although nothing came of it since an earthquake destroyed the foundations which had just been laid.

Relying on divine providence, Julian—who now saw himself as following in the footsteps of Alexander the Great—launched a campaign against the Persians in 363. As would be expected from a man of his generalship, the emperor prepared this campaign thoroughly and assembled numerous elite units. Covered by an army protecting his flanks, Julian advanced to the enemy capital of Ctesiphon but was unable to capture it. On the march back home, the Romans were hard-pressed by the Persians on a terrain which favoured their use of archers, elephants and a superior cavalry. Julian, who rushed into the midst of the fighting, was fatally wounded in one of these skirmishes. On the same field of battle, Jovian, the commander of

Reconstruction of the Germanic and Rhaetian limes

the bodyguard (*primicerius domesticorum*), was proclaimed the new emperor. He was a man of only average ability who immediately concluded peace with the Persians on unfavourable terms. Admittedly, through Julian's lack of success, the frontier areas along the upper reaches of the Tigris now remained in Persian hands and Armenia was abandoned to the Sassanids.

Only under Valentinian I (364–375) were vigorous efforts made again to consolidate Roman rule. He was also the founder of the last dynasty which may be said to have still been all-Roman (up to 455). The son of an officer, he himself had advanced to the rank of tribune. He soon made his brother Valens co-regent and the latter headed the eastern part of the empire until 378. Both emperors were Christian and lent their support—even if with some reserve—to their fellow-believers, Valens being particularly strong in his furtherance of the Arians. This had a certain effect on various Barbarian groups, especially Gothic ones who had been converted to Christianity by the missionary bishop Wulfila (Ulfilas) in the middle of the 4th century—the author of the famous translation of the Bible into Gothic. Dating from the time of Valentinian and Valens, certain religious and ideological differences can be identified between the Eastern and the Western empire and these ultimately helped to play a part in the division of the empire in 395 which was carried out for political and military reasons. The West—with the exception of North Africa which initially continued to remain Donatist—became Catholic, while the East was first confronted with Arianism and then with Monophysitic and other movements. And towards the end of the 4th century, at the latest, these questions became so important for ordinary people that Bishop Gregory of Nyssa (382) criticized the atmosphere in Constantinople in the following words: "The city is full of people who talk inconceivable and incomprehensible things—in every street and market-hall, at every square and crossing. When I buy something in a shop and ask how much I have to pay, I get a philosophical lecture about the begotten or not begotten Son of the Father. If I ask the price of bread in a bakery, the baker answers that the Father is without doubt greater than the Son (basic doctrine of Arianism; the author). And when I ask at the thermal springs if I can take a bath, the attendant tries to prove to me that the Son without doubt came from the void." This humourous observation nevertheless reveals the great interest of the population in religious and even abstruse theological matters. This was obviously even too much for the theologian and showed the uselessness of any kind of indoctrination. Of course, all this discussion may also be regarded as a successful ruse by the leading political circles to distract the attention of the ordinary man from the fundamental problems of life, assistance in this being provided by the senior dignitaries of the Church. As Julian's attempts at reform had amply demonstrated, paganism was no longer in a position to perform such an ideological function—even if it was only as a diversion—so that the Christian Church had to be given support in an increasingly more exclusive manner. Accordingly, the pagan opposition was increasingly forced into a defensive posture and largely restricted itself to the more high-born senatorial circles, mostly at Rome itself, who were economically independent, were at odds with almost every government and, in closed communities, maintained the old-style education and culture. Even Valentinian's sycophants had taken rigorous action against these groups but, headed by men like Symmachus, they had retained their influence for decades to come. Indirectly, these anti-aristocratic actions of Valentinian's government may be connected with a reform of the administration which was once again due and which benefited above all the subordinate officers and officials. They could now easily attain senatorial rank—which must have seemed like discrimination of the older and "nobler" members of the Senate. Something of the same kind happened when Valentinian strengthened the organization of the *defensores* (*civitatis*) which had been set up for the protection of the urban curiae and population and took vigorous action against the patrocinate movement through which previously free peasants had become dependent on the big landowners. Nevertheless, this movement—which was remotely comparable with the colonate system—remained important in social practice and, with little change, continued to exist among some of the migration states. It would naturally be wrong to view the action taken against the patrocinate movement as merely reflecting the concern of the emperor for the threatened free rural population. It was mainly a question here of the interest of the State in its subjects who were liable to taxation. In order to escape the demands of the authorities, many peasants voluntarily entered a patrocinate and were given back their property by the new landlord as a kind of loan when various rights and obligations had been agreed. This then freed them at least from their direct obligations towards the State.

The government of Valentinian, his brother Valens and his son Gratian, who was raised to the rank of Augustus when only eight years old, was likewise overshadowed by numerous wars and attacks from wandering Barbarian tribes. Britain was threatened from the North and West by the Picts and Scots and by the Saxons coming across the North Sea. The Comes Theodosius, a Spanish landowner and the father of the later Emperor Theodosius I, brought security again to the island as far north as Hadrian's Wall. In the meantime, from bases at Paris and Trier, the emperor launched a campaign against the Saxons and the Franks who had swarmed over Northern Gaul. Cities such as Mayence (Mogontiacum) which had been captured by the Alemans were soon restored to Roman rule. After extensive preparations which were co-ordinated from Trier, Valentinian also carried out various offensive thrusts into the area on the right bank of the Rhine. It is true that he failed in his efforts to go beyond the deterrent action carried out by Julian and to restore the old limes but the Rhine frontier was kept intact and many improvements made to the fortifications (bridgeheads as additional strong-points since Constantine the Great, as at Cologne-Deutz).

North Africa, too, which had once again passed through a crisis following the spread in the power of the Berber leader Firmus who was supported by the Donatists, was again firmly under Roman control by the time of Valentinian's death.

For the time being, it was more from the East that there was a military threat to the existence of the empire. Admittedly, the still strong Eastern army under Valens and his generals maintained Roman influence in Armenia until about 378 and won a

14 Giant head of Constantine the Great in the courtyard of the Palazzo dei Conservatori, Rome. It was part of a statue about 18 m high which once adorned the Basilica of Constantine. From the iconographic viewpoint, the bold and monumental head, which seems to incorporate realistic features, presents many a riddle. It is clear that it was intended to enhance the glory of the emperor who introduced a new epoch, even though the origin of the work is unknown.

15 Basilica of Constantine on the Forum Romanum in Rome. The "Imperial Hall", begun by Maxentius and completed by Constantine the Great, was one of the most monumental buildings of late Rome. Occupying an area of 6,000 sq.m., it consisted of a middle aisle with cross-vaulting about 35 m in height and with side-aisles spanned by barrel-vaulting about 25 m high. The middle aisle was carried on four mighty columns and coloured marble was used for the floor slabs. Constantine added a four-column portico to the long south side and a new apse to the side-aisle on the northern side where, seated on a throne, he carried out the official business with the magistrates. In the west apse of the structure, there stood the colossus of the emperor, about 18 m in height, the head of which is now in the Palazzo dei Conservatori. From its dimensions and architectural structure, the building can be regarded as typically Late Antique. The influence of the basilica-type structure on church architecture can only be noted here.

16 The Arch of Constantine in Rome—one of the latest and most impressive triumphal arches—was erected by the Senate after Constantine the Great's victory at Milvian Bridge (Ponte Molle). The sculptured ornamentation was mostly taken from edifices erected by Trajan, Hadrian and Marcus Aurelius, the heads often being remoulded in the style of the late period and iconographically modified. The long reliefs above the side-arches were carved specifically for this monument and are clearly of late Antique style. At any rate, with its height of 12 m, the arch is an impressive sight and presents an organic whole.

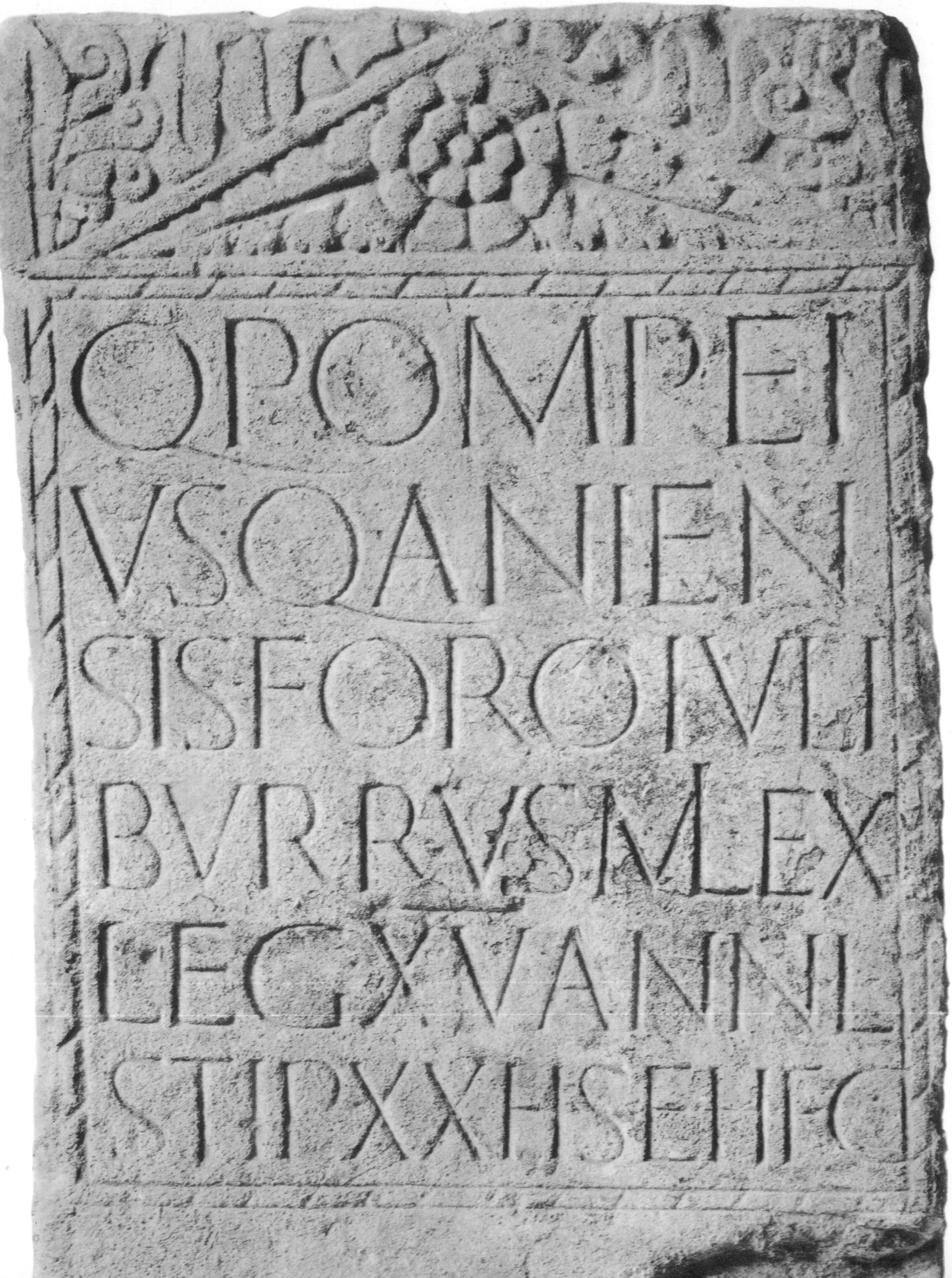

O POMPEI
VS Q ANIEN
SIS F ORO IVLI
BVRRVS M L EX
LEG X VANNI
STIP XXII S E H E C

17 Classical Roman capitals on the tombstone of a warrior from the 1st century (Römisch-Germanisches Museum, Cologne).

18 Bridge in Trier known as the "Römerbrücke". Five of the seven pillars of the present bridge date back to the 4th century when Trier was still one of the residences of the emperors of Western Rome.

19 Porta San Sebastiano in Rome, one of the fortress-like gate structures of the Aurelian wall which was built after 270. The walls of smaller cities had similar gates but on a lesser scale (see Ill. 10, Hissar). This structure, once called the Porta Appia from the road which entered it, is a mighty edifice in three storeys. Of rectangular outline at the base, the towers are crowned by a round superstructure with pinnacles. In the many struggles for Rome, fighting often centred on these gates.

20/21 Porta Nigra in Trier. This was the north gate (built about 300) of the Late Roman perimeter wall which was 6.5 km in length. The structure, which reaches a height of 30 m and reinforced the defensive capability of the town in the face of many Barbarian attacks, was called the "Black Gate" from the patina of the heavy sandstone ashlar which was laid without mortar.

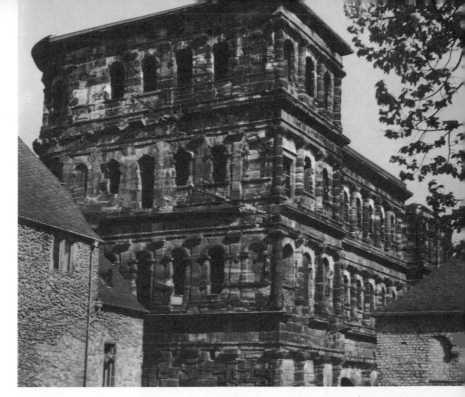

Preceding two pages:

22 Ludovisi battle sarcophagus depicting struggle between Romans and Barbarians (Thermae Museum in Rome). This work is the subject of controversy as regards its date and the significance of the details. It depicts a typical scene from the violent fighting which went on continually between the Romans and the Barbarians, something which was already familiar to everyone in the 3rd century. This well-known work of art, which in many aspects recalls the column of Marcus Aurelius but otherwise has a number of expressionistic features, shows a victorious general, doubtlessly an emperor, in the midst of his courageously fighting troops (probably bodyguards, the protectores, who were then coming to the fore). Even in their facial expressions, the Romans are depicted as superior and on a higher level—almost proof that they were no longer quite so sure of this superiority. The relief with its artistic composition exploits all the resources of Classic art but is lacking perspective and presents a confusing array of individual episodes so that it assumes "Barbarian" traits itself.

23 The Rotunda of St. George in Sofia—probably built on the site of an early Christian martyry from the beginning of the 4th century. Only a part of the entire complex is visible today since much of it lies under the walls of the Balkantourist Hotel. It was originally thought that thermal baths were situated here but this theory has now been abandoned in the light of recent excavations indicating that this site was a martyry. Towards the end of the 4th century, it was converted into a baptistery church. After the frightful devastations of the Hun raids in the 5th century, the complex was rebuilt, the central part then being used as a church dedicated to St. George. Under Turkish rule, the building was used as a mosque.

24 East Gate of the city-wall of Serdica (Sofia). Recent excavations on Lenin Square in front of the Party building: masonry technique and finds have confirmed that it dates from the Constantine period.

25 Amphitheatre (arena) of Verona—built under Diocletian about 290. The outer wall, originally three storeys high, enclosed one of the largest arenas for gladiator and animal contests. The mediaeval saga of the Nibelungen regarded this building as the castle of Dietrich of Bern (= Theodoric the Great).

26 Imperial villa in Piazza Armerina near Enna (Sicily). This famous villa with its many rooms in Central Sicily was built in the last decade of the 3rd century on the instructions of Emperor Maximianus (286 to 305). Its mighty walls, marble columns and magnificent mosaic floors still bear witness to the splendour of this Late Antique hunting-lodge, part of which was subsequently inhabited by the Normans. The illustration shows part of one of the numerous mosaic hunting scenes found here, the "Diaeta of the chase for small game". It is true that there are no wild animals of Africa here, as on other mosaics of this villa, but the episodes depicted in five scenes (our picture shows the 5th on the right) nevertheless tell a great deal. The chase takes place on a wooded plain, in mountainous terrain and in a forest of cypress, oak and laurel trees. The hunters with their dogs are pursuing small game such as hares, foxes and also wild boar. The falconry symbolizes a hunter, lying in wait for thrushes (3rd zone). The picture depicts in realistic fashion a hunter lying on the ground and being attacked by a wild boar; two companions fight the beast with a thrusting spear and a piece of rock. The hunters, some of whom are mounted, wear belted tunics and a kind of puttee wrapped around the leg up to the knee.

27 Mosaic (c. 432—440) from the main aisle of Santa Maria Maggiore, Rome. This famous Roman basilica, erected on a former pagan cult site, was built in 352. Under Pope Sixtus III the building was renovated and decorated with mosaics depicting Biblical motifs. The battle scenes—as the conquest of Jericho represented here—show Late Antique characteristics. Weapons and fortifications give a true picture of the Migration period.

28 Barbario inscription from Trier. This early Christian inscription, which has not yet been accurately dated, is on a white marble slab which was found to the northeast of the Church of St. Paulin (now Landesmuseum, Trier). It is dedicated to a boy named Barbario, who was only eight months and 24 days old when he died.

29 Tomb of the Longidieni family in Ravenna (Museo Nazionale d'Antichità, formerly the Cloister of San Vitale). Of interest is the inscription in high-relief which refers to the picture of the ship's carpenter. It reads: "Publius Longidienus, son of Publius, hurries to his work" (P. LONGIDIENUS, P. F., AD ONUS PROPERAT).

P·LONGIDIENVS·P·L·RVFIO
P·LONGIDIENVS·P·L·PILADES·PO
INPENSA·A·PRONO·DEDERVNT

P·LONGIDIENVS
P·F·AD·ONVS
PROPERAT

number of victories over Persian forces. It was then, however, that the events taking place in the area of the Lower Danube forced the empire to give up its claims at various points. Retreating in the face of the superiority of the Huns after 376, the Visigoths had asked permission to settle in Roman territory south of the Danube. In return for undertaking to defend the frontier, they were in fact granted a settlement treaty, thus entering into a federate relationship with Rome. The Visigoths settled in the province of Moesia but it was not long before they had trouble with the Roman bureaucracy which took advantage of the serious food situation. Many of the Barbarians or members of their families were forced to become slaves in return for food. Resentment increased until at last a rebellion broke out which was joined not only by large numbers of other Goths but also by oppressed slaves, coloni and miners. In this situation, on the eve of the Battle of Adrianople, it seemed likely that there would be an alliance between the enemies of Rome within and without the empire. After an Eastern Roman army had been soundly defeated by Fritigern, Valens postponed a campaign against the Persians, assembled an army and also requested military support from his nephew Gratian. Fritigern, a talented leader, soon appreciated the danger of being encircled by possibly superior Roman forces and opened negotiations with Valens, promising to refrain from any hostile action in return for the province of Thracia. With these conditions, he obviously wanted to make a definite alliance with Valens and to guarantee the military security of the Danube line. At the same time, however, the Gothic leader had taken up a strong position, covered by a ring of waggons and other defences, at Jamboli north of Adrianople. He believed that, if he had to and with the aid of various detachments, he could prevent the union of the Eastern and Western armies of Rome. Valens refused to negotiate any further but also decided not to wait for the relief army since he was irritated by the success of Gratian against the Alemans. On 9 August 378, a very hot day, he had his forces march out of Adrianople. It was not until mid-day that the Roman advance-guard sighted the Gothic positions. Valens had difficulty in hurriedly changing over from marching order to battle order but he launched an

attack without waiting for all his troops to reach the field of battle. Initial successes caused the Roman line of battle to be split up even more before the last units had arrived on the scene. The mounted forces of the Goths tore apart the left flank of the Roman cavalry and forced the infantry back onto difficult terrain. Valens was unable to re-form his troops or to fall back to a base position. Deserted by his bodyguard, he met his death as an ordinary warrior at the end of the battle. The Goths did not stop at winning the battle but immediately set out in pursuit of the remnants of the Roman army and also attempted to overrun Adrianople. But their fast-moving forces, specializing almost entirely in mounted actions, were unable to make much impact against the mighty fortifications. Despite this, Fritigern's success was not only of great tactical importance but also of strategic and operational significance. Without having ambitious plans in mind and not even disposing of the complete contingent of a large tribe or people, the Gothic leader had defeated a fully intact Roman army and—as subsequent events were to show—caused a military vacuum in the Eastern part of the empire. The only limits to this success of the Barbarians were their weakness and their inexperience, especially in siege techniques, so that the Romans, behind the great bulwarks of their fortifications, were gradually able to build up their forces again. Nevertheless, Roman attacks against the Barbarians could not be contemplated for decades and even defensive engagements were often matters of very great seriousness. In addition, it has been proved by modern research that the armies recruited in the Eastern and Western parts of the empire now consisted to a very large extent of Barbarians. Even before Adrianople, the percentage of Barbarians in the army and even among the officers had risen slowly but steadily so that from now on new and reinforced units have to be regarded as very largely—if not exclusively—Barbarian. From the origin of the ordinary soldiers and officers and also from many features of their weapons and combat techniques, these were quite simply Barbarian armies fighting in the name of Rome. Of course, they were still commanded by the emperors or their generals and were trained and led according to established principles. These armies were essentially of a mixed type

30 Ivory diptych of Stilicho and his wife Serena (c. 400; height 32.2 cm, width 16.2 cm; cathedral treasure in Monza). The illustrious Germanic general and son-in-law of Theodosius the Great is shown dressed in a chlamys with lance and shield, next to his wife with their son Honorius. On the shield there is the double portrait of the sons of Theodosius, the emperor of the Eastern and Western empire—Honorius and Arcadius; the allusion to Stilicho's loyalty to the ruling dynasty is unmistakable.

and the myth of Roman invincibility, still maintained albeit with difficulty, was due from now on to Barbarian rather than Roman elements. Thus it was only with the aid of newly-recruited Gothic mercenaries and Frankish commanders such as Bauto and Arbogast that Theodosius, the new emperor appointed by Gratian, succeeded in driving back Fritigern across the Balkans, and even this at the cost of severe losses. It was only in 380/81 that peace was officially concluded, parts of the Roman provinces in the Balkans being allocated to the Visigoths of Fritigern as federates in return for an undertaking to defend the frontiers. This was certainly a compromise for both sides but the concession made by the Romans was greater than that made by the Goths and other tribes were gradually encouraged to do likewise. At this time, the conditions for fairly large federate groups of the kind described were quite advantageous since they remained under their own commanders, who had not only military functions but also civil ones, especially as judges, and, apart from exemption from taxes, also received pay. Groups which were particularly useful from the Roman viewpoint were even incorporated in the official forces when this was considered expedient. Small groups in particular had the chance to serve as *buccellarii (satellites ; comites)* on extremely good terms in the bodyguards of the generals in question. These bodyguards or retainers represented the core of every army and, to an increasing degree, many of the senior officers were drawn from their ranks.

To round off the picture, the line of development must be followed at least as far as 455. Up to 395, the scene was dominated by the still energetic defensive actions of Theodosius the Great who, for a short time, brought the entire empire under the control of a single person once more. He also dealt successfully with dangerous adversaries at home, such as the anti-emperor Eugenius, who was supported by the leading circles of the pagan senators (394).

The battle by the Frigidus, which marked the defeat of Eugenius and of his Frankish general, Arbogast, who was still a pagan, was not only a notable event in military history but also marked a particular climax in political and cultural matters. Although this victory was won with troops of Barbarian origin

who were still mostly of pagan or Arian faith, the party of Theodosius had the support of the Pope and of Bishop Ambrosius of Milan and from now on it was clear that Rome would follow a policy clearly in favour of the Catholic Orthodox Church. A long period of intellectual and ideological conflict thus drew to a close. Initially, Gratian and Theodosius had been obliged to use pressure to bring about a union of the various Christian factions before the latter could devote his energies to the defeat of paganism. As early as 380, the two emperors had ordered their subjects to accept the doctrine of Nicaea (of 325). The second Ecumenical Council of 381 consolidated this position. Bishops who now insisted that the relationship of Christ to the Father was "homoiousian" and not "consubstantial"—this was the main point of contention between Arians and Catholics—had to leave their pulpits. Even Gregory of Naziantium, one of the most brilliant advocates of the Nicene Creed, was compelled to withdraw his candidacy for the See of Constantinople which had been promised to him and to return to a remote provincial town. Not by chance, it was precisely Gregory, considered as "the most fertile and remarkable poet of this period" (Wilamowitz), who provided a sharply critical picture of the events of Constantinople. In the different conditions of the West, the policies followed often combined both anti-Arian and anti-pagan aspects. Gratian dropped the pontifex maximus title and was the last emperor to use it. Henceforth, it designated the occupant of the Holy See. The Victoria Altar, which had been returned to its original site by Julian, was once again removed from the curia of the Senate by Gratian. But his anti-pagan programme was also directed against the material basis of the pagan cults and the colleges of the priests not only lost their exemption from taxes and their allowances from the State but also had their estates confiscated. Even before his death (25 August 383), however, there was new unrest in domestic and ecclesiastical affairs. After the movement of the Priscillianists had been destroyed—above all by the usurper Magnus Maximus who resided for years in Gaul—trouble again broke out between the Arians and the Catholics, mainly in the residence-city of Milan. The widow of Valentinian I, Justina, who reigned on behalf of her young

son Valentinian II, was influenced by pagan and Arian officers and consequently gave resolute support to the Arianists, who had many followers among the Germanic and other Barbarian troops. It can be appreciated that even pagan commanders, whether for ideological or political reasons, were more inclined to support Arianism than Catholicism and it is understandable that a weak government in particular would take account of their wishes. Bishop Ambrosius of Milan, one of the outstanding churchmen of his day, was instrumental in defeating Arianism in the "quarrel of the basilicas", which was aimed at transferring some of the Catholic churches to the Arians. By his adroit handling of people plus a touch of demagogy, Ambrosius even managed to win over some of the troops of the "child-emperor", Valentinian II, to his side. Even though Arianism was condemned to insignificance almost overnight—its subsequent revival in the Barbarian states is worth a separate examination—pagan influence was still maintained by the tenacious commitment of senatorial circles in the city of Rome in particular. At first, even Theodosius I was forced to make certain concessions to men like Praetextatus, Symmachus and Flavianus. He conferred high offices on them, especially that of the consulate which now had little influence but was still regarded as an exceptional honour. In return, the senators proclaimed their loyalty to the emperor and also openly declared that they were the real patriots of Rome, extolling in extravagant manner the fame of the Eternal City and patronizing men like Ammianus Marcellinus, the leading historian of the epoch. Something of a mystery is the connection between the pagan senators and the work of the Imperial historians (*Scriptores Historiae Augustae*), a collection of the biographies of the emperors from Hadrian to Carinus. There is such a marked agreement between the anti-Christian and socio-conservative views of its author (or authors) and the attitude of the group around Symmachus that modern researchers have assumed close factual and personal contacts but this has not been proved by documentary evidence.

The group headed by Symmachus cherished the heritage of a great past by publishing new editions or commentaries of works by classical authors such as Virgil and Livy in particular.

To be sure, this attention given to philology was only a means to an end, i.e., the revival of the great pagan traditions of Rome. The best way to make people forget the shameful present was by recalling the outstanding political and military achievements of the past and this, of course, was the aim of the group around Symmachus. Ultimately they supported, as much as they could, the usurpation by the former rhetorician Eugenius, who was almost one of them, in the final stage of his struggle against Theodosius. The activities of this circle are also of particular historical interest from the education viewpoint since they saved many classic works from oblivion and, had it not been for their efforts, education would certainly have been even more restricted during this period. However, their principal endeavours were concentrated on establishing counter-positions to Christianity which was now becoming all-powerful and in linking the Roman cause as inseparably as possible with Stoic and Neo-Platonic thinking which permitted not only the inclusion of the Roman ideal but also consideration of humane ideas. The advocacy of the human rights of slaves was not forgotten either. Of course, all this had much in common with the reform instituted by Julian and, to some extent, included its impenetrable demagogic aims. However, most of the letters of Symmachus, who corresponded with a large number of the important personalities of the time, are remarkably mild and human, giving the impression of a good-humoured and almost serene character. Serious problems are not avoided, it is true, but in general he only makes a gentle reference to them as if they were not really so important. This attitude is hard to overlook and explains, at least in part, the lack of success of the intellectual and cultural efforts of the group as a whole. Forced into a hopeless situation, they no longer took other people—nor themselves—very seriously and, at most, tried to save what they could with the means at their disposal. In the intellectual sphere, this meant with the means of irony and often only with mild ridicule as compared to the usually sharp polemics from their Christian opponents of the time (Ambrosius, Hieronymus, Augustine). Tolerance was even one of the chief characteristics of this late phase of paganism whereas Christianity was generally very intolerant at that time.

Admittedly, under Eugenius, who must have been confident of victory before the battle by the Frigidus, there were also pagan excesses in the spirit of the measures once taken by Julian. However, the battle by the Frigidus marked the beginning of the end. Many distinguished pagans now followed the ruling trend and came to terms with the government which, in turn, attached importance to support from illustrious families. Theodosius and Stilicho, who governed the Western empire for the boy-emperor Honorius and was himself a man of partly Barbarian origin, were naturally not able to bring about a settlement between paganism and Christianity. But they did want to utilize as much as possible of that potential which up till now had been pagan to counter the constant Barbarian threat to the empire of which the new State Church was an integral part. Paganism increasingly lost ground through this and was ultimately restricted to a few senatorial families, small groups of Neo-Platonic philosophers and a minority of the peasant population, especially in the frontier provinces. Anyone with ambition now had to be a Christian, at least formally. Nevertheless, there were still marked pagan elements in the writers of this changing epoch, even in the work of bishops such as Synesius of Cyrene († about 413).

The following years were characterized by unrest in Africa, where the military commander Gildo vainly attempted to establish independent rule with Donatist help and the support of Berber tribes, and by new Barbarian raids on the northern frontiers of the empire. Following the death of Theodosius, when the empire came under the rule of his sons Arcadius and Honorius, there began the final division into two halves, something which seemed almost natural. A unified system of defence, which had existed at least as a basic concept until the battle of Adrianople, became increasingly more difficult and often even impossible in actual fact. The West tried to divert the Barbarian invasions towards the East and vice-versa. In these circumstances, a large army, consisting mainly of Ostrogoths, swept into Italy in 405. Stilicho was able to inflict a crushing defeat on the main body of this force at Fiesole in August 406 but, prior to this, had been obliged to greatly reduce the frontier troops. So it was that at the very beginning of 406 a motley force of Alans, Vandals and Suebi of great strength was able to cross the Upper Rhine and ravage Gaul and then the Iberian peninsula. This advance also marked the start of a new stage in the Barbarian invasions, leading to the establishment of an empire by the Vandals, Suebi and Visigoths in North Africa and Spain. This was the outward sign of the now imminent disintegration of the Roman Empire in the West.

Such invasions by strong but heterogeneous Barbarian bands, mostly under irregular leadership, into the central areas of the empire might still have been prevented if the government of the day had made efforts to set up a unified system of defence but there was no question of even this. Time and again, it proved possible to persuade certain groups of these Barbarians to change sides—either by capture or direct recruitment—and, as federates or even as *buccellarii*, to fight against their own tribes. Using the old principle of *divide et impera*, it was possible to throw back the enemy temporarily with the assistance of the enemy himself or that of his near "relations" and these purely defensive successes were considered good enough by the ruling circles. Perhaps the government also believed that it was making a virtue of necessity when Barbarians who were no longer needed were eliminated in good time and replaced by Romans. This happened, for instance, after the fall of Stilicho (408) which, probably unexpected by the government, led to a power vacuum. This in turn attracted Alaric, the king of the Visigoths, to Italy, an unnerved and starving Rome falling to him on 24 August 410. After collecting much booty and taking with him Galla Placidia, the sister of the emperor, as a hostage, he left the country again. The people of Rome and Italy were able to count themselves lucky that the Visigoths left the land at all to initially set up a state in southern Gaul which was still nominally subject to the emperor (Tolosanic empire).

The political and intellectual effects of the capture of Rome were immeasurable and certainly went beyond the bare fact that the capital had been briefly occupied and looted by the enemy. Fugitives spread the news of the horror of this event throughout the empire and the consequences of it were discussed with emotion everywhere by Christians and pagans, by the apologists

of the eternal rule of Rome and by their opponents. Hardest hit were the pagan elite who regarded the humiliation of Rome as a just punishment imposed by the ancient gods. Thoughts on this were written down by Christian authors such as Hieronymus, Augustine (354–430) and Orosius, the latter two with a passionate defence of their new Christian view of history. Under the shock of a defeat which affected them, too, they attempted, on the one hand, to camouflage and minimize the decline associated with it and, on the other, they belittled the role of Rome in the history of the world. The Roman Empire, regarded by public opinion at that time as the last of the four empires of the world, is overshadowed in Augustine's argumentation by the realm of God *(civitas Dei)*, its role as the last world-power being almost disregarded. This cleared the way for a new approach to history which was mainly metaphysical in character and regarded the history of mankind as guided by God. Naturally, there were different opinions about this and a further restriction of the historical horizon was not really threatened. Augustine and

Orosius, who was somewhat younger, enlarged the historical material step by step by recognizing the Barbarians as active participants in an historical process taking place in this world, in accordance with the prophecy in Matth. 28, 19f. Orosius supplemented *Civitas Dei*, the monumental historical and theological work of his master, with a "History against the pagans" (*Historia adversum paganos*). The line they took was continued by the outstanding men of letters of the following period, such as Salvian, Prosper Tiro, Cassiodorus, Jordanes and Isidore of Seville. Naturally enough, there were constant disputes between the metaphysical chiliastic basic concept of the Christian framework of history and the chronological and chronicled description of what really happened. In the face of the fanatical patriotism of the pagans of Rome, Augustine and Orosius still recognized Rome's role although it was not of first importance for them. In the course of the further development of the science of history, however, its position continued to decline. Even Augustine had occasionally appeared to echo elements of the oft-proclaimed

Construction of plank-paths from moors in Northwest Germany

official programme about a "renewal of the empire" (*renovatio imperii*) but such opinions were soon seldom heard. Subsequently, when reference was made to Rome, it was often not even the emperor or the empire which was meant now but the Papacy which had absorbed many Roman elements and soon claimed on a large scale the Roman attitudes to power (Papal Primacy; Pontifical State). For the beginning of the 5th century, however, the works of Augustine and his followers provided numerous standpoints which again contributed to a stabilization of the empire. They did not glorify the Barbarians at all and considered them just as critically as they did the representatives of Rome. Like other Fathers of the Church, Augustine likewise recommended the military and economic use of the Barbarians in the sense of the traditional *pax romana*. This reflected a markedly conservative attitude which was also characteristic of the social doctrine of this man who, through his great literary activity, is better known to us than any other author of Antiquity (important works: apart from numerous letters, sermons and the *Civitas Dei*, there are the *Confessiones* and numerous ethic, exegetic, dogmatic and polemic tracts in which paganism and heresies are sharply attacked).

Despite a completely independent standpoint which was restricted to the Church sphere and of which various arguments still provoke lively discussion among present-day researchers, Augustine was the last major ideological representative of Rome and what it stood for and up to the Vandal invasion of 429 must be regarded as the protagonist of Roman civilization against the Barbarians and heretics of North Africa. His attitude and similar opinions expressed by his followers also reflect very clearly the modest upswing which occurred again in the western part of the empire soon after 410. The socio-economic position was stabilized—as before by way of the colonate and patrocinate systems—and the defensive positions of the bureaucracy and the army were extended further. The rulers (Honorius, Valentinian III, Galla Placidia) who resided at the small town of Ravenna, which was regarded as impregnable, had little ability, and in actual fact it was the high court officials and military commanders who governed for them. Men such as Flavius Constantius and, later,

Aetius tried to prevent more Barbarians from streaming into the territory of the empire and to supervise the federates who had already settled there, using Visigoths, Vandals and Suebi from time to time for the defence of the frontiers. Administrative and fiscal reforms, as reflected above all in the *Codex Theodosianus* published in 438, which also applied to the Western empire, and its various supplements, reveal just how difficult it had now become to safeguard the shrinking territory of the empire from its enemies at home and abroad. There is also a hint of the intensive measures taken in the *Notitia Dignitatum*, a list of all the military and civil offices compiled between 400 and 425. Incidentally, this State handbook is of great interest in many different aspects. More effectively than even the laws of this time, it provides an insight into even the smallest details of Late Roman bureaucracy, in which Byzantine features are already apparent, and throws light, in its way, on the hierarchical organization of State and society. Here and there, one might even speak of a caste-like paralysis of the system in which the lower officials, for example, had scarcely any chance of promotion whereas the ordinary soldiers were in a better position. Even officials with a higher education were normally glad if, in the course of decades, they were able to aspire to the respected and highly paid post of a leading official in a government department or of a provincial governor. On account of the greater risks, a military career offered better opportunities. Even the *Notitia*, in association with other sources, proves that simple Barbarians or at least the commanders of Barbarian auxiliaries or even robber-bands could attain the rank of a staff officer (*praefectus, praepositus*) or even a general (*dux, comes, magister militum*) often within an astonishingly short time. Of particular interest is the fact that the *Notitia*, in the form in which it is known to us, is heterogeneous in its composition. Thus at many places and for many frontier areas it is the system of defences at the end of the 4th century which is outlined whilst at others it is the conditions prevailing in the 5th century which have been inserted at a later date.

The rich pictorial decoration of this handbook is also of cultural interest. The chapters in question are headed by illustrations showing officials' insignia of rank, vignettes of fortresses,

badges of military units and so on; here and there, even first hints of landscape painting are visible. The combination of pictures and words occasionally provides a vivid cartographic description.

The legal works mentioned above and the Imperial measures frequently reflected in them are sufficient evidence that there was no intention of allowing the Barbarians to take over or even permanently keep the military and political initiative. For long after 410 and at least until the end of the Valentinian dynasty (455), the Western empire also maintained its claims to power. Admittedly, these claims were modified and, with the increase in the de facto independence of the Federate states, became less and less noticeable. With the recognition of the sovereign state of the Vandals by Ravenna in 442, a stage was reached which seemed to indicate that the Western empire had voluntarily renounced its rights to the central areas of North Africa. Since the Visigoths had likewise established a de facto sovereign state and Ravenna— disregarding Italy—only continued to exercise direct authority over a few areas in Spain, Gaul and the Alps, a kind of co-existence between the Western empire and the new Barbarian states can now be identified. Of course, there was a constant shift in power relations and in the years after 440 it seemed as if Western and Eastern Rome might be crushed by a possible coalition between the Huns, the Vandals and other new states which had emerged. Even Byzantium had to pay tribute to Attila's realm in Pannonia. However, personal links between the various rulers and dynastic ambitions enabled the Western Roman general Aetius to forge a strong alliance in 451 against Attila, the king of the Huns, who was pushing forward into Gaul. At the Battle of Châlons, he was compelled to retreat and the mighty empire of the Huns rapidly disintegrated soon after his death in 453. Subjugated tribes and peoples such as the Ostrogoths, Gepidae and Alans freed themselves from the tyranny of the Huns and, in the period that followed, again turned towards areas ruled by Eastern and Western Rome.

For the development of the subsequent phase (lasting at least until 500), two facts must be given special emphasis: the final replacement of Western Roman rule by Germanic power (Odoacer deposed Emperor Romulus Augustulus in 476 and assumed actual power in Italy) and the slow stabilization of the Eastern Roman-Byzantine Empire.

At first sight, it may seem surprising that Byzantium was able to consolidate itself again at the same time as its Western Roman "partner-state"—which is how it can be described despite the postulate of the time of a united Imperium Romanum Christianum—was falling apart but there were various reasons for this. To begin with, it is clear that the Barbarian invasions were increasingly directed towards the West, especially after the collapse of the Hun empire. This was partly spontaneous and partly due to the manipulations of Byzantium which was in need of peace and quiet. The result was that only peripheral areas of the Byzantine Empire, such as the southern Balkan area or the Oriental frontier zones, were affected by the inroads of invading tribes. The rulers of Byzantium also succeeded in subordinating to the interests of the State the Barbarians, such as the Isaurians, who settled in the central districts of Asia Minor. However, the principal explanation for the survival of the Eastern Roman-Byzantine Empire must be sought in certain socio-economic aspects. The old village community had been able to maintain itself better in the Byzantine area than in the West of the empire and it was here, too, that there were more free coloni who had a profound and enduring interest in high productivity. Also of importance for stability seems to be the fact that there were fewer big estates with exemption from taxes in the East than in the West, where the proliferation of latifundia (as in North Africa and Gaul) practically crippled the State administration and taxation system and caused a continuing reduction in the rights and labour productivity of the coloni. Another important factor in the stabilization of the Eastern empire was the large number of towns with skilled craftsmen and flourishing commercial activities. Apart from the major centres of production such as Constantinople, Thessalonica, Smyrna, Antioch, Damascus and Alexandria, there was a host of small towns with large numbers of artisans, working not only in the usual trades but often in luxury branches as well (woollen and silk fabrics, metalworking: Damascus swords). The surplus product derived from commerce and trade benefited not only the upper strata of the towns but also the State. This helps to explain why it was that Byzantium, in contrast to Ravenna, was able to halt the incursions of the Barbarians at its frontiers and eventually was able to pursue not only a repressive home policy but an active and aggressive foreign policy. Already under Emperor Anastasios I (491–517) but especially under Justinian I (527–565), Byzantium had very largely overcome the crisis which had arisen with the Great Migration. It now went over to the offensive in its turn against the newly emerged states and won notable successes against the empires of the Vandals, Visigoths and Ostrogoths in the course of struggles which continued for many years.

The Principal Peoples
of the Great Migration and Their Aims

THE REASONS FOR THE BARBARIAN MIGRATIONS were many, as is apparent from the research on the subject right down to the present day. News of the crisis and growing weakness of the Roman Empire had spread throughout almost the whole of the known world and innumerable bands of young warriors with an appetite for adventure and even entire tribal contingents had been attracted by the prospects of gain and booty on Roman soil or even by the idea of settling permanently there. From at least the time of the Cimbri and the Teutons, rumours had spread through Northern and Eastern Europe of rich and sunny areas in the South where one could live in ease and safety. In many of the Barbarian legends, the joys of life in the Mediterranean area were probably so exaggerated that they became increasingly envious of these fertile regions, especially when the at best meagre harvests of the North were unable to provide enough food for the growing numbers of the tribe following changes for the worse in weather or climate. The poor quality of the soil and inadequate tillage of the land also led to migration in many places. People retreated in the face of hunger and other misfortunes and sought better places where they could settle. This frequently involved lengthy detours and travels, various neighbouring or more remote tribes being caught up in the process as if in a chain reaction.

For several reasons, the examination of the Barbarian migrations from the standpoint of the principal peoples concerned is best begun not with the Germanic tribes but with the Alans and the Huns.

The Alans

The Alans were a tribal group of Scythian-Sarmatic origin who had initially lived as nomads in Central Asia and Eastern Europe. In the years after 350, some of them had been subjugated by the Huns while others had united with the Vandals and Suebi who were moving westwards. They were introduced to Roman readers by Ammianus Marcellinus (XXXI, 2, 17–25) in the following words: "The Alans, whose various tribes it is unnecessary to list, are distributed through both parts of the world. But even if they are separated from each other by wide areas and as nomads wander through immeasurable areas, they have nevertheless gradually acquired a *single* name and are all called Alans on account of their customs, their wild way of life and the uniformity of their weapons. Huts or plough-shares are unknown to them and it is rather the case that they live from meat and milk, of which they have an abundance. They set off on their waggons, which they cover with curved bark from trees, and drive thus through limitless wildernesses. When they find pastures, they arrange the waggons in a circle and seek food like wild animals. When the food is exhausted, everything is put back on the waggons and they move on. It is there that the men couple with the women and there, too, the children are born and brought up. The waggons are their dwellings and this is why they feel at home wherever they are. Their livestock is driven in front of them, no attempt being made to keep large and small creatures in separate groups. They have a particular preference for horses. The plains there are always green and there are also regions with a profusion of fruit. Thus they nowhere suffer from a lack of food or fodder which is available in abundance due to the moist soil and the numerous rivers. All those who cannot fight because of age or sex remain by the waggons and do light work. The boys practise riding from an early age and even consider it despicable to go on foot. Trained in a variety of disciplines, all are practised warriors (this is why the Persians, also Scythians by origin, are also very experienced warriors). Almost all Alans are slim and good-looking people with medium-blond hair and quite a wild look in their eyes. They are agile in the use of their light weapons. They are very like the Huns in everything but more moderate in their whole way of life. Robbing and hunting, they venture as far as the Palus Meotis and to the Cimmerian Bosporus (Strait of Kerch) but likewise to Armenia and Media. While quiet and peaceful people wish for leisure, they find pleasure in war and danger. Only he is considered fortunate who breathes his last in battle. He who becomes old and leaves this world by a natural death is reviled by them as degenerate and cowardly. They con-

sider it particularly laudable to kill a man, to cut off his head and remove his skin, which they hang on their horses as a decoration. They have no temples and no sacred places; not even a rush-covered hut can be seen anywhere. In accordance with Barbarian custom, it is rather the case that they thrust a drawn sword into the ground which they honour as the god of war and the protector of their homes. In a strange way, they attempt to explore the future. Thus they collect straight branches of willow and put these in a certain order at a particular time, reciting secret magic formulas. They then know exactly what is predicted for them. Slaves are unknown to them since they are all of noble race. As their leaders (chiefs), they still choose men who enjoy respect through long experience of war."

Ammianus thus provides a vivid and basically accurate picture of a nomadic tribe still living in the conditions of a primitive society in which there are no divisions of class. The remarks about the "noble" origin of all and the non-existence of slaves really are evidence of an egalitarian structure which was only gradually modified by features of a military democracy. Naturally enough, subjugation by the Huns and their travels westward

Cicada fibulae from the period of the Great Migration

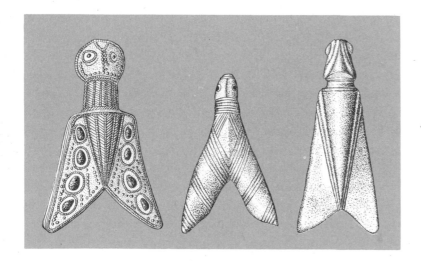

caused a rapid advance in their social development so that the branch of the Alans which united with the Vandals in Spain and then participated in the forming of a state in North Africa attained a level within a few decades which already combined characteristics of a slave-owning society with those of an early feudal order. This was a vastly accelerated process which would have been unthinkable without fairly close contact and confrontations with the forms of society which had emerged in the Imperium Romanum and with the Mediterranean mode of production and development of civilization. It can already be seen from this part of the story of the Alans to what a great extent external factors can accelerate or restrict social development. A whole series of tribes which took part in the Barbarian migrations and which had already passed beyond the level of development of the Alans as described by Ammianus but were caught up in the migrations at a later stage or only little by little, made the transition to a class society and to the establishment of a state-structure at an appreciably later date. This applies, for instance, to tribes and peoples on German soil such as the Saxons or Thuringians. The fact that these tribes were mostly able to create a more independent and stronger civilization in the course of a slower process of transformation is another story to which an occasional reference is made later.

The Huns

More attention has to be paid to the Huns, who were far more important for the beginning and early stages of the Barbarian migrations. They were a group of nomadic tribes which, like the Mongols of Genghis Khan, probably originated in the eastern part of Central Asia. Theirs was only a loose association and it was only the writers of the day who grouped them under the designation of Huns on account of certain outward features that they had in common. In Chinese sources, their appearance on the scene dates from the end of the 3rd century B.C. at the latest under the name of Hung-no (or Hsiungnu). After B.C. 214, the Great Wall was erected as a defence against them and Chinese armies later succeeded in annexing part of the Hun territory. The vigorous resistance encountered in the East may have encouraged the Huns to turn towards the West. Their structure must have remained at an early stage for a long time but it also acquired elements of a military democracy. The extent to which they had already for a temporary period given up their nomadic habits and adopted the Chinese life-style is outside the scope of the present book. After the middle of the 4th century, large groups of those tribes which from now on went down in history as the Huns appeared in the area around the Caspian Sea and the Sea of Azov. From here, they had the choice of advancing southwards through the Caucasus or taking the offensive in a westerly direction. In actual fact, thrusts were made in both directions but it was only the gradual build-up (after 370) of the massive advance through Southern Russia and into Central Europe and the Balkans that achieved epoch-making dimensions. From that moment when the Huns appeared in the district around the Sea of Azov and subjugated Alans and Goths, they naturally also arrived on the horizon of the authors of late Antiquity who, confronted with a strange and particularly repulsive people, characterized them accordingly. Of the various forceful reports about the Huns by Jordanes, Zosimus, Hieronymus, Ammianus Marcellinus and others, it is that by Ammianus which is without doubt the most revealing. XXXI, 2 contains the following description: "The people of the Huns, practically unknown from the older sources, dwells on the other side of the swamps around the Palus Meotis near the Polar Sea and is of incredible wildness. Since deep lines are cut with a knife in the cheeks of the children immediately after birth so that the beard which grows after a certain time is checked by wrinkled scars, they age without a beard and, like eunuchs, have to do without this decoration. They all have stumpy, powerful legs and a muscular neck but are so disfigured and bent that they could be taken for two-legged beasts or roughly hewn figures such as are found to the right and left of bridges. Although they are of human form, they have become so hardened by their way of life that they need no fire or seasoned food but live on the roots of wild plants and the half-raw meat of any animal which they place between their thigh and

the back of their horse for a short time to warm it up. They never stay under a firm roof but avoid houses like graves which are divorced from life. They do not even have a rush-covered hut but wander aimlessly through the mountains and forests and from their early years are accustomed to enduring cold, hunger and thirst. Only in extreme cases of distress do they go under a sheltering roof, so insecure do they feel there. They clothe themselves in linen or mouse-skins. There is no special clothing for inside or outside. Once they have put their head through such a shirt of dirty hue, they only take it off or change it when it is worn out and falls to pieces. They cover their head with a round cap and their hairy legs with goatskin. Their shoes are not made on lasts and hinder them from walking freely. Thus they are no good at all at fighting on foot but are perfectly at home on their tough and ugly horses, which they sometimes ride side-saddle when they relieve themselves. It is on horseback that each one of this people buys and sells, eats and drinks and, bent across the narrow neck of his steed, takes a deep sleep, filled with pleasant dreams. In this posture, they also hold joint discussions about public matters. They do not allow themselves to be ruled by strict kings but are content with an improvised leadership by their chiefs and in this way overcome every problem. They sometimes challenge their adversaries to do battle and they fight in a wedge-shaped battle-order, uttering a penetrating hue and cry. Since they are lightly armed and can rapidly perform unexpected manoeuvres, they sometimes ride out in a fan-like formation and attack without keeping to a pre-determined order. Causing fearful slaughter, they gallop to and fro and, due to their fleetness, they are scarcely seen when they penetrate a stronghold or plunder an enemy camp. They might be called the most fearful of all warriors since they fight from a distance with darts which have a skilfully fitted bone in place of the usual metal tip ... but fight man against man without regard to their own life. They avoid dangerous sword-thrusts but capture their enemies with braided lassoes, entangling the arms and legs of those resisting them and preventing them from riding or running. None of them ploughs or ever touches a plough since they have no permanent dwellings but roam around without a home, laws or an

Type of the Przewalski horse

ordered way of life, in flight with their waggons, as it were. This is where their women sew their dirty garments, sleep with their men, bring their children into the world and bring up their boys until adolescence. None can answer the question of whence he comes since he was conceived at one place, born at another and brought up at a third and even more remote one.—Faithless in treaties, they change their mind according to the wind, are easily excited and yield to every passion. Like animals without the gift of reason, they know neither honour nor perfidy, are ambiguous and have respect neither for a religion nor for even mere superstition. Yet they burn with a limitless greed for gold. They are so inconsistent and excitable that they often, on one and the same day, part from their comrades and then make it up with them again just as quickly without anyone having calmed them down."

The wide-ranging ethnological description of the Huns included by Ammianus in his history of the first years of the Bar-

barian invasions provides food for thought in many respects. As in his portrait of the Alans, this historian based his remarks on contemporary sources, some of which were good while others were somewhat unreliable. It was clear, of course, that soldiers and officials who somehow had come into contact with the Huns or had even been defeated by them would accordingly exaggerate the wildness and total invincibility of these enemies who had newly arrived on the Roman scene. Taking account of the contemporary taste of his readers at Rome itself in particular, Ammianus himself embellished this picture of the Barbarians accordingly, using descriptions given in earlier sources. To some extent, his account follows on from the first classic description of the Scythians and Sarmatians in Herodotus (Book IV), which seemed reasonable since it was certainly a question of tribal groups which were threatening Roman civilization from the Northeast. Thus the picture of the Huns presented by Ammianus and other historians of Late Antiquity is to be seen as part of a more general Barbarian typology in which there are many common features. In actual fact, all these tribes possessed the common feature of being primitive and wild in the Barbarian manner and incomprehensible from the viewpoint of classical education since they were naturally unsophisticated. The specific features of the Huns—most of which are historically authentic—are the following: their way of life, especially their clothing (even the men kept their legs covered), food, weapons (especially their much-feared composite bow), hunting and their combat techniques. Extreme even for primitive tribal conditions, these corresponded to what was possible for a people of mounted nomads who really had adapted themselves to the conditions of being constantly on the move and constantly in conflict with settled populations of the most diverse kinds. Ammianus and other sources, too, describe the Alans and other nomadic tribes as typically having more understanding and being more emotionally perceptive than the Huns, which was due to the situation which had largely been created after 375 or thereabouts. If it was not the ideological opponent—normally rebellious slaves and coloni or the last representatives of paganism—who was disparaged in the atmosphere of the ever-present crisis, then the entire blame for the present adversity and for the destruction of material and intellectual values was heaped on the so-called Barbarians and primarily on the Huns. This is shown even more clearly by a few lines from the Court poet, Claudius Claudianus (end of 4th century) than by the words of Ammianus, although they echo the same feeling. In the first poem, "In Rufinum", I, 323 ff., it reads as follows: "Far away in the extreme East, in Scythia, there dwells a people on the other side of the icy Tanais; there never lived in the North a more infamous one; cruel are its customs, dreadful its appearance. It has never been accustomed to toil. Its food is what it can take. It knows neither seed nor harvest. They consider it honourable and beautiful to cruelly wound the cheeks and the forehead and to swear oaths by their murdered parents. The cloud-born Centaurs are not more closely joined to the bodies of horses than they. Unsurpassed in fleetness, they attack abruptly from their place of concealment."

The most serious error in the ancient assessment of the Barbarians in general and the Huns in particular was, of course, that these groups were considered incapable of development. The frequent comparison with animals, which is of particular interest for the history of religion, illustrates in an especially dramatic manner just how gravely people tried to deceive themselves about the dangers associated with these "Barbarians". It was their outward characteristics, such as savageness, their speed in battle and, at best, also their treacherousness which were stressed whereas little attention was paid to the capability of very rapid social, political and cultural development displayed by most of these tribes. Thus some of the Huns soon left the fully nomadic stage behind them. Under Alan and Germanic influence, a consolidation took place of the social differences which had certainly emerged during the time they were in contact with the Chinese empire. It was not long before numerous "noble families" began to appear among the Huns, chiefs with large followings and herds of animals and, with the transition to an early form of State with many feudal traits, even kings. Special variations emerged, such as the dual kinship of two brothers (Bleda and Attila), while the speed of social development depended on other differentiating factors from outside in the form of Roman influences and from within via the partly subjugated Germanic and Iranian tribes. It was possible that many of the smaller Hun tribes, which had helped Attila to set up his Pannonian empire, were slow in developing beyond the nomadic stage with its strong links with animals, and particularly the horse, as reflected in the animal-style of many of their ornaments. Others passed through this process more rapidly since they provided officers, officials or envoys whose task it was to supervise the subjugated tribes and to carry out negotiations with the Romans. Certain traits of a warrior caste must have continued to develop both in the area held by the Huns and among those in the service of Rome. There is frequent mention of Hun chiefs and *buccellarii* in Western Rome and in Byzantium. Next to the Goths, they even provided the main contingent of the mercenaries who had to still hold up the reeling Imperium in this or that manner. The divergent development of the Huns is the result of a very rapid process, almost constantly accelerating

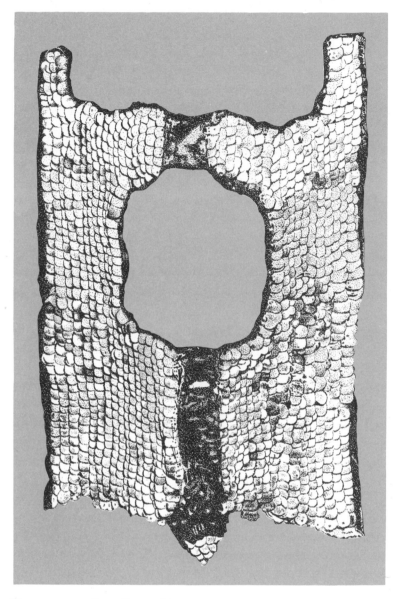

Horse-armour from Doura-Europos

and lasting to the mid-5th century, which affected not only other Turkish and Mongolian tribes but also Germanic peoples such as the Gepidae, Ostrogoths and Burgundians.

At the centre of the emergent Pannonian empire of the Huns, the basic features of this development were as follows. The earlier social basis of the Huns in the form of clans and tribes gradually declined, a major change resulting from the absorption of people from other tribes and a powerful influx of slaves. Under Attila, at any rate, whose residence by the Theiss resembled a shanty town more than anything else, a new stratum developed side-by-side and over the old structure. Characterized by the Byzantine historian Priscos as *logádes*, this stratum can be understood as a kind of bureaucratic nobility, of which there were similar groups in the other Barbarian states. These retainers of the king, some of whom were Huns while the remainder came from other tribes, had to carry out all the major functions essential for the running of the large and rapidly emerging empire which at one time extended from the Baltic to the lower reaches of the Danube. They were generals and officers, tax-collectors, envoys and members of the Royal staff. In this connection, attention has been correctly drawn (F. Altheim) to the importance of the scribes and the emergent bureaucracy in the Hun empire, short-lived as it was. It is likely that the illiterate Huns—to recall the remarks of Ammianus—first learned the art of writing from their Iranian neighbours. For official requirements and perhaps also for literary and commercial purposes, there was a sudden increase in the demand for people who could write and, if possible, knew several languages. Priscos reports that Hun scribes read out to the king the notes that they had taken in their own language but there were also officials who had to speak Gothic, Latin and probably Greek as well. Attila was in communication with almost all the states and tribes within reach and had to be concerned with establishing an efficient system of correspondence and a continuous flow of information, a basic condition for all the political and diplomatic moves by which he played a weighty role in the "concert" of the great powers of the time. The written form also contributed of course to an efficient system of domination over the Huns and the numerous allied and subjugated tribes. With the aid of this bureaucracy and a constantly updated military organization—archery tactics were greatly modified and some mounted units were equipped as cuirassiers—Attila succeeded in consolidating the internal structure of his new state and its relations with other powers. He kept a personal check on as much as possible, being assisted in this by his relations, who were also given the right of secundo-geniture. In other respects, an important part was played by the system of *logádes* since these retainers, unlike the vassals of a more advanced feudalism, remained absolutely dependent on the king. Even if they themselves had retainers and slaves and large domains, they were nevertheless always dependent on further allowances. Thus they always had to be available for the king who, in his turn, by exerting pressure on the frontier areas and the two Roman states which paid him tribute in a hardly disguised way, provided a steady supply of gold and booty for the "shareholders" in his empire. The parasitic activities of Attila naturally led to a further stage of exhaustion in the Roman economy and, on the other hand, also restricted the economic development of the areas under the direct rule of the Huns. It is true that most of the invading nomads, gradually becoming settled, changed over to an intensive system of livestock keeping and even tillage but this process was again delayed by the frequent wars and their far-reaching military obligations for the male subjects of Attila. The rapid disintegration of the empire caused at least some of the Huns and the tribes which had freed themselves to return to a nomadic or semi-nomadic life.

It was already clear that the assertion of the Late Antique sources that the Huns had no culture or religion was a pure invention, although, of course, this statement was made in good faith by the historians concerned. It must be stressed, however, that in one respect they were more or less correct. The Hun culture and religion was indeed largely based on something strange, on the adoption, assimilation and propagation of achievements from all over the world, beginning with obscure events which took place in the confrontation with China. Naturally, there were also completely independent elements in this which turcologists and scholars in related fields such as archaeology and comparative religion are now attempting to identify. Alliterative sayings and early sagas of the Huns going back to the time before they had a written language are certainly original and in most cases are probably the common heritage of many Turki tribes. To say the least, the nomadic style of life had a long tradition. The writers of Late Antiquity considered that the Huns had practically no ethical or religious background. It is precisely this alien character, so unlike Antique humanity, which makes it easy to recognize this background. This is to be understood primarily as the peculiar belief, with marked magical traits, of Asiatic hunting and horse-riding peoples which may still be best designated as shamanism. However, the shamanist ecstatics also had totemistic traits. In all cases, a close relation with the animal world can be found, not only with game creatures (bear, elk, stag, various birds) but also riding animals (horse). In this imaginary world, the line between man and beast is indistinct. Through long training and the use of certain psycho-physical techniques such as drug-taking and dancing, the shaman is able to put himself in an ecstatic state in which he loses his substantiality, establishes contact with spirits or even identifies himself with them. This identification mainly refers to animals which were regarded as divine animal forbears. Even Genghis Khan believed a grey wolf was his ancestor while his wife thought she was descended from a white hind. Such beliefs often became shallow and superficial and it is hard to say whether golden wolf heads, which are said in Chinese reports to have been placed above their banners by certain groups of Huns, still signified a credo or whether they were only symbolic or even only a mark of identification. Nevertheless, it is significant that animal motifs continued to be used on craft products, especially weapons and equipment. Foreign smiths and other metalworkers, particularly Chinese, Iranian and Teuton, aided the Huns in this, but it was the latter who encouraged and ordered the widespread depiction of animals. Animal symbolism on weapons, fibulae, belt-clasps, felt appliqué or woollen embroidery work mostly depicts a great deal of movement, especially when friezes or sometimes whole groups of animals are shown fighting or being hunted. Of considerable artistic merit are the pictures of animals on pots and

31 Pommel in horsehead form (Jankovich Collection, Hungarian National Museum, Budapest). This dates from the 7th century and is from the "second Germanic animal style period". An interesting detail are the almandine or carnelian inlays marking the eye and ear.

32 Gold goblet from the Avarian "princely treasure" of Bócsa (Hungarian National Museum, Budapest). This magnificent vessel was part of a find which also included a gold belt, a quiver with gold mountings, a sword, a drinking horn and 25 arrow-tips, from which conclusions may be drawn regarding the life-style and level of culture of its owner.

33 Bronze kettle from Törtel (Hungarian National Museum, Budapest). The rim is decorated with semi-circular, fibula-like drooping ornaments. Vessels of this kind, which have been found as far as the Rhine, were closely related to the Hun invasion.

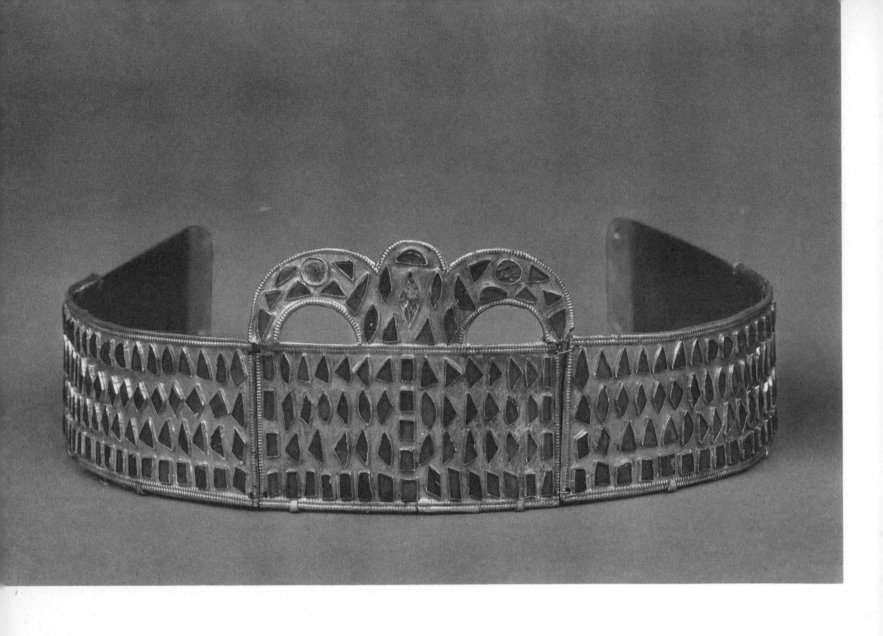

34 Crown (diadem) from Kerch (Römisch-Germanisches Museum, Cologne). This magnificent work of art comes from the civilization of the Crimean Goths. The arch-shaped upper part above the centre of the crown is obviously intended to represent two eagles' heads, the eyes of which are marked by lustrous green inlays.

35 Sword (spatha) with fragment of sheath (Badisches Landes-museum, Karlsruhe). This 56.9 cm long weapon was found in a grave at Altlussheim/Mannheim and dates from the middle of the 5th century. The handle and the sheath fragment are of fine workmanship (gold foil and gold mountings with almandine inlays). The buckle with almandine cellular work is of unknown origin, dates from the 5th or 6th centuries and is now in the Römisch-Germanisches Zentral-museum in Mainz.

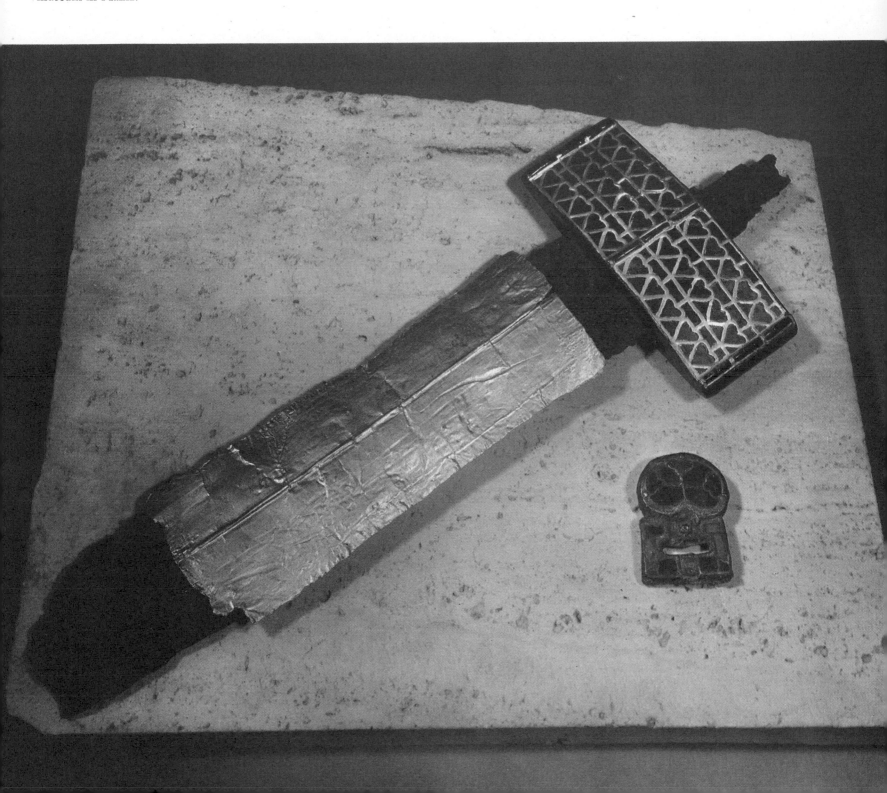

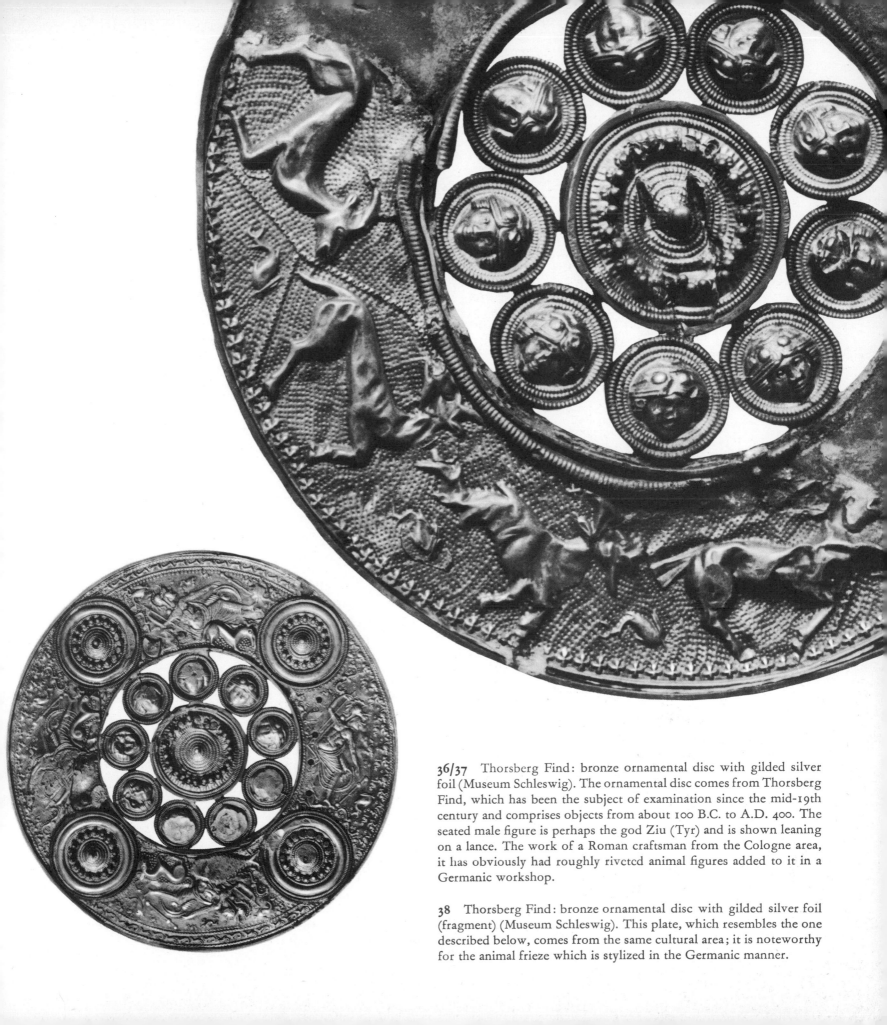

36/37 Thorsberg Find: bronze ornamental disc with gilded silver foil (Museum Schleswig). The ornamental disc comes from Thorsberg Find, which has been the subject of examination since the mid-19th century and comprises objects from about 100 B.C. to A.D. 400. The seated male figure is perhaps the god Ziu (Tyr) and is shown leaning on a lance. The work of a Roman craftsman from the Cologne area, it has obviously had roughly riveted animal figures added to it in a Germanic workshop.

38 Thorsberg Find: bronze ornamental disc with gilded silver foil (fragment) (Museum Schleswig). This plate, which resembles the one described below, comes from the same cultural area; it is noteworthy for the animal frieze which is stylized in the Germanic manner.

drinking vessels of Teutonic and Avarian origin, which are mostly of a later date but go back to the same source.

The age of Attila shows that the shamanistic animal creed had not totally died out at all, although in the meantime the Huns had come into contact with numerous alien religions and faiths. Huns who joined the Romans—which the king tried to prevent by draconian punishments and political pressure—became Christians, others probably adopted Iranian religions such as Manichaeism, still in its early stages at that time. That Attila, astute politician and diplomat that he was, could still adhere to the old beliefs may seem astonishing but there is considerable evidence which proves it. He stressed to his people that a cow had led to the recovery of a divine sword, through the possession of which he felt himself appointed as the ruler of the world. Before the battle of Châlons, Attila consulted the oracles in a manner which was still current until fairly recently among many Mongols, the Hun priests reading the future from the entrails of sacrificial animals, in particular from the tripes, and from the marks on bones from which the flesh has been removed. On this occasion, they prophesied the defeat of Attila but also the death of the enemy commander, whereupon Attila opened the battle. In his last campaign against Italy, he was also obviously influenced by a bird omen. While out surveying the position, the king observed that storks which had nested on the roofs of Aquileia were taking their young into the countryside for safety. His commanders had not been able to agree on the siege of the town, considering the heavy losses to be expected. Attila now told his army of what he had seen as a prophecy of the imminent fall of the besieged town and it was not long before the fortress was actually in his hands. Even assuming that political astuteness and convincing demagoguery played a part in all this, it is certain that Attila was only able to assert his viewpoint because he believed in his mission which, in such a strange manner, continued the ancient tradition of sacrifices and animal observations. To say the least, the thinking of the Huns at that time was still largely theriomorphic. They were consistent only in seeing animals as leaders which could find the right way or reveal the future. Thus the apparently primitive approach of the Huns re-flected an ancient tradition of hunters and nomads who depended for their existence on animals, around which the whole of their life was centred. On the other hand, it also mirrored a consistently developed stage of civilization in which the attempt was made to link the domination of animals with ascendancy over as many subject peoples as possible.

The scope of all this which was associated with the word "Hunnish", when regarded from this point of view, was astonishing and almost prompts the question whether it would be more accurate, for the epoch of Attila, to speak of the emergence of a new world empire with a significant standard even in the sphere of civilization. However, no clear answer can be given since too many elements had been borrowed from other peoples while his political ascendancy was too brief and unstable. The structure of the Hun empire was much looser than that of the Imperium Romanum, with which it is inevitably compared. Despite the bureaucracy of the Hun empire and its budding feudal elements, it was still founded to a much greater extent on force and the parasitic appropriation of a social product other than its own than that of Rome. To round off this picture of the Huns, it must also be remarked that the giant camp, made up of wooden palaces, tents and waggons, from which Attila ruled his empire, was totally unsuitable as a centre for a stable state and, indeed, even in the archaeological sphere, no significant trace of this state has survived.

The Germanic Tribes

If the Arab invasion of the Middle East and North Africa for the most part is disregarded, the principal peoples concerned in the Great Migration were the Germanic tribes which were followed, of course, by early Slav groups. Thus it is first a question of the early Germanic tribes and then of the larger Indo-Germanic group. The origin and first home of the Indo-Germanic peoples is much disputed. Apart from the makers of corded pottery of Central Germany, the *Bandkeramik* potters (pottery

39 Curved fibula from the grave of the Aleman princess of Wittislingen (Bayerisches Nationalmuseum, Munich). Of the curved fibulae of the Merovingian period, this example from the first half of the 7th century is particularly noteworthy. Of gilded silver with cellular inlay work, niello and filigree ornamentation, it is characterized by plait strips and animal decoration in the Germanic-Pontic animal style. On the reverse side with the inscription "UFFILA VIVAT IN DEO FELIX..." (May Uffila live joyfully in God) is the mark of the goldsmith Wigerig.

decorated with banded lines in scratch technique) of the Danube area may also perhaps be regarded as members of the Indo-Germanic group. Evidence from the spheres of comparative linguistics and archaeology points to an early division of the Indo-Germanic (or Indo-European) peoples. At the present level of research, it is difficult and often impossible to draw linguistic and archaeological lines of division between the Germanic tribes and their Celtic, Illyrian and even Veneti neighbours. The first Germanic consonant shift from the 1st century B.C. shows, for instance, that the separation from Celtic had just taken place and that numerous loan-words from Celtic were needed (helmet from Negau). As even Tacitus in his *Germania* testifies, the very name "Germanic" is probably Celtic in origin or at least transferred under Celtic influence from a single tribe to the whole group. However, both the Celtic and the Germanic interpretation of the name itself as "the fierce ones", "the bawlers", "the friends", "the Thing comrades" or "the outstanding ones" presents problems so that the Veneti or the Illyrians may also have had a hand in the origin of the name. In the far distant and common past, Germanic had close links with all the other related Indo-European linguistic spheres, especially within the Centum group. However, we are more concerned here with the cultural interrelations in the period of the Great Migration itself.

Archaeological and linguistic criteria indicate that the Teutons originally came from Southern Scandinavia and Jutland, although parts of Northern Germany also played a part in the process of development of the Germanic tribes.

A process of ethnogeny covering many centuries culminated for most tribes in the stage of military democracy which was retained up to the period of the Great Migration. This took different forms and the tribes moving eastwards (mostly the East Germanic tribes) had already introduced a kingship confined to certain families while the western tribes merely had a warrior nobility heading the broad mass of the common freemen. However, even Tacitus in his *Germania* indicates that a rapid further differentiation took place in this nobility through contact with the Romans and through "dynastic" family relations. A particular characteristic of the warrior nobility of higher

rank was their following or retinue, an institution which was also common among the Celts, in which younger warriors, bound by oath, acquired warlike qualities in the service of a proven leader. These followings, often with an internal structure, frequently consisted of hundreds of men and naturally enhanced the power and reputation of their individual chiefs who, in many cases, was also the commander of a tribal contingent (*dux*) or, with the development of larger tribes, even king (*rex*). Finally, the following continued to exist in the shape of the buccellarii units already mentioned.

The social pyramid now comprised also a gradually increasing stratum of slaves and freedmen who—in line with the character of the stage of development—lived in a specific form of patriarchal slavery. At first they may have been dependants of the patriarchal clans which now increasingly broke up into individual families. The smaller family groups then achieved economic independence since they acquired land and livestock according to the rank and importance of the head of the family. Despite the patriarchal social structure, a major part was played by the womenfolk. Monogamy was the normal state of affairs and, although the tribal nobility and the priesthood were dominated exclusively by men, great importance was nevertheless attached to the counsel of women, especially the soothsayers.

Domestic personal possessions also included slaves and freedmen although many of these had their own farms and only had to deliver a part of the surplus product. The slaves were naturally excluded from voting in the public assemblies.

The more the power of the tribal nobility or certain groups within this nobility increased, the greater the decline in the importance of the public assembly or Thing, as it was termed. The selection of the head of the tribe, decisions about war and peace and similar important competences passed more and more into the hands of the tribal nobility which also acquired an increasingly greater share in the means of production and articles of trade than the mass of the common freedmen. Not least under the influence of the retainers, who had become more important since the beginning of the Great Migration by reason of their military function and who, as service nobility, scorned any

Marcomanni round-house

The more that metalworking techniques became widespread —often under Roman influence—the more intensive became the manner in which agriculture and the crafts were pursued. Bigger yields of corn and vegetables (peas, beans, carrots, turnips) and hemp and flax were obtained by the use of the harrow, the iron ploughshare and manuring with marl. Wine-growing and the cultivation of new kinds of fruit (cherry, plum, peach) spread here and especially in the Rhine-Danube area from the South and Southeast. From the Latin loan-words in Germanic and German, it is possible to trace the spread not only of certain plants and animals but also of many techniques, trade designations and names in some detail in many cases, and occasionally it is even possible to fix the date of their adoption. From the time of the first contact with Rome and the Roman advance to the Rhine-Danube line, words appeared such as *kaupo* (merchant), *kaiser* (Caesar), *kapillon* (haircutting), *militon* (to serve as a soldier) and many others. Since the traditional wooden mode of construction with wattle walls covered with plaster was largely replaced by stone masonry techniques, people naturally adopted the corresponding loan-words such as *Ziegel, Mauer, Kalk, Mörtel, Estrich, Pflaster, Keller, Speicher, Kammer, Fenster* or *Pforte*. Even the Roman cuisine, with the high standard it had already achieved, is reflected in words such as *Koch, Kessel, Schüssel, Pfanne, Becher, Bottich, Bütte, Flasche* or *Kelch* and the plants associated with it in *Kohl, Rettich, Kürbis, Zwiebel, Kümmel, Fenchel, Baldrian, Enzian, Kamille* and so on. The same applies to *Winzer, Kelter, Presse, Spund, Trichter* and *Kufe*. The trade carried on or influenced by Rome can be found in terms such as *Kiste, Sack, Zins, Zoll, Münze, Pfund, Esel, Saum* or *Maultier*. In connection with this, mention can be made of words which were first associated with military applications and then with the communications network and its role in commerce (*Strasse, Pfosten, Pfahl, Wall,* etc.). Nevertheless, it would be wrong to over-emphasize the influence of Antique Roman culture on Germanic as well as on Celtic, Illyrian and Slav civilizations. Most of the achievements of these groups in the sphere of material civilization were of an independent nature or resulted from exchange within the same stage of culture. In general, it was only the improved

kind of productive work, serious contradictions emerged in the individual Germanic communities. There was a big gap between the slaves and the prosperous ploughmen who kept livestock and grew not only grain but also vegetables. Differences on a considerably greater scale, however, existed between the leaders of mighty followings and the smaller peasants, merchants and free artisans who often could only achieve a certain social and economic security under the patronage of more powerful persons. The actual migrations tended to accentuate these differences rather than mitigate them since even the parasitic appropriation of Roman property mainly benefited the nobility and its followings.

techniques and processed raw materials which were adopted from the South and these were used to raise the local mode of production which was already of a respectable standard.

Thus—to mention only two examples—the forbears of the Teutons had already achieved a noteworthy standard in textile production and metalworking in the course of the Bronze Age. There was a steady decline in traditional clothing made from skins or leather. Linen underclothes were worn and looms were used to produce the woollen fabrics for making coats, smocks, caps and other garments. With the development of horse-riding, trousers (Old High German *bosa* or *bruch*—in English "hose" or "breeches") came into use, obviously from the example of the Eastern mounted peoples. In women's clothing, there appeared not only the fabric and cord skirt but also the bodice and hair-net. Weaving, fulling and garment-making exercised a mutual influence on each other and were certainly carried on as "home industries". Woodworking and to some extent pottery, too, were also the results of individual activities.

In the casting and forging of metals, however, the expert was of prime importance. It was not long before the rapidly specialized techniques, associated with a variety of tools and raw materials, could only be utilized by specially trained craftsmen who were of high social standing in consequence. Even in the period of the Great Migration, smiths were frequently the subject of quarrels in the tribal nobility and this is reflected in the heroic sagas. Thus the legendary smith Wieland in the *Edda* is indeed a divine Alb (according to another version he is at least descended from a giant) but at the same time he is nevertheless the prisoner of King Nithuthr. To stop him from escaping, the king has him lamed but Wieland takes a fearsome revenge. He decapitates the two sons of the king and makes tools from their bones. He then rapes the king's daughter and makes his escape through the air after describing his revenge to the now powerless king. It is true that the *Edda* was written at a fairly late date but many of its details are derived from earlier events and developments. Early "parallels" of Wieland in the *Edda* can be quoted without difficulty. In his *Vita Severini*, written about 511, Eugippius tells of wandering goldsmiths who were forced to work for a Rugian queen in the Danube area of Austria (*Vita Sev.* 8). They made a hostage of the young prince Friedrich and in this way gained their freedom. Perhaps this incident was the inspiration for the *Wieland Saga*.

After the appearance of the iron ploughshare, the lowly peasants also needed a smith who could make implements such as scythes, axes, hammers, chisels and saws. The making of weapons was likewise a matter of first importance for metalworkers. There was a great demand for cast bronze swords, daggers and battle-axes, partly because a certain quantity of these were also exported. Initially, the most popular weapon was the battle-axe which had been developed from the Neolithic stone-axes. Its place was subsequently taken by a variety of spears and swords with skilfully shaped hilts, most of which were finely decorated even at this stage. As yet, there were not many helmets but shields (round shields of bronze) were very widely used as a defensive weapon. Once smiths had acquired the skill of making exquisite parade weapons, they were naturally also prepared to make small bronze ornaments and then articles of precious metals. Brooches, necklets and ornamental clasps bear witness to the constant progress in techniques and in artistic appreciation. Geometrical decoration characterizes most of the small objets d'art but later the animal motifs of the East also appeared.

There is a notably sharp divergence of opinions concerning the intellectual civilization of the Teutons both overall and in the individual spheres (poetry, religion). This starts with the question of runic writing which was formerly thought to date back to 100 B.C. However, the earliest proven examples only go back to the 3rd century A.D. and are associated with a North Italian alphabet. The first known runic alphabet, the older Futhark as it is known, contains 24 signs, like Latin, but was only used as secret writing for magical purposes. The Nordic runic alphabet, consisting of 16 signs and in use around A.D. 800, was also used for profane records. The entire complex of Germanic ideology and religion, which cannot be examined in every detail here and must be restricted to a period of up to A.D. 500 at the latest, presents a similar picture to that of corresponding phenomena among the Huns. The dependence on developments

of neighbouring tribal groups (Celts, Illyrians) was considerable and often it is not possible to draw a clear line between them.

Thus the many survivals of Totemism and Shamanism which are found among the Germanic tribes of the Bronze and Iron Ages must have come from the common past of the Indo-European peoples. The supposed descent of individual families and even entire tribes from sacred animals (stag, boar, wolf) also recalls a far-reaching Eurasian tradition, just like the etiological legends according to which certain groups of people were descended from trees or water spirits. It is possible that the ancient veneration of animals is linked with ancestor worship which can be associated both with cremation and intact burial. Homage to the dead also included the often sumptuous articles placed in the graves of high-ranking persons, especially in the so-called "princely" graves. Here there are parallels with other civilizations, such as the Scythian kurgans of Eastern Europe or even the cupola tombs of Mycenae.

Little by little, a Germanic "pantheon" developed, which was probably centred around tribal tutelary deities. They seldom had temples dedicated to them but were usually worshipped in sacred groves, where people gathered at appointed times for religious ceremonies which frequently still included human sacrifices (especially prisoners of war and unsuccessful kings who had lost their charisma or kingly status). These were dominated by the priests, often members of the tribal nobility, who usually put their own interests first, however. They alone performed the sacrifices, condemned offenders and tried to divine the future with the aid of oracles (by the drawing of lots or by the interpretation of entrails). These human sacrifices, like many of the customs of the Alans described by Ammianus Marcellinus or of the Huns, derived from an ancient tradition of cannibalism which was unrecognized for the most part since it had been upgraded. The original purpose of such practices can still be identified, however, when it is realized that the idea was to gain an indirect benefit from these bloody sacrifices by strengthening the gods and then hoping for assistance from these deities who were already widely regarded as anthropomorphic. The Roman *do, ut des* is certainly still valid for this stage of Germanic polytheism.

Incidentally and as a reflection of the social development, this divine heaven was dominated by a small number of personages who claimed absolute priority. Wodan (or Odin in North Germanic) was a personification of the forces of Nature and especially of the storm but, with the advance of a belief in a life after death, he emerged also as the leader of souls and the god of the dead. For the Northern Germanic peoples, Odin was the lord of Valhalla, to which the souls of warriors slain in battle

Germanic weaving techniques

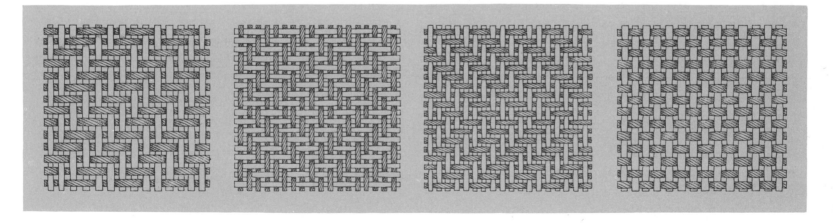

were led by Valkyries, the "choosers of the slain". "For those who come to Odin, the house is easy to recognize from its outward appearance. The house is covered with shafts, the hall is covered with shields, the benches are strewn with coats of mail and a wolf hangs to the west of the door, over which an eagle lowers its pinions"—thus reads the description of Valhalla, the heaven of this bellicose society, in the *Edda*. Everything here is dedicated to the glorification of the feats of the dead who in this way have achieved fulfilment or liberation. Wodan, however, had still other functions, being regarded as a sorcerer, with knowledge of the runes, as a god of healing, as the Prince of the Aesir and as the Lord of Heaven and Earth. He thus represented a step towards monotheism, which must have helped the Germanic tribes from the 4th century onwards to make the transition to Christianity in the Arianistic form, in which God the Father is regarded as being of first importance. Like other prominent Germanic deities (Donar = Thor, Freyr, Freya), Wodan likewise had very human traits, including furtiveness and unpredictability in particular. His subsequent decline to the "Wild Huntsman" is probably associated with his original function as god of the storm. Among the lower sections of the population, Wodan and the other high deities were without doubt not very popular, this being confirmed by the small number of relicts found. The majority of the poor preferred to honour the deities of vegetation and fertility who populated the home and farmyard, fields and forests, springs and mountains. There was an exceptional local diversity, female deities, such as the fertility-cult matrons of the Rhineland, being generally favoured. Many of these have endured right up to the present in the form of folklore and poetry (Frau Holle).

The crisis and decline of the Germanic religion is reflected in the myths about Baldr, son of Odin, who was the dying and resurgent god of fertility, and especially in the apocalyptic of the end of the world as described in the *Völuspa*, a part of the *Edda*. In this, the aspirations of the warriors unite with those of the broad masses who were opposed to the constant warlike ventures and the whole narrative is naturally already permeated with the Christian critique of these inadequate and much too human gods.

Typical of this is that in the "twilight of the gods" (Ragnarök) of the *Edda* the defeated gods also drag down their enemies to destruction with them. Thus room is made for a brighter future for the supernatural powers themselves.

The Goths

Here, too, the first question that has to be asked concerns the homeland and origins of these people who had such a decisive influence on important phases of the Great Migration. Jordanes, an historian of the 6th century writing in Latin and himself a descendant of a noble Gothic family, had this to say in his history of the Goths (Geten) which was based on a lost book by the Senator Cassiodorus (1 ff.): "In the North, in the salt floods of the ocean, there lies Scandinavia, a great island. It is the shape of a lemon-leaf with indented sides, long and compact ... Pomponius Mela reports that it lies in the Kattegat, into which the ocean pours. Its nearer coast lies opposite the Vistula which springs from the mountains of Sarmatia, flows into the ocean in three mouths facing Scandinavia and separates Germania and Scythia. In the East, this island has a vast inland sea, from which the Vagus flows as from a belly and rolls its watery masses to the ocean. In the West, there extends an immeasurable sea which also encircles the island in the North—but here it is unnavigable. From there, an arm branches out, curving far and forming the Germanic Sea. There are also many small islands here. On account of the bitter cold, the sea freezes in winter and this is how wolves come on these islands and lose their sight there. Thus this land is not only inhospitable for humans but even fearful for wild beasts.

On Scandinavia, of which we speak, there exist many different peoples but Ptolemy only gives the names of seven ... In the northerly regions, there lives a folk called Adogit where it is said that in mid-summer it is as bright as day for forty days and nights without interruption, in return, there are as many days and nights in winter without sunshine.

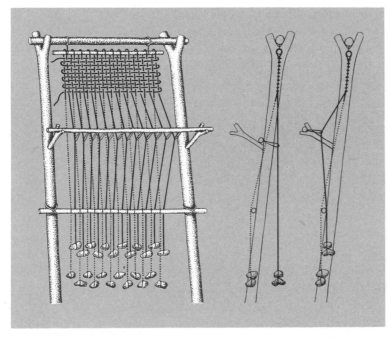

Schematic representation of a vertical loom and its mode of operation

Another people there are the Skrerefenni who do not live on corn but on game and birds' eggs; there are namely so many of these in the marshes that the birds multiply enough even when entire tribes eat their fill from them. Then there live in that place the Svear [the name refers to the Swedes, the author] who, like the Thuringians, breed excellent horses. From them there come, too, the sappherine skins to Rome which are particularly famed for their beautiful, deep black, although these are first obtained by trading with innumerable other tribes. Wretched as the life of the people of these regions otherwise is, they are nevertheless richly dressed. The district of the Svear borders that of a host of different peoples, namely the Theusti, Wagothi, Bergiones, Hallines and Liothides, who all inhabit fertile plains and are thus exposed to raids by other tribes. These tribes are followed by the Ahelmiles, the Finnaithi, the Ferviri and the Gauthi (the Goths), wild and warlike people. They all live in caves hewn in the rocks

like in castles, in the manner of wild beasts . . . According to old reports, it was from this island of Scandinavia, as if from a workshop or rather from a mother's lap that once the Goths under their King Berig came forth. They gave the name to that country which they trod on leaving their ships; for it is still called Gotiskandza today [the area referred to is between the mouths of the Oder and Vistula, the author]. From here they advanced to the lands of the Ulmerugi who at that time dwelt by the shores of the ocean, setting up their camps there and expelling the latter from their homeland. They also conquered and subjugated the neighbours of these people, the Vandals. As their numbers continued to increase, the Goths decided in the reign of Filimer, the son of Cadarig and the fifth king after Berig, to leave this place with their warriors and with their entire families. In the quest for a suitable homeland, they came into the country of the Scythians which they called Oium. Those of the Goths who crossed the river with Filimer and came to Oium took possession of the land desired. They soon came across the tribe of the Spali, whom they fought and conquered. As victors, they now advanced to the furthest frontiers of Scythia, bordering on the Black Sea. In their lays, the Goths record this with historical accuracy."

The last sentence is significant for the understanding of this text which to some extent recalls Ammianus and other ancient historians and "ethnologists". Via his middlemen, Jordanes—himself a Goth—goes back to the earliest Gothic traditions and thus, to a certain degree at least, reflects the matter-of-factness of earlier Goths and the surviving tribal groups of his time. He without doubt confused much of the surviving material at his disposal or, via the medium of Cassiodorus, at least made changes in it. Thus some of the ethnological data and even the tribal names that he lists are incorrect or inexact. His geographical information is likewise not very reliable since it was based on the beliefs of his time which had not advanced beyond the classical geography of Strabo and Ptolemy. Accurate knowledge, based on surveys and territorial explorations, was available only for the Mediterranean area itself and even this was known only in part to the best-known writers of the time, as is apparent even from the encyclopaedic work of Isidore of Seville.

As reported by Jordanes, the Goths and the Gepidae left Scandinavia (including the island of Gotland) in boats they had built themselves and arrived in the Vistula area. At that time—about the beginning of the Christian era—they already possessed a higher social and cultural level than that described by the chroniclers. Neolithic finds are rare and, seen as a whole, weapons and ornaments of bronze predominate, these being found in numerous burial places. Incidentally, from their homeland the Goths brought the custom of burying the bodies of their dead and this now began to replace the tradition of urn burial which had hitherto been customary in the Vistula district. To discuss the new attitude towards the dead that this implies would be too speculative here. The chief practical advantage of the new custom from the archaeological viewpoint is that many specific biological features can be checked from the remains of skeletons and confirmation obtained about the use of brooches, belt-clasps and other ornaments. For instance, amber necklaces with gold filigree beads have been found which, like bronze armbands and characteristic examples of embossed helmets, have revealed craftsmanship of a high standard. It is a significant fact that weapons are seldom found in the graves of the men and only their spurs were buried with them. It is likely that there is an association here with the cult of Nerthus which was also widespread among the Goths and for which there is also linguistic evidence. Nerthus, the mother-goddess, was regarded as essentially peaceful and when her cult-image was taken through the countryside on a waggon hauled by cattle, fighting ceased everywhere, a fact recorded even by Tacitus (*Germania* 40). However, it must be admitted that slaves were sacrificed to her.

The standard of house-building corresponded approximately to that of metalworking and ship and waggon construction. Houses were normally built of stakes with mud-covered wattle walls and a saddle roof. They averaged four or five metres by six metres in size but extensions often increased the actual floor area, at least for the storage of provisions. Every dwelling naturally had a hearth and paved ways facilitated communication within the hamlets or villages. The Gothic settlements in the new Southeastern European territory must have varied in appearance

since the same building materials were not available everywhere and there was also, of course, a strong two-way influence between the Goths and the tribes they subjugated, such as the Bastarni, Skiri, Alans and early Slav tribes. Some buildings of considerable size have been found, recalling those of Gotland where a site with four buildings has been excavated, the largest of which—comprising the residential quarters and the great hall—was 40 m long and 13 m wide. Linked with this but correspondingly smaller were a kitchen, storehouse and dormitory. Limestone was the building material here but considerable use was made of earth for filling. There was a partial upper storey as well, even at this date. In Southern Russia, it was the Goths of the Crimea in particular who achieved steady progress in domestic comfort. They split off from the main body of the tribe at an early date and isolated groups survived down to modern times. They soon established town-like settlements and buried their dead in the princely graves, as they are sometimes termed. These graves often closely resemble the earlier Scythian kurgans, consisting of large mounds containing burial shafts, chambers and niches. It is precisely these large graves and the many objects buried with the dead that provide a great deal of information about methods of construction and how these people lived. As in other civilizations, they reflect the life of at least the upper stratum of the population in a fairly complete manner.

Seen in its entirety, the material legacy of the South Russian period is indeed considerable. In ceramics and metalworking, numerous ideas were borrowed from the Iranian-Eurasian mounted peoples and from the Graeco-Roman sphere of influence. Many of these borrowings were developed further in a creative manner. This is shown not only by the transition from geometrical spiral forms and looped bands to the plaited band but also by the use of exquisite material (precious and semi-precious stones) and the introduction of new techniques such as filigree and granulation. One can speak of a mixed culture which was particularly advanced and apparent in metal articles since both Romano-Hellenistic motifs and forms, such as the diadem and the mitre-shaped helmets or ornamental fibulae, and an increasing number of animal-style objects, imitated from those

of the Eastern mounted peoples, were produced. This certainly evolved step by step as depictions of animals scarcely ever figured in the art of the older Germanic culture despite its totemistic and theriomorphic associations. The Germanic preference for the complexity of intertwined lines now became fused with the nomadic art of the animal style, generating a profusion of new themes and possibilities. Animals and animal heads appeared on belt clasps and buckles, "eagle" clasps being characteristic. Animal motifs were often used for fibulae as well and weapons were decorated not only with symbolic signs and magical runes but also with animal ornamentation.

This is obviously all embodied in the stage of civilization attained in Southern Russia which, admittedly, was not of a uniform nature. Above all, it was the peasant element, based on a settled life and peaceful cults such as that of Nerthus, which contrasted with the bellicose life-style deriving largely from the mounted nomads. There is clear evidence that weapons were adopted from the Iranian and Turkish peoples. The Goths introduced the cavalry lance (*contus*) and adopted from the East side-piece helmets and chain-mail. The Goths obviously passed on chain-mail reinforced with iron bars to the North since it also appeared in the district of Uppsala. Whereas the Goths in the Vistula area at the time of Tacitus fought with the short sword, in Southern Russia they used a long sword developed from a type of weapon used by the Sarmatians and Alans. The mounted warriors also used the lasso while the infantry forces, which were otherwise declining in importance, were equipped with the bow. Up to the 6th and 7th centuries, there is evidence of the decisive superiority of the Gothic cavalry—and of the Vandal and Alan mounted forces, too—which were practically unrivalled after the collapse of the Hun empire. In open battle, they were regarded as invincible.

These cultural and military achievements would have been unthinkable without corresponding developments in the social sphere. It can be shown that the military democracy of the Goths in Southern Russia soon experienced a vigorous development which proceeded side-by-side with the emergence of the kingship idea—Jordanes, of course, attributes the institution of kingship to Scandinavian emigrants. The tribal society was soon only reflected by a few surviving features since, in view of the increasing numbers of subjugated Bastarni, Skiri, Scythians, Sarmatians and Alans and the increasing pressure of unconquered tribes and peoples, a process of differentiation took place among the Goths themselves. In the course of this, the free Gothic peasants—who only occasionally took part in warlike campaigns—remained as such but the hereditary and warrior nobility acquired a superior social status which became increasingly more marked. The defensive struggles of the early South Russian period initiated this process which gained in momentum from the 3rd century onwards. After the Goths under their legendary King Ostrogotha had conquered the districts between the Don and the Dnieper and the Dniester, they advanced further in the direction of the Danube. During the 3rd century, so critical for Rome, they also launched numerous plundering expeditions which, often crossing the sea, took them deep into the Balkans as far as Greece and Asia Minor. The reasons for these far-ranging expeditions must have been largely of an economic nature. It is likely that the area in Southern Russia, which was inhabited by numerous other tribes, no longer provided enough food by the 3rd century, at least not for a society which did not cultivate the land to any great extent and needed vast pastures for its herds of cattle and horses. Perhaps a population explosion had occurred even at this early stage since it was a fact that the numerous Gothic districts could no longer be contained in an integrated state structure, even as loose as that in question. Thus the two large groups of the Ostrogoths (Grutungi, Austrogoti) and the Visigoths (Tervingi, Visigoti) took on a definite shape. Reference has already been made to the Crimean Goths. Other groups split off later, at least from the Visigoths, such as the so-called "Little Goths", who settled as peaceful herdsmen in the northern foothills of the Balkans. Although the early Gothic raids on cities north of the Black Sea (Olbia, Tomi) were expeditions by individual followings and districts, many of the invasions of the Roman Empire were certainly large-scale plundering campaigns and attempts to establish settlements, admittedly without co-ordinated planning or leadership. Thus, according to the exaggerated details of ancient historians, a giant column of 320,000 persons—warriors and their families, complete with waggons and herds of livestock —advanced southwards from the Dniester in 269/270. Although this land force was allegedly supported by a fleet of 2,000 vessels, only modest successes were achieved. Hampered by storms, the force did indeed pass through the Bosporus but could not take cities such as Byzantium or Kyzikos. The coasts of Greece and the islands of the Eastern Mediterranean were laid waste but no fortified city was captured, even though siege engines were employed. The intervention of the energetic Emperor Claudius II was a catastrophe for the Goths and their allies, the invaders being defeated by the Romans at Naissus (Nish) in a pitched battle. The numerous prisoners taken were enrolled in the legions, allocated to Roman legionaries or settled as coloni. The Gothic units and waggon-trains which survived were decimated still further by plagues and practically destroyed. The emperor could now justly assume the title of Gothicus Maximus since the Gothic pressure on the Imperial frontiers now ceased for a long time.

Despite this, the aggressive spirit of the Goths of this time remained unbroken. The followings of the kings and other members of the nobility often launched campaigns of a fairly modest nature to obtain booty, mostly in the form of gold and silver and slaves from alien tribes.

All this encouraged the development of a differentiated Gothic society which, to be sure, was halted again by the onrush of the Huns. The details of this process are even more difficult to reconstruct than the history of settlement of the late 3rd and 4th centuries which, for the Gothic area, shows at least as much if not more activity than that of the Germanic-Roman frontier districts along the Rhine where, in the meantime, the Alemans and Franks had moved over to the offensive.

By about 300, a considerable area was in the hands of the various Gothic groups. Large parts of Wallachia and Transylvania were occupied by the Visigoths while the Taifalae and the Gepidae, likewise Goths, had settled in other parts of these regions. Constantine the Great had difficulty in resisting the Gothic pressure along the frontier of the Lower Danube which was refortified and provided with a number of bridge-heads (e.g.

Oescus). Following an appeal for help from the Sarmatians living in the Banat, an army commanded by Constantine II in 332 defeated a part of these Goths, who now became firm federative allies of Rome for some 35 years. In return for annual payments, they undertook to defend the Danube frontier and the northern foreland. Large numbers of them at least finally adopted a settled, peasant way of life, this development being reinforced among many of these Visigoths by the process of Christianization which is closely associated with the name of Wulfila (Ulfilas).

Wulfila was not the first missionary on Gothic soil since as early as 325 there existed a diocese of Gothia under an Orthodox bishop by the name of Theophilus. This was clearly the area of the Crimean Goths who, in keeping with their geographical position, were the first to come under Christian and specifically Catholic influence. However, the efforts of Wulfila were incomparably more successful. Not everything is known about the life of this famous missionary bishop and translator of the Bible and he must have been the descendant of Cappadocian prisoners of war captured in one of the raids mentioned before. However, his father was certainly a Goth. Born about 310, he received a sound education, probably outside Gothic territory, which fitted him for a clerical office, at least as a lector. At any event, between 335 and 337 at the latest, he was a member of a delegation which was sent by the Goths to Constantine the Great. He now came under the influence of the Patriarch Eusebius of Constantinople, who must have been primarily responsible for his profession of homoiousian Arianism. He was consecrated evangelist bishop of the land of the Goths by the same Prince of the Church, probably in 341. Up to 348, he carried out his mission in the area north of the Danube but was then forced by a persecution of the Christians in this locality to seek refuge with his community in the Roman district south of the river. From here, he continued to carry on his work and it seems likely that he even gained influence over Fritigern, the prince of the district, and his retinue. The principal achievement of Wulfila, who died in 383, was not so much his work as a missionary, which was restricted to the Little Goths, but his translation of the Bible into Gothic, for which he had to start from the very beginning by creating an alphabet.

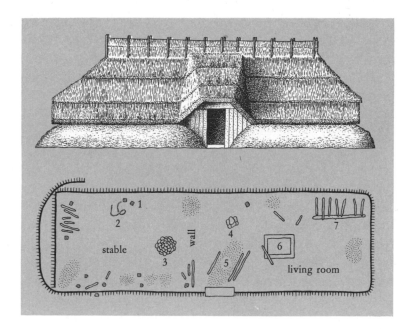

Ground-plan and elevation of a mud-walled house in Ginderup
(North Jutland):
1 peg, 2 rope, 3 hearth, 4 stone for grinding cereals, 5 wickerwork,
6 hearth, 7 bed

Although only fragments of the Gothic translation of the Bible have survived, it is known that Wulfila also covered the Old Testament (with the exception of Kings 1 and 2). Of his other extensive theological writings, which would now be of great interest from the viewpoint of the history of civilization, nothing has survived apart from a baptism and mass symbol in Latin which was passed on by Auxentius, Bishop of Durostorum, and a pupil of Wulfila. Nevertheless, even these fragments supply considerable information about the Gothic culture of that time and of the religious and ideological situation. Wulfila did not leave a harsh Arian confession as his legacy—strict Arianism had already been abandoned by this time—but rather an intermediary credo which coincided in the essential points with the confession of the Synod of Rimini (359). However, his views were far removed from the Catholic doctrine decreed at Nicaea in 325 since he obviously knew how to forge a link be-

tween moderate Arianism and the religious ideas of the still pagan Goths. Unlike the Catholic doctrine of the Holy Trinity, Christ was presented as the SON OF GOD, admittedly being Lord and God—for mankind—but still dependent on the Father. Modern theologians see in this a reflection of the Germanic status of the king's sons who ranked above all the members of the tribe but still owed obedience and service to their father. Be this as it may, the followers of Wulfila may have seen two related gods in the Father and the Son. The acceptance of the idea of the Holy Ghost, deriving from the Graeco-Hellenistic logos concept, was incomparably more difficult for the Germanic imagination, and for this reason he was regarded as the true servant of Christ and not as a god. Incidentally, this is also indicative of the unspeculative and non-dialectical approach of Wulfila which ultimately leads to a strict—or, if one will, narrow—Biblicism. He relies expressly on the traditional Christian legacy which he simply tries to preserve, rejecting any theological analysis: just as the runes and oracles were regarded with respect in the past and taken as a guide, he now demanded the same for the old Biblical faith which the Catholic Church had changed by constant exegesis and casuistical application. Thus it was not so much a difference in the basic standpoint as a divergence in the understanding of the Scriptures and a quite different approach to religion which led to the Catholicism evolved within the empire and the Arianism adopted by the Goths and other Germanic peoples becoming two entirely disparate forces.

Much of the social and cultural condition of the Goths at this time is reflected more or less directly in Wulfila's translation of the Bible. The contradiction between the Christian and Antique world on the one hand and the pagan Gothic background on the other is even apparent in linguistic subtleties. It was naturally in keeping with Wulfila's character that he often tried to take the middle way and find a compromise. There is a marked Germanic accent, for instance, in the translation of the Greek *makários* (in Luther: "selig"—blissful, blessed) by "audags" (diligent, happy). Matthew 5, 24 "first be reconciled to thy brother" is rendered by "Go and make a kinship bond with thy brother". This is a reminder that peace and friendship naturally prevailed among kith and kin and that the disturbance of this from outside the family was severely punished—even by vendetta. The Kingdom of God is portrayed as the *thiudangardi* (king's court), to which the people (*thiuda*) and the king (*thiudans*) are linked by loyalty and affection. Characteristically, Wulfila uses the word *reiks*, which was associated with something like despotism, only for the designation of the rule of Satan. The New Testament word *kýrios* (Lord) is translated by *hulths* (Mod. German *hold* = kind [person]). *Mystérion* (Sacrament) is reproduced by *runa*, clear evidence that the runes were regarded as something sacred and closely associated with the godhead.

An aspect which is also of importance concerns the terms referring to guilt, sin, conscience and so on. It would be superficial to explain the lack of terms such as these in Gothic or Germanic in general by the moral standards of these Barbarian tribes as stated by many Antique historians, including high-ranking ecclesiastics. It is true that in the Germanic laws up to the period of the Great Migration considerable importance was attached to morality and ethical cleanliness. Exceptional offences—such as adultery by a woman—carried Draconian penalties. The literary evidence of Late Antiquity, which goes back at least as far as Tacitus, should nevertheless not be accepted so uncritically since there is a clear tendency for the Germanic and other Barbarian societies to be portrayed to the decadent Romans as models of virtue. The exaggerated songs of praise extolling Barbarian chastity, honesty and simple bravery naturally fade a little in the face of a critical examination. These were qualities which, to be sure, were more likely to survive in a military democracy than in a slave-owning society which was becoming increasingly degenerate and moving far beyond its natural tribal and ethnological ties. However, particular caution is appropriate in this respect before any judgement is made. If Gothic did not have such words as "conscience" or "sin", then this is due not so much to the complete non-existence of what they are used to describe but rather to the incomplete state of development of the language. Since the Gothic language still reflected social and natural reality by a narrow and simple realism—Schiller's expression "naive" could be applied here—it was not able to communicate transcendental and abstract concepts in an adequate manner. Consequently, when the Goths were ignorant of terms which had already become well-established in other languages, this was rather a reflection of the actual logical and philosophical level of development than the expression of moral perfection. Of interest here, too, is the linguistic result. For "sin" (Greek *hamartía*), Wulfila used the word *frawaurhts* (something like "forfeiture") and translated "damn" (Greek *katakrínein*) by *gawargjan* (meaning: to declare some-one a wolf, to outlaw somebody). These examples give an indication of the cultural achievement which Wulfila's translation of the Bible doubtlessly represents and of the trends in linguistic, cultural and social development which were emerging from the Christian mission to the Goths and other Germanic tribes. The translation of the Bible was only a beginning, through which the Visigoths and, in the course of time, the other Gothic tribes and communities came into closer and closer contact with the Antique sphere of civilization. The regional differences in this development can only be demonstrated by a few examples here.

Mention has already been made of the Catholic Crimean Goths, who were mainly exposed to Graeco-Hellenistic influence. It is the continuity of their development which is the chief point of interest here since this tiny facet of civilization survived up till modern times, even if it was only as an isolated group of people. From the time of Bishop Theophilus, it was the Greek Orthodox doctrine of the Eastern Church that prevailed here but among the Danubian Goths it was the creed of Audianism that was widespread for a time. This heretical offshoot had originated in Mesopotamia and prescribed asceticism of a strict order. Since the founder of this heresy, Audius, had been banished by the emperor to Scythia, he achieved notable success as a missionary there—possibly at the same time as Wulfila, although this cannot be clearly proved from the few sources available. Why the Goths flocked to Audius in great numbers can only be conjectured. Perhaps the force of his personality made him appear to many of them as a liege lord of a new type. A point worth considering, however, is that the great majority of the Goths he converted no longer had any meaningful links with their tribal background

40/41 Collection of finds from Visigothic Spain (Museo Arqueológico Nacional, Madrid). The eagle fibula of cast bronze with incrustations of coloured glass paste comes from Calatayud and dates from the first half of the 6th century. The belt clasp, the disc of which is richly decorated with almandines, was found in the necropolis of Carpio de Tajo and was probably made during the second half of the 6th century.

42 Pendant cross of gold with cloisonné and tiny almandine discs,
c. 800 (Bayerisches Nationalmuseum, Munich).

43 Disc-type fibula from the grave of the Aleman princess of Wittislingen (Bayerisches Nationalmuseum, Munich). This round Aleman
fibula from the first half of the 7th century reveals both Aleman and
Lombard influence. The gold foil is ornamented not only with filigree
decoration but also with almandines in cellular mountings, forming
snake-like pairs of creatures which are intertwined in a cross.

Following two pages:
44 Agilulf plate (Bargello, Florence). This gilded copper plate,
which may have graced the front section of a Germanic helmet, presents an interesting picture in relief of the Lombard king who ruled
from 591–616. More details about the picture and its interpretation
are given in the text on page 204.

45 Frankish disc- or circular fibulae (Römisch-Germanisches Museum, Cologne). The fibulae, the centre part of which forms a cross in each case, are of gold with almandines in cellular mountings. The cross is of filigree work and is marked with precious stones and green glass-paste. These fibulae were made during the first half of the 6th century.

46 Part of the Codex Argenteus with excerpt from the translation of the Bible made by Wulfila (University Library, Uppsala), 5th/6th century, forms part of the Gospel according to St. Matthew (6,5–16, 9–13; Our Father). As can be seen, the Gothic alphabet created by Wulfila and used in the Codex Argenteus is based on the Latin and Greek alphabets but used runic letters.

Following two pages:

47 North Germanic curved fibula (gilded silver) from Foss, Amt Lyngdal, Vest-Agder, Norway (Oldsaksamling, University of Oslo, Norway). The animal head ornamentation and the animal plait on the square-edged head-plate are characteristic.

48 Germanic shield-centre mountings (Lombard) from Ischl/Alz near Traunstein/Upper Bavaria (Prähistorische Staatssammlung, Munich). The mountings of gilded, punched bronze foil date from the 7th century and were found in 1905 in a warrior's grave. At the top and in the centre there is a crouching eagle while at the bottom a leaping lion is depicted.

weihnai namo þein· qimai þiudi-
nassus þeins· wairþai wilja
þeins· swe in himina jah ana
airþai· hlaif unsarana þana sin-
teinan gif uns himma daga· jah
aflet uns þatei skulans sijai-
ma· swaswe jah weis afletam þaim
skulam unsaraim· jah ni brig-
gais uns in fraistubnjai· ak lau-
sei uns af þamma ubilin· unte
þeina ist þiudangardi· jah mahts
jah wulþus in aiwins· amen·
ΜΔ unte jabai afletiþ mannam
missadedins ize· afletiþ jah
izwis atta izwar sa ufar himinam·
iþ jabai ni afletiþ mannam missadedins ize· ni þau atta izwar afletiþ missadedins izwa-
ΜΕ ros:: aþþan biþe fastaiþ ni wair-
þaiþ swaswe þai liutans gaurai·

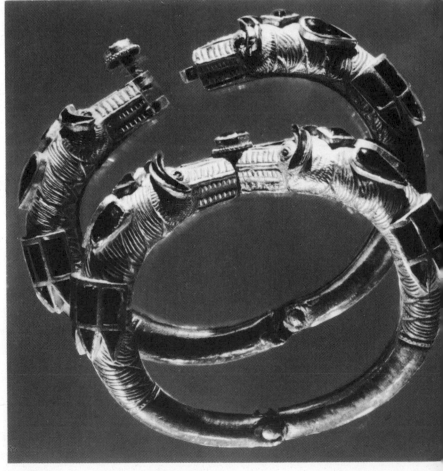

49/50 Bracelets of the supposedly Skyrian princess of Bakodpuszta (Hungarian National Museum, Budapest). Diameter 8–8.8 cm. They indicate the preservation of the best Pontic-South Russian traditions in the art of the Germanic cellular goldwork technique.

51/52 Thorsberg Find: Bronze belt-fitting (Schleswig Museum). The rectangular bronze fitting, curved in a semi-circular shape, is lined with gilded silver foil at the front. It is not known what purpose it served. The rectangular centre area with its counter-clockwise animal frieze is of gilded silver foil and was made from a wooden matrix. It shows a hippocampus, a horned sea creature, a boar, a bird and a tiger (?). The centre part is enclosed on each of the long sides by a row of human heads turned to the right, these having been produced by the punch technique.

53 Frankish spouted cup (Römisch-Germanisches Museum, Cologne). The Frankish glass-makers did indeed use Roman techniques but they also developed many forms of their own, such as the bell-shaped spouted cups. As here, the most popular material was greenish glass containing sprinklings of a different colour. A characteristic feature are the hollow, drooping spouts which appeared in the 5th century.

54 Aleman Find from Lörrach (Baden). An Ostrogothic curved fibula, a hair-pin, an ear-ring (gilded silver with niello work) and a finger-ring (gold with garnet inlays).

55 Frankish (?) finds from Andernach and Gondorf. The bracteate fibula with Roma (!) on a throne is in the Late Antique tradition. The richly decorated golden pins and rings also unmistakably reveal the marked influence of the Roman craftsmanship which flourished in the Rhine district in particular.

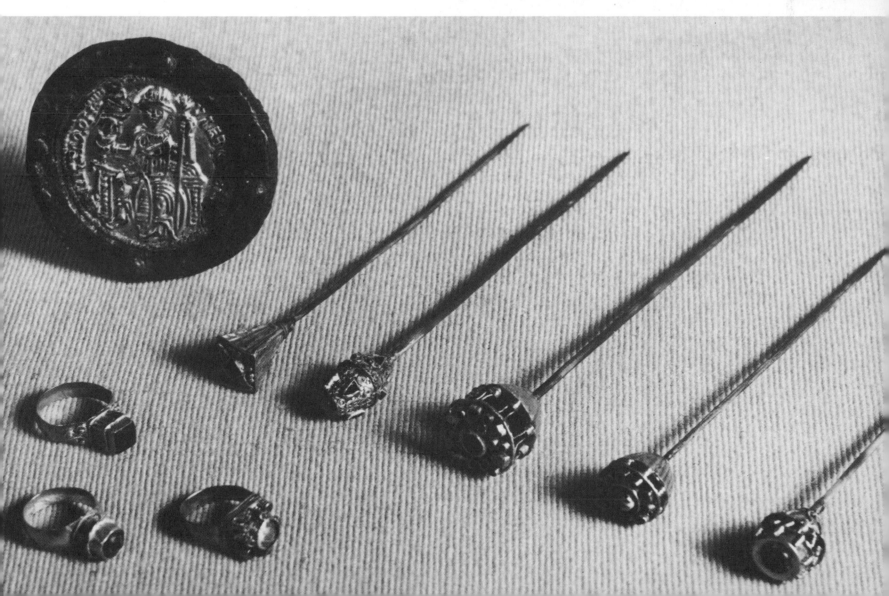

56 Avarian imitations of Byzantine gold coins (solidi) (Hungarian National Museum, Budapest). Although of equivalent weight, in style they are Barbarian imitations of 7th century coins bearing the image of the emperor.

57 Late Avarian belt-tongue from Klárafalva (Móra Ferenz Museum, Szeged). The galloping, arrow-shooting hunter recalls Iranian models.

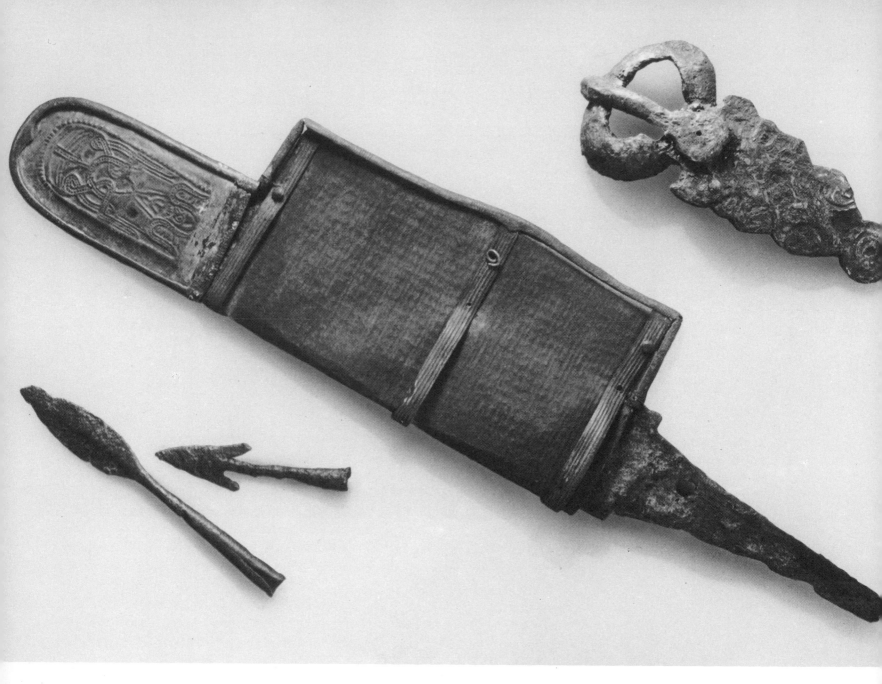

58 These finds from Oberflacht, Urach, Wurmlingen and Waiblingen consist of a broad sax, two arrow-heads and a belt-buckle and are of average quality (Altertümersammlung, Stuttgart).

59 Frankish finds from the warrior-grave of Daseburg, Warburg district (Landesmuseum Münster); earthenware vessel, iron shield centre and grips of iron, sword, lance-tip, fragments of horse-harness and comb.

60 Aleman spear-tips from Murr, Sindelfingen and Wurmlingen (Altertümersammlung, Stuttgart). The four spear-tips are evidence of the high level of development of weapon-making attained in the course of the Great Migration. The second tip from the right bears a runic inscription.

61 Aleman find from the burial field of Basel-Kleinhüningen (Historisches Museum, Basle). Iron sword (spatha) with handle of gold foil, silver mountings and amber ball.

62 Aleman find from the "grave-line" burial field at Schretzheim. Four golden bracteates with attachment rings.

63 Two Aleman decorative bronze discs and a circular fibula (iron and silver) from Karlich (Rheinisches Landesmuseum, Bonn). The intertwined animal ornament on the left decorative disc is worth noting; the other disc almost looks like a swastika. Despite their simplicity, both discs have a markedly dynamic quality.

64 Celtic shield from Battersea (bronze, originally gilded; length 77 cm), dating from the 2nd century A.D. (?) (British Museum, London). Characteristic of this splendid object are the scroll decorations and the coloured enamel inlays. Roman influence cannot be excluded, apart from others.

65/66 Anglo-Saxon reliquary boxes of walrus ivory from the Gandersheim Stift (Herzog Anton Ulrich Museum, Brunswick). The boxes are scarcely comparable with the numerous fine reliquaries of the Carolingian period. Nevertheless, the animal and plaited strip decorations and the runic inscriptions on the underside, representing a mixture of pagan and Christian elements, are an unusual feature.

67/68 The illustrations show two Aleman gold-leaf crosses with plait strip ornamentation; one appears to depict a human head (?), (Ulm, Adelfingen).

Reconstruction of the oldest marshland settlement, Ezinge near Groningen

so that they found a substitute for this in the monastic communities where each was required to perform manual work as laid down by the founder.

The persecution by Athanaric, the leader of the pagan Visigoths, which drove the Arian followers of Fritigern and Wulfila into Roman territory and thus provoked the beginning of the main phase of the Great Migration, also affected the Audians. Like many other splinter groups, in all likelihood they were now scattered. Incidentally, this confrontation proves that the pagan Visigoths, subject to scarcely any Roman influence, certainly had the upper hand in the tribal association until about 370. However, this was soon to change when the flourishing empire of the Ostrogoths under King Ermanaric fell victim to the sudden onrush of the Huns. Ermanaric himself committed suicide, his successor was slain in the battle, the territory of this state fell into the hands of Huns advancing westwards and large numbers of its Gothic and non-Gothic population were henceforth obliged to serve in the Hun armies. Some of the Ostrogoths evaded this, however, and many splinter-groups must have joined the Crimean Goths or settled in the Caucasus where they are recalled by the Ingushes still surviving in the 20th century. Others joined the Visigoths who, before the battle of Adrianople as well as in the following years, were already exerting considerable pressure on the Roman frontier. From the political and military viewpoint, this development has already been considered. From the viewpoint of the history of civilization, however, there is another factor which was particularly significant for this phase of the constant latent aggression of Visigoths against the Imperium Romanum, namely the growing influence of Roman civilization on these enemies, who were always fluctuating between a state of alliance and a military confrontation with Rome. This was apparent in the time of Fritigern and Alaric but it became even more marked after the emergence of the Tolosanic empire in Southern France. Paulus Orosius, to whom reference has already been made, provides some interesting information about this, especially concerning the reign of King Athaulf.

As the successor of Alaric, Athaulf forced the princess Galla Placidia to marry him. She was the sister of Honorius, the reigning emperor of Western Rome, and had been taken by the Goths as a hostage. Despite this dynastic link with an illustrious Impe-

69 Belt-buckle from the Sutton Hoo ship burial of the 7th century (British Museum, London).

rial family, which not only enhanced the prestige of the Barbarian king but also gave him a legitimate claim to sovereignty, he is said to have toyed with much more ambitious plans. At least, it is asserted by Orosius (VII, 43) that he wanted to set up a Gothic empire in place of the Roman one with himself as emperor. However, the Barbarian lack of discipline of his tribal comrades thwarted this plan so that he had to be content with being the restorer *(restitutor)* of Rome. This report, which certainly seems credible, reflects the many possibilities which the then state of the disintegrating empire and the potential of the impatient Barbarian peoples might at least have suggested to ambitious and power-hungry princes. And it can be assumed that Athaulf only put into words that which had already passed through the mind of Alaric and, under apparently even more favourable conditions, had appeared as a dream within reach to men such as Attila and Geiseric.

Incidentally, this highly official political contact, as it were, was not the only rapprochement feasible at that time between the new Barbarian rulers and the Roman state. The same Paulus Orosius also mentions the constantly changing relations between the invading Barbarians and the resident population of the Roman provinces. He was not unaware of the mutual hostility but he also indicates the possibility and even reality of fairly rapid contact which he himself must have noticed before his flight from the Iberian peninsula. In VII, 41, 7 he says that the Barbarians "cursed" their swords, made the ploughshare their own and regarded the Romans who still remained as their friends and allies. However, it was often the case that the latter preferred to share an impoverished freedom with the Barbarians than to be at the mercy of the Roman tax-collectors any longer. This development, which is confirmed by other authors such as Salvian of Massilia, is significant in a number of aspects. This echo of Isaiah (2,4), where in the future kingdom of peace swords were to be made into ploughshares, may be interpreted one way or another but Orosius certainly had a positive vision of significance for the future when he already saw the feared Barbarians as allies and friends. This was because he did not regard them from the viewpoint of state policy but saw them with the eyes of large sections of the population and was not afraid to criticize the Roman system of government. This can be taken further since even Orosius realized that there was no great divide between the mass of the Barbarians and the local population and that slaves, coloni and other oppressed groups, who had nothing to lose, really did regard the newcomers as liberators. To a large extent, at least, he shared this opinion since he could not have foreseen that many of the still intact ruling class in the Roman provinces would soon amalgamate with the ruling circles of the Barbarians and establish a new order of exploitation which, with its early feudal features, was indeed less oppressive than the old system. He himself obviously thought that the aspirations of the Barbarians in respect of equality and liberty were more advanced than they actually were.

The two-way process of assimilation indicated by Orosius can be easily documented in another field, that of family and place names. In Southern France and the Iberian peninsula, Gothic influence and the fusion of the Gothic and Provincial Roman sections of the population is reflected even today by the many "goti" names, names ending in -ville (villa) and -ingôs and family names of the most diverse formation (other Barbarian groups were also involved in this). Only a brief reference is possible here to the complicated process of the intermingling of culture and population, many details of which are still disputed. The Romanization of the Goths and of their language often went hand in hand with the Barbarization of the Latin Roman substratum. This is clearly illustrated by the "ville" place-names since here the Latin ending "villa" was preferred to the Gothic "haim" but was regularly attached to the Germanic personal name, normally regarded as that of the founder of the settlement. Similar phenomena are found in the Frankish and Burgundian settlement areas. The total number of place and personal names formed in this way amounts to several hundred at least, which underlines the extent to which language and culture of each group mingled with that of the other. Only in conjunction with an intensive analysis of the late Visigoth empire would it be possible to examine the highly interesting development associated with the spread of Vulgar Latin and the emergence of the

Romance languages. However, it is not possible here to go into further details concerning the realm of the Visigoths which survived until 711 or that of the Ostrogoths which, in the struggle with Byzantium, lasted until 554/555. In connection with the development of kingship, Church and culture, a further reference is made in Chapter 4 to some interesting phenomena which were characteristic of these Gothic states. Further information is given in the chronological table.

The Vandals

It is not only the example of the Goths which illustrates the major role of the East Germanic tribes in the Great Migration, although the Goths and their close relations—the Gepidae and the Heruli—were responsible for particularly notable and far-reaching advances and subsequently were even able to found states. The only "competition" that they encountered was from the Burgundians and, even more, from the Vandals who, by their trail of conquest to North Africa, have provided an exceptional stimulus for historical fantasy. The Germanic tribes from the Elbe area, such as the Alemans, Hermunduri and Thuringians, and from the Weser-Rhine district, such as the Franks and their predecessors, the Bructeri, Chamavi and Salians, did not move so far away from their point of origin as the East Germanic groups but were able to keep possession of the land they took for much longer and to settle it in a more intensive manner. In many ways, the advance of the Vandals can be compared with the spread of the Anglo-Saxons across Britain or with the later inroads of the Vikings.

The first mention of the Vandals (as the Vandilii) is by early Imperial authors such as Tacitus. They were often associated with the Cimbri and the Teutons since they originally came from the same area—Jutland (North Jutland is still known as Vendsyssel and Cape Skagen was formerly called Vandilsskagi) and the district around Oslo Bight. Many similarities of a cultural and linguistic nature with the Gothic tribes have already been noted. Although hardly any written documents of the Vandals survive, an approximate identity of the Vandal language with Gothic must be postulated, due to the close relationship which originally existed between them. Already by about 100 B.C., there was a clearly defined "Vandal" civilization appearing in Silesia and to a lesser degree around the mouths of the Oder and Vistula, the influence of this being subsequently traced as far afield as Hungary and Slovakia. The name Silesia, probably through the intermediary of the Slavs, is thought to be associated with the Silingi, a tribal formation of the Vandals. In the confrontation with the ancient Celtic population, the tribal formations of the Vandals, probably mixed with other groups from this early migratory period, founded the confederacy of the Lugii, an association which might be best regarded as a confederacy for the purpose of certain practical and political aims and held together by the common veneration of two gods (dioscuric deities). The confederacy of the Lugii soon asserted itself and, in alliance with the Hermunduric Bohemian realm of Marbod, proved capable of overwhelming Vannius and his so-called empire in A. D. 50. There was a continuity of settlement up to the 4th century in Silesia itself, leading to a fairly intensive development of the land. Archaeologically, there is much that recalls the Goths but the Vandal civilization must have had a more marked farming orientation. Both in agriculture and in the crafts (jewellery, arms manufacture, minting of coinage), much was adopted from the Celts, whose forms of settlement must have influenced the Vandals for a time at least. The town-like *oppida* of the Celts, frequently developed from strongholds used as a place of refuge, were sometimes found in Vandal territory, too, although the village or hamlet with its small wooden buildings and combined structures, 15 to 30 m long, for man and beast must have been the typical form of settlement, as it was among the other Germanic tribes. Instead of cremation (crematory trench) as was the usual custom, some of the Vandals adopted the Celtic practice of burying their dead, which has provided more accurate information about clothing and other articles buried with them. The Vandal civilization of that time reached a climax in what are sometimes known as the "princely courts", which must have been the centres of political life and of social display. Evidence of this is provided by lavish skeleton graves, three of which have been excavated at Sacrau alone, near Wrocław. M. Jahn described them (p. 1000) in the following words: "These are true burial vaults with walls of fieldstone a yard thick, enclosing burial chambers up to five yards long, three yards wide and at least seven feet in height. These graves probably had a wooden ceiling. It is very likely that the furnishings of these burial chambers—beds, little tables, chairs and other domestic articles—were also of wood, of which only slight traces have survived. Thus not only was clothing, ornaments, food and drink placed in the grave with the dead of this princely family, as was usual, but their burial chambers were arranged as comfortably as for the living." While the graves of ordinary warriors, often arranged as urn-graves in burial fields and alternating with skeleton graves, contained only simple weapons and requisites, persons of princely rank were thus buried with a profusion of domestic articles and in particular the jewellery buried with them reveals good taste and luxury of an almost unnaturally exaggerated kind. This includes local products as well as articles imported from the Roman area, such as millefiori bowls or Roman silver beakers, alternating with gold ornaments of Vandal manufacture. A collapsible bronze drinking-table, decorated with sculptured Dionysian motifs, is an outstanding example of this Vandal art. Fibulae with double and triple spirals and various gold pendants with filigree decoration likewise bear testimony to a high standard of craftsmanship and artistic appreciation and throw a very positive light on this early Vandal art. The bronze and iron weapons and requisites are correspondingly simpler, of course. Nevertheless, with the smelting of local ores, metalworking had already attained a high level and the trade of the smith, under Roman and perhaps Celtic influence, was well-developed. Pottery was mostly decorated with meandrian patterns or undulating lines with impressed markings and, as finds have shown, was usually moulded on the potter's wheel and fired in closed kilns.

In the 4th century and in conjunction with the other crafts, pottery-making experienced a phase of marked development. At this time, just before the beginning of the population movements known as the Great Migration, the social differentiation among the Vandals must already have been considerable, as indicated, above all, by the differences in the appointments of the graves. The power and wealth of the occupant of the grave was reflected not only in the quantity of the objects buried with him but also by their quality. It was a matter of some importance whether luxury articles and other treasures of foreign origin predominated in the princely graves or pottery of local manufacture, plain weapons and spurs—as in many of the warrior graves.

Naturally, the number of articles buried with the dead and their standard of craftsmanship also reflect ethnic differences, to which attention has recently been drawn by J. Filip and others on the basis of investigations by J. Kostrzewski. The Polish school of Kostrzewski has lately spoken of the Przeworsk culture which is regarded as the southern branch of the Wendish culture and derived from the Western Slavic peoples associated with the Lusatian culture. It is considered that it also included the settlement areas of the Vandals in Silesia as well. In Filip's view, the controversy can most easily be explained by the existence—in the Silesia of Imperial times, for instance—of a certain (and already fairly high) standard of civilization, the components of which—naturally in the ethnic sense, too—were of varying origin. This explanation is worthy of serious consideration.

Indeed, there can be no doubt that the Vandals and Silingi settled in Silesia, just as it is equally certain that the other main group of the Vandals, the Hasdingi, established themselves at the mouth of the Vistula and in Masuria. Under pressure from the Goths and other tribes, the Hasdingi invaded Dacia in 171 and were allocated territory there by Rome. In the 4th century, large numbers of them moved to Slovakia and Hungary (Pannonia). Without leaving much archaeological evidence behind them, they must have developed here as a nation of herdsmen and horsemen, which they still were when they appeared on the African scene. There is no reliable evidence of confrontations with the Goths and Romans until, in association with other events in the history of the Great Migration at the beginning of the 5th century, the emergence of the Vandals also came about. In 401, the Hasdingi were enlisted as federate allies by Stilicho,

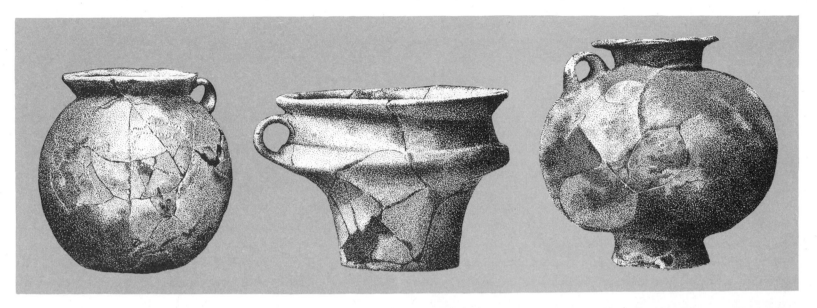

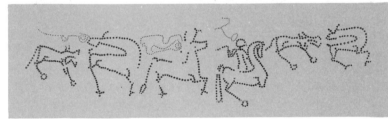

Vandal earthenware vessels from North Jutland; the drawing opposite shows animal and horseman motifs from the vessel at left

who was of partly Barbarian origin, in Noricum. However, as early as 406, they took advantage of the particular weakness of the Western Roman Empire, which had been obliged to withdraw most of its forces from along the Rhine in order to rally troops for resisting the Gothic threat to Italy, to form a strong migratory confederacy with Silesian Vandals (Silingi) and groups of Quadi, Suebi and Alans and invade Gaul. The principal motive for this invasion, which soon spread to Spain as well, must have been the advance of the Huns, in the face of which the united tribes—or tribal formations, since many groups had remained in the former homeland areas—fell back to the almost undefended Roman territory.

The following years were marked by devastation and pillage which affected large areas of Southern Gaul as far as the Pyre-

nean frontier. The Vandals and their allies met with scarcely any resistance in the flat countryside and it may even be assumed that they were joined by Bagaudae and other resistance-fighters. Only a few large towns, such as Tolosa, remained unscathed. It is true that Constantine III, a soldier proclaimed as emperor by the Britannic legions, organized resistance to the Germanic incursions and once again reinforced the Rhine frontier but in 409 the Vandals and their allies crossed the Pyrenees and took possession of new homelands in the Iberian Peninsula. This use of force was soon legitimized since the government at Ravenna recognized the settlements of the Hasdingi and Suebi in Galicia, the Silingi in Baetica and the Alans in Lusitania and the region of Carthage by a federate treaty (411). While the Suebi consolidated their settlements in the north-west of the peninsula—

initially by various aggressive and defensive wars—and established an empire (one of the smallest created by the tribes involved in the Great Migration) which maintained its independence till 585 (when it fell to the Visigoths), the Vandals and Alans embarked on a course of development which was much more hazardous. Harassed at Roman instigation by Visigoths, Suebi and also Roman contingents, they suffered such severe losses in 418 that it seemed that survival was only possible through a closely-knit union of the Hasdingi, Silingi and Alans under Gunderic, the king of the Hasdingi at the time. The institution of Kingship, which had been continued from the past but which cannot be described in more detail until about 400, thus became firmly established and tended to reduce the authority of the tribal nobility. Clear evidence of this is provided by the title "Rex Vandalorum et Alanorum" which was more than just a personal union.

In Spain at the latest and perhaps even during their previous migrations, most of the Vandals had adopted the Arian creed of Christianity. Even considering the ideological "leap forward" accomplished by the Huns and Goths, as noted in the preceding pages, this development seems to have been rapid since there is no report in existence of activities by men such as Wulfila or Audius among the Vandals. The transition from a polytheism necessitated by the course of development and centred here around two deities, which in earlier periods were probably mirrored in a kind of dual kingdom, to Arian Christianity was completed without any particular complication. Perhaps they simply put the Bible in the place of the objects previously venerated, once the ineffectiveness of the runic spears, wooden idols or solar symbols had been amply demonstrated. The concepts of the Vandals in this respect were still highly influenced by magical and fetishist ideas and they appear to have worshipped cosmic powers as well. At least, this is the impression conveyed by a note of Salvian, the ecclesiastical writer, who stresses that the Vandals owed their victory in Spain to their faith since the Bible had been carried in front of their troops (as a kind of military symbol—VII, 11, 46). At any rate, it was not long before the Vandals and Alans were completely converted to

Arianism. Indeed, the Vandal kings subsequently held tenaciously to this heresy since it provided them with ideological ammunition to use against the strictly Catholic Roman upper classes of Spain and North Africa.

The political experiment of Geiseric, who founded in North Africa a despotically guided state with many early feudal features, illustrates on a large scale the role that Arianism could play even in the establishment of an absolute monarchy. From this aspect, too, the conquest of North Africa, which took place in stages between 429 and 455, marked a definite turning-point for Rome, for the provincial Romans in Africa and for the Vandals and Alans themselves. Rome lost not only an important economic area but also political and ideological prestige since from now on it was exposed to constant threats from the West and South and had to tolerate a sovereign state on territory that had once belonged to Carthage. The fact that the Vandals soon attempted to establish a legitimate link with the dynasty of Valentinian III was of no great significance for the government of the Western empire since simultaneously with this Geiseric was vigorously combating everything Roman in his own sphere of authority. This tactic of two directions of attack reveals political acuteness of a high order. A merciless struggle was declared against the Roman landowners on the one hand and the Catholic Church on the other, as the principal moral and ideological backbone of the old order. By 442, the year of the first peace treaty between Geiseric and Western Rome, the Vandal king had fully asserted his will in internal affairs. Imperial, private and Church estates were confiscated and taken over by Geiseric, his tribal associates or the Arian clergy. Those who had not yet fallen victim to the "new order" were condemned to forced labour or fled. The landed property acquired in this way fell into the hands or the king or the apparently flourishing Arian Church which, surpassing the example given by Wulfila, became a national or even State Church of the Vandals. By assuming as much as possible of the institutional character of the Catholic Church, it also acquired its claim to authority which, under Geiseric and Huneric, was even taken much further so that ultimately persecution was extended not only to the Catho-

lic clergy but at times also to the whole Catholic population as well. Under Geiseric's son Huneric, religious intolerance went so far that the very existence of Catholicism in Africa was threatened since it was systematically persecuted by the Vandals and many of the Berber tribes allied with them. However, in the late Vandal period, various forms of compromise prevailed. The Catholic churches recovered and flourished, an outstanding part in this being played by Fulgentius of Ruspe, the well-known successor of Augustine. Even the monastic orders took root and numerous new monasteries were founded which endured until the coming of the Arabs. Geiseric, who soon openly revealed his despotic ambitions, took drastic action against the Roman administration. Only a few of the judicial and fiscal authorities, indispensable for the supervision of the provincial population and the management of the State, were tolerated or restored after appropriate reorganization. Within the politically incapacitated and socially declassed provincial population, the slave-owning structure was maintained, this lasting into the Byzantine period. Of course, the Vandals also possessed slaves who had come from the ranks of prisoners of war and, under their direct influence, various groupings of coloni, forced labourers and other persons of low status were formed, too. The development of the Sortes Vandalorum, a compact Vandal settlement area to the northwest of Carthage, favoured the emergence of a new kind of socio-economic structure, the details of which are unfortunately not known. Since the tribal nobility of the Vandals and Alans had been decimated in an uprising against Geiseric, a service aristocracy (of ministerials or stewards) was able to emerge, the development of which was probably closely associated with the agrarian structure of the Sortes Vandalorum. The extent to which these influential men exercised and combined socio-economic, political and military functions can only be surmised. An authoritative intermediate position between the kings and the free commoners of the Vandals was occupied by the *millenarii*. Since their title indicates a command of a thousand men, it may be supposed that theirs was primarily a military function. However, they certainly had civil functions as well and exercised considerable influence through the size of their estates, which were cultivated by numerous servants and must frequently have been administered from lavishly furnished villas. A well-known mosaic from Bordj-Djedid Hill in Carthage obviously depicts a horseman from this landowner class: he has just left his stately, castle-like villa and is setting off for the chase, as indicated by his clothing—sleeved jersey and closely fitting trousers. His long hair shows that he is a Vandal and it is possible that alien and non-African influences are reflected in the cross-shaped symbol—which certainly is of apotropaic secondary significance—on the hind-quarter of the horse. This new and largely Vandal nobility, together with the kings and their relations—who represented the real elite in the Vandal despotism with its stress on the principle of seniority—, played a considerable part in determining developments in North Africa. They outranked by far the ordinary Vandals and even more so the provincial Romans who had formerly had such an important voice in affairs. It was only in the Catholic Church of the late Vandal period and in the broad sphere of education and intellectual life that the local people were able to retain or recover their positions.

The culture of Vandal Africa was consequently only marked to a slight extent by the ruling stratum itself which usually only encouraged or commissioned projects in the sphere of art. Vandal influence is most apparent in the manufacture of weapons and the production of fibulae, rings, circlets and necklaces in Pontic-Gothic style, especially when these objects were intended for the royal treasure. In the construction of buildings, the only reports of which are in the form of a few inscriptions and an occasional literary reference, there must naturally have been co-operation between the Vandals and the provincial population, the former playing the role of patrons, of course. This would have concerned such buildings as the palaces and thermal baths extolled by the court poets.

Even more modest was the role of the Vandals in the intellectual life of North Africa. As in the past, a knowledge of Latin, which was taught in the schools of the grammarians and rhetoricians, was essential for anyone wishing to take part in this. It is true that Dracontius, one of the best-known African writers of this time, and the author of a Christian didactic poem and an apology addressed to King Gunthamund, reports that in the school of Felicianus, his teacher, Romans and Barbarians alike received instruction. It thus appears that Vandal boys, too, were taught Latin and introduced to the fundamentals of the "free arts". However, in practice, this privilege of education was certainly restricted to the children of the hereditary and service aristocracy in preparation for important functions in the State and in the Arian Church. For purely practical reasons, Latin had to be retained in the State administration—even in communications with Berbers from the border areas of the Vandal empire—while the Arian Church, which continued to use the Vandal language for its services, likewise had to pursue the theological confrontation with the Catholics in Latin. In this connection, there resulted interesting controversies which, in reality, are more revealing than the pronouncements of profane literature dating from the same period. The writers Luxorius, Flavius Felix or Florentinus, who are correctly regarded as court poets, were not even remotely capable of representing Latin literature as well as their predecessors from the Late Antique period who were much closer to the Classical Age. When they discuss mythological themes or extol the virtues of the Vandal rulers, especially the magnanimity and interest in education of Thrasamund, their concoctions lack originality, often even any commitment and thus conviction. Only Dracontius, who was thrown into prison—probably because of his sympathy for the Byzantine emperor, is on a different level. The theologically or ecclesiastically oriented literature which resulted directly from the antagonism between the Arians and Catholics is of a different quality. Unfortunately, the works in Latin of the Arian priests Cyrila, Pinta and Abragila have been lost and can only be reconstructed to a slight extent from the corresponding Catholic polemics. At any rate, they were theologically less effective than these. The Orthodox clerics and bishops, men such as Eugenius of Carthage, Victor of Vita and especially Fulgentius of Ruspe, were better educated and, with the whole weight of their dialectical and casuistical training, defended the standpoint of Augustine, who continued to influence the theology of the West. Direct controversies between Fulgentius and King Thrasamund and his theological advisers show that the Catholic theologians in this daunting situation were able to assert themselves with great circumspection and consistency. At any rate, the arguments of the Arians, which were little more than those of Wulfila, did not prove convincing in the public confrontation. The special situation of Africa in the history of thought also explains how it was that monastic and hagiographic literature flourished at this time, pointing the way in many respects (imitation of the Passion of Christ) to the Middle Ages.

Mention must still be made here of another factor. In addition to the Vandals and the Provincials with their mixed Roman-Punic cultural background, it was the Berbers who were becoming steadily more influential in this period. Most of these tribes were still at the stage of nomadic or semi-nomadic horsemen and herdsmen. Taking advantage of the gradual decline and sudden collapse of Roman rule, they moved forward from their base areas and into the cultural sphere of the settled populations. They came into Roman or Vandal territory from the edge of the Sahara, from Kabylia, from the divide of Hodna and from the Aures Mountains, often mounted on camels, and they ultimately even settled down in the Dorsale area in Central Tunisia. In the Late Roman period, their chiefs and their followers were frequently enlisted as *gentiles* for the defence of the frontiers and, from the settlement centres of the *centenaria* (small citadels), stimulated a specific form of Roman-Barbarian mixed culture. These chiefs now became the princes and kings of independent states which—partly with and partly against the Vandal empire—began to consolidate themselves. The resident population was disturbed by the penetration of the Berbers but the continuing antagonism between Arianism and Catholicism must have led many of them to sympathize with the Berber tribes, who were gradually becoming converted to Catholicism, rather than with the Vandals. This was a fact which contributed to the rapid conquest of the Vandal empire by the Byzantine general Belisarius in 533/534. Under Byzantine rule, the relations between the settled populations and the semi-nomads again deteriorated. The clearest evidence of this is that walls were built around all the towns

still in existence, the centres of which were often fortified like fortresses. The Berbers and the Arabs who followed them in the middle of the 7th century had great difficulty in taking possession of these last refuges of the Romanized population of North Africa.

The Burgundians

Together with the other East Germanic tribes, the Burgundians also had a not unimportant share in the Great Migration and early mythology *(Nibelungenlied)* even put them firmly in the centre of the confrontations. Although they are mentioned by writers such as Pliny the Elder and Ptolemy, there are differences of opinion about their origin and homeland, too. The designation of the island of Bornholm in mediaeval sources as Borgundarholm is a pointer but not more than this. Just as Rügen is believed to have been a "staging post" for the Rugians, who were related to the Burgundians, Bornholm may have performed the same function for the Burgundians on their way southeastwards from their probable home in Southern Norway. From their origin and original culture, they can be classified somewhere between the Goths and the Vandals. From the linguistic evidence, particularly a nasalization which was retained for a long time, it seems that they must have come down from the North at an even earlier date than the Goths, although it must be appreciated of course that some of the tribes remained behind in Southern Norway and on Bornholm. After a period of settlement along the middle reaches and at the mouth of the Vistula, they were driven away from here by the Gepidae in about A.D. 200. In place of the Burgundian crematory trench graves (in which swords, decorated lance-tips, shields and spears with barbed hooks have been found), there then appeared, at any rate, burial fields of the Gepid type, thus confirming information reported by Jordanes that speaks of the destruction of this Burgundian group. Lusatia was the next settlement area of this only moderately large tribe which, instead of a king, initially had only a

Wooden pail with bronze fittings from the grave of a Vandal woman of the 4th century (from Széke/Slovakia)

kind of regional duke, an arrangement which allowed sufficient scope for the influence of the popular assembly. After coming into conflict with Lombards, who are reported to have subjugated some of the tribe, the Burgundians pushed forward in a westerly direction. The possibly slow trek westwards, which may have been associated with the formation of the tribe of the Alemans at this time, reached the area where the Main and Rhine join by the middle or end of the 4th century at the latest. Burgundian graves have been identified between Würzburg, Mayence and Wiesbaden. The Burgundians utilized the situation resulting from the withdrawal of the Roman troops and the advance of the Vandals and Alans to take possession of the districts around Worms and Speyer. Under Gundahar, the Gunther of the *Nibelungen Saga*, some of the Burgundians became federate allies of Rome after this and were stationed in towns on the left bank of the Rhine. Taking advantage of the precarious state of affairs which had developed for Rome, the Burgundians moved forward into Gallic territory as well after 413. In the years following, the legendary city of Worms must really have been the capital of the first Burgundian empire which emerged in the midst of Roman, Hun and Frankish spheres of influence. In this situation and in order to withstand the threats from all sides, it was natural and necessary that a central kingship should take the place of a still undeveloped military democracy. However, it is scarcely possible to say anything about the standard of organization of this "empire". The Burgundians were still pagan around 370 but they were converted to Christianity during the time that Worms was their capital, although the question of whether they adopted the Catholic or Arian creed has not yet been resolved and the inscriptions that have been found on graves do not throw any light on this, either.

In the course of time, the Burgundians attempted to expand their territory at the expense of Belgica, which was still a Roman province. They were defeated by the Roman general Aetius who, after the conclusion of a formal peace treaty, also arranged for these troublesome neighbours to be attacked by a Hun formation. This defeat of 436, in which Gundahar and his brothers perished, provided the historical nucleus for the Nibe-

lungen Epic in which, with poetic licence, Attila himself is placed at the centre of the events. The "Song of the Nibelungs" has justly been described as "one of the mightiest tragic poems of German literature". It was evolved in the course of a long period of time and mirrors the outlooks of various social formations. Whereas the nucleus—the *Siegfried Saga* which became the most popular German folk-tale—places the ethos of the "legendary" pre-feudal age in the foreground, there are numerous elements of the mediaeval world—such as the minstrels, court pomp and circumstances and Christian customs—in the other parts. As a whole, many of the happenings of Late Antiquity are echoed in the story and especially in the fall of the Nibelungs. This refers to the alliances and conflicts of the various Germanic and non-Germanic peoples (Huns) and major, more or less historical figures (Attila = Etzel, Dietrich of Bern = Theodoric the Great, Gunther, Hagen, Siegfried, Brunhild, Kriemhild).

Weakened from the defeat by the Huns, the Burgundians along the left bank of the Rhine at least came again under Roman influence to a more marked degree. Aetius again enlisted them as federate allies and in 443 allocated them rights of settlement in Sapaudia, later known as Savoy. Their primary function here was to defend the frontier against the Alemans advancing into Switzerland. In 451, they took part in the defensive battle against Attila, suffering heavy losses. Although formally still under Roman hegemony, Burgundy nevertheless became increasingly independent in the following years. Finally the reins of power in the emergent state between Geneva and Lyons passed from the hands of Roman officers to native kings who were related to the Visigoths and Franks. Despite periods of friendly relations with the Franks, with whom many Burgundians also shared a common Catholic faith, the smaller empire was exposed to increasing pressure from its northern neighbour even from A.D. 500 onwards. In 534 it was incorporated in the Frankish empire so that the period of political and cultural independence was not very long at all.

Thus the role of the Burgundians can be outlined in relatively few words. They were settled in accordance with the Roman law on billeting which applied both to federate allies and to sol-

diers of the regular army. One-third—and in Burgundy perhaps even one-half—of the available houses and land was taken for the king, the nobles and the free commoners of the Burgundians. This compulsory sharing, however, does not indicate sharp hostility between the neo-Latin population and the Germans— as in the Vandal empire, for instance—since the two "nations" were rather regarded as being equal. The Arian King Gundobad (480–516) thus had a codification of the two bodies of laws carried out. It was in the course of this conscientiously implemented project that numerous Roman elements—without doubt to be attributed to the king's legal experts from Lyons—were incorporated in the *Lex Burgundionum* which, in the words of Beyerle, stands "in the twilight between Germanic Antiquity and Late Antiquity". The *Lex Romana Burgundionum* (506), as it is termed, largely combines older Roman legislation with common law components. Naturally, the process of Romanization influenced not only laws and legislation; it is rather the case that its penetration of the legal sphere was a reflection of actual developments and trends. In contrast to other states associated with the Great Migration, in the realm of the Burgundians, Romans (neo-Latins) were also liable for military service and there were no restrictions at all prohibiting marriage between members of the two "nations". The Visigoths, for example, attained such a level of development only in the course of the 6th or even 7th century. In order to be more independent of its own tribal nobility, the Burgundian form of kingship was based on Roman and Antique roots also in the ideological sense and even claimed for itself an hereditary right. The emergent despotism was no longer under the control of any popular assembly but had to come to terms, however, with an assembly of notables (*Conventus Burgundionum*), the advisory function of which should not be underestimated.

Burgundian inscriptions with Latin capitals, runic alphabets (clasp from Charnay) and numerous Burgundian place-names reveal the influence exercised by this tribe for a fairly long time in Southeastern France. Burgundian loan-words also appeared in Provençal. As in the other states of the Great Migration, the Burgundian area can best be described as having possessed a mixed culture. The ruling class and the upper strata of the population became noticeably Romanized—when they were not of neo-Latin origin in the first place. The impact of the Latin language and Antique customs on the ordinary Burgundians came later and was less marked. In many cases, it is likely that it was only due to the constantly growing influence of the Catholic Church. As regards clothes, for instance, Barbarian styles remained in favour for a long time. The men wore a smock, knee-length trousers and high laced boots. Sword belts were in use. Female clothing consisted of an under-garment and a mantle, held together by clasps, brooches and pins, often of exquisite workmanship and ornamented with precious stones. The decorative articles worn often reflected South Russian and Gothic influence but, understandably, Christian motifs ("prophet buckles" with Daniel in the lions' den) later appeared in increasing numbers. Thus a blend of Antique and Barbarian elements can be observed which is probably even more characteristic for Burgundy than for the bigger states which emerged after the fall of the Imperium Romanum.

The Alemans

This tribe or federation of tribes, since the translation of the name as "all men" would seem to indicate something of this kind, was the first group of the Germanic tribes along the Elbe to appear on the scene. Like the related Suebi, Hermunduri, Thuringians, Bavarians and Lombards, they were somewhat less prominent than the East Germanic peoples in the confrontation with Rome. In comparison, their wanderings were fairly modest, but their origins are not less mysterious than those of the other tribes. There must have been certain connections between the Suebi of Ariovist, who were thrown back by Caesar, and the Alemans who appeared in South Germany in A.D. 200 or thereabouts. On the other hand, they were also associated with the Semnoni confederacy, whose religious—and also for a time political—centre was situated in the Marches of Brandenburg. From here, raids were launched to the Southeast and

South by followings and sometimes by entire tribes—for instance, the advance into Bohemia of the Marcomanni and Suebi just before the start of the Christian era. The beginnings, at least, of a kind of planning can be identified here. Under the leadership of their tribal aristocracy, the Suebi and some of the Alemans from about A.D. 200 pushed forward to the Main and the Upper Germanic-Rhaetian limes, against which continuing attacks were launched. Thrown back by Emperor Caracalla in 213, they still persisted in their attacks time and again. About 260, Rome was forced to give up not only the province of Dacia but also the territory between the Rhine, the Danube and the limes to the Alemans and, in the North, to the Franks (in Latin called the *agri decumates*), which subsequently proved to be a "launching pad" of vital importance for the later Barbarian invasions. In the following decades, the Alemans—sometimes with the support of the Jutungi, who were related to them—attempted to expand their territory still further in the southern and western directions and sent expeditions into Italy. As already noted, the counter-offensives of the Emperors Julian and Valentinian I could only slow up this process and retard the occupation of land in Alsace and large areas of Switzerland. Even Augsburg, Regensburg and Passau belonged for a time to the loosely-knit state structure which emerged in the 5th century under Aleman dukes. Before long—as in the dispute over Trier—violent quarrels broke out with the Franks, in the course of which the entire area of the Alemans eventually became Frankish. The last duke, Lantfrid, died in 730. The Duchy of Swabia was set up in the former area of the Alemans in 911.

The development of the Alemans and the tribes related to them up to the time of the Great Migration was very similar to that of the East Germanic tribes, particularly in the cultural sphere. As specific features, mention may be made of a more marked cultivation of the old traditions and pagan habits which is explained by the thorough development of the land in settlement areas, once these had been conquered. Thus there only remained certain neo-Latin and Celtic residual populations, especially in the towns. The open countryside was re-settled to a very considerable extent by Alemannic warrior-peasants, as can

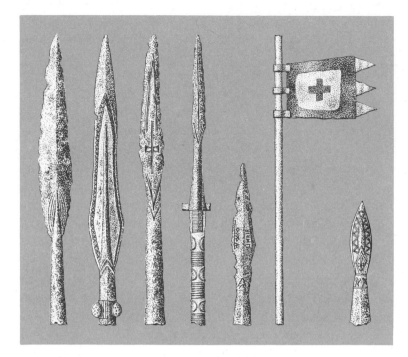

Richly decorated lance-heads and a flag-stave from Aleman graves

be seen from numerous place-names ending in -ing, -heim, -weiler, -feld, -hausen or -dorf, and in Switzerland also -ikon. These were large hamlet and village settlements, judging from the urn-fields. The fortified settlements, some of which were of Celtic origin, usually functioned as the political and cultural centres of the Alemannic districts. Names such as Berchta, Frigga or Hulda, apart from the fact of their Germanic origin, also indicate that up till the 6th century at least the ancient polytheistic beliefs continued to be maintained. Maternal deities (known as "matrones" and possibly of pre-Germanic origin, e.g., Celtic) played an outstanding role in this, side-by-side with other gods (Wodan). Only after the Alemans became subordinate to the already Catholic Franks did Christian influences become stronger—and from the Northwest, not from the South. Missionaries of Frankish or Irish-Scottish origin, such as Saint

Columba, Gallus and Pirminius were active among the Alemans and founded the monasteries at Bregenz, St. Gallen and Reichenau. By about 715, the Catholic Church with the bishoprics of Chur, Basle, Constance, Strasbourg and Augsburg had become firmly established among the Alemans, too.

The Franks

The details concerning the origin of the Franks, who occupy an important place both in German and French history, have been much disputed. Although the original Germanic tribes of the Weser-Rhine area from which the West Germanic confederacy of the Franks emerged did not move very far away from their point of origin, there is by no means unanimity of opinion about the exact time at which the Bructeri, Amsivarii, Chamavi, Tubanti, Ubii, Sugambri and other tribes became "Franks". It is not possible to give an accurate indication, either, of the extent to which these small tribes participated in the forming of the larger tribal confederacy; many of the older tribes later lost their names completely while others kept theirs longer, as is evident from the "competition" between the name Salians (Salii) or Ripuarians (Ripuarii = riverside Franks) and the designation for the tribe as a whole.

Some of these tribes, such as the Ubii who settled in the Cologne area, were exposed to the influences of Roman colonization along the Rhine at an early date. On the one hand, this led to social levelling but on the other these influences contributed to the emergence of an antagonistic class-society. Other tribes retained the old tribal character for a longer time. The militant attitude associated with many Germanic tribes at the stage of military democracy was retained for a considerable period by the tribes along the right bank of the Rhine and at the mouth of that river (Salians, Batavians) in particular. They were feared by the Romans but were included as far as possible in Roman defensive strategy on the principle of *divide et impera*. Thus for a long time the Franks, who were pushing forward on

land and—to a certain degree—engaging in piratical activities at sea, were unable to establish permanent settlements in Northern Gaul, at least not as independent units. Until the 3rd and even 4th century, the Romans always succeeded in repelling Frankish contingents who were seeking new settlement areas or in settling captured Franks in depopulated areas. A particular problem in this connection are the *laetes*, as they were known. These were Barbarians who served as regular units in the Roman army but mostly under the command of tribal leaders having the rank of

Stylized human figures from the Aleman area

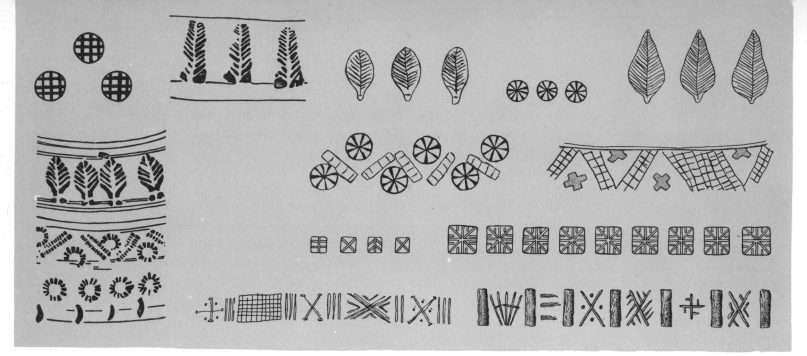

Frankish decorative patterns

prefect under their own law and were spread over large areas of Gaul and Italy. At least one Frankish laetes unit is even mentioned in the State Handbook of the *Notitia Dignitatum*. However, the large number of non-Frankish laetes formations indicates that it was precisely this new Gallo-Italic defence system which was designed to hold back the Franks from the right bank of the Rhine and similar tribal confederacies. At the same time, of course, it was intended to control the Bagaudae movement which was dangerous for the central government. The connection of the "grave-line" civilization in Northern Gaul and Belgium with the laetes is still disputed but these burial fields are clearly linked with a Germanic population. Despite such defensive strategies of the 4th century and the continuous modifications to them by such capable emperors as Julian and Valentinian I, the base of the "free" Franks on the right bank of the Lower Rhine remained strong and was known by the name of Francia even before the time of Ammianus Marcellinus (XXX, 3, 7). Depending on the situation, the tribal potential there launched small- or large-scale attacks on Roman territory or on the areas of the neighbouring Alemans or Burgundians. To begin with, it was generally the open countryside which was ravaged but by the time of Julian they were also attacking cities such

as Cologne and Trier. The first agrarian settlements of the Franks, and specifically of the Salians, were established in Toxandria, in the district between the Meuse and the Scheldt, which may also be regarded as the point of origin of the Merovingian empire. Even such an imperially minded general as Aetius had to concede the acquisition of various tracts of land by the Franks, this being not least in conjunction with the containment of the invading Huns under Attila. It was at this time, when the differentiation of the tribal nobility and the decline of the authority of the popular assemblies of the individual tribes were taking place, that kings (minor kings) also appeared upon the scene, succeeding and replacing the older ducal power or the district principes. In some places, their residences were already of an urban character, especially of course when they established permanent settlements in former Roman cities such as Cologne, Metz or Tournai which had not been totally destroyed. The formal dependence of these minor kings and states on Rome was still maintained, however, until the time of Childeric, the father of Clovis, who defended what remained of Roman authority in Gaul against the Visigoths who even in the formal sense were not subjects of Rome. It was not until the time of Clovis that a crushing defeat was inflicted in 486 on Syagrius, the last Roman ruler, at Soissons.

On the basis of the successes against Rome and other states (Visigoths, Burgundians, Alemans), he was then able to establish an integrated Frankish empire of great territorial extent which absorbed the former tribes. The individual features of the tribes then survived only in certain names and, to a certain degree, in the judicial system *(Lex Salica, Lex Ribuaria)*. Of epochal significance was also the conversion of Clovis to Catholic Christianity, which gave the Frankish empire a more certain future than the Arian creed of other Germanic tribes. The contradiction between the Franks and the Romans, the majority of whom were long since Catholic, was thus totally eliminated. And thus the way gradually became free for the creation of a great early feudal state under the rule of the Merovingians and their Carolingian seneschals and successors. Under the predecessors of Charlemagne, this state already began to prepare for the confrontation with the Byzantine empire and the great Islamic states and in the "Carolingian Renaissance", which produced men like Alcuin, Einhard or Hrabanus, forward-looking cultural elements of the most diverse origin fused with Antique intellectual achievements to form a synthesis of a new kind in the empire of the Franks.

The Anglo-Saxons

The tribes of the Angles, Saxons and Jutes were members of the North Sea group of the Western Germanic people and, after engaging in plundering and exploration, they established themselves in most of Britain (England) in the years after 449. Although the Venerable Bede, himself an Angle, only reports these events in the 8th century, there is not much doubt about the date quoted. After 407, Roman troops were withdrawn from Britain for the urgent defence of Gaul and Italy. Taking advantage of the resultant power-vacuum, inroads were made by the Picts and the Scots, much to the dismay of the more or less Romanized Britons in the South of the island. Some of the Britons and remaining Romans withdrew to the Armorican peninsula, now known as Brittany, while others turned to the Angles

and Saxons for help. A militia army was established with the support of the Emperor Honorius for the defence of many of the fortified towns and walled estates, evidence of which has recently been found in the form of weapons and remainders of clothing (such as belt-buckles). In the long term, however, it could not retain control of the situation. The actual process of settlement of the North Sea tribes took place under the auspices of the mythical brothers Hengist and Horsa, who—as their names indicate—were dioscuric brothers but also reflected a widespread equine cult at the same time. By the end of the 5th century, the following picture had emerged: the Jutes from around the mouth of the Rhine settled in Kent and the Isle of Wight; the Saxons advancing from the Lower Elbe occupied Sussex, Essex and Wessex while the Angles from Schleswig-Holstein took over Suffolk, Norfolk, Mercia and Northumbria. Attack and defence followed this occupation of land since not only the Picts—against whom a wall was built in the North—and the Scots remained enemies of the Anglo-Saxons but also some of the Britons, who were not prepared to accept the newcomers as their masters. Those that were able to avoid subjugation withdrew to Cornwall and Wales. Procopius in the mid-6th century reports on an Angle empire but also mentions the existence of other smaller realms. In the constant confrontation with the Celtic Britons, which is still mirrored in the varying origin of place- and river-names, 824 may be quoted as the date of emergence of the first national state, which was associated with King Egbert of Wessex.

It might be assumed that the wild and warlike Angles and Saxons were practically untouched by the influence of a fairly advanced civilization. This, however, is only true to a certain extent, as will be seen after a brief digression about the name of the latter people. It seems that this must be associated with the *sax* (Sahs), the single-edged sword regarded as a kind of national weapon, which also gave the name of their chief deity, Sahsnot (the Sword-swinger). To begin with, the Anglo-Saxon civilization in Britain largely followed their traditional pattern. This is apparent from the simple settlements and houses, the humped and pierced vessels and the fibulae with equal arms or in the shape of a cross which have been found both on the mainland

and in Southeast Britain. More difficult to classify are the belt-buckles known only from certain warrior-graves which from the Late Roman period—and probably up to at least 500—point to close relations with the Gallo-Frankish area. The various related aspects of the mode of burial are also subject to varying interpretations. However, many new developments and mixed forms with the cultural values of the earlier Romano-British population soon emerged.

This is most clearly indicated by the Christianization of the pagan Anglo-Saxons, all of whom had hitherto been polytheistic and, in addition to Sahsnot, also venerated an Earth-Mother *(eorthan modor)*. Most of them were converted by Roman monks, sent under the Abbot Augustinus to Canterbury in 597 by Pope Gregory I. King Ethelbert of Kent was the first who had himself baptized by the Benedictines but after 604 they were also successful in Essex (London). In the following decades, their missionary activity spread over the whole of the Anglo-Saxon area and they established a kind of national Church which, admittedly, was closely dependent on Rome. This development was not, however, so straightforward as it might appear since the Irish-Scottish monks originating from Ireland had also tried to convert the Anglo-Saxons. From the mid-7th century, considerable efforts were invested in the founding of churches and religious houses (Synod of Streaneshalch 664) and education and science flourished in the Anglo-Saxon monasteries (Aldhelm, Bede). On the other hand, both the Irish-Scottish and the Anglo-Saxon monks soon sent missionaries to the mainland, particularly to the Friesian area (Willibrord, Boniface). These wandering bishops even reached the Middle Rhine and Upper Danube districts (Emmeram, Corbinian, Rupert of Worms).

The Lombards

Appropriately enough, the Lombards come almost at the end of this review since they were latecomers in the Great Migration and it was only after the mid-6th century that they invaded for-mer Imperial territory. However, in many respects they merit more interest than the Thuringians, for instance, or the Avars and Slavs, who were likewise involved in the events at a late date but—even in the geographical aspect—remained on the edge of the happenings associated with the Great Migration.

The older and newer Lombard traditions were noted by Paulus Diaconus who, living for a time in the vicinity of Charlemagne, wrote a history of the Lombards in addition to works on the history of the Church. A Lombard himself, he found himself in a similar situation to that of Jordanes since his people had already lost their political independence. Originating from Southern Scandinavia like many other Germanic tribes, the Lombards must have been related to the Goths. In the course of conflicts with the Vandals, a detailed account of which was provided by Paulus Diaconus, they came to the area of the Lower Elbe. During their long settlement on Lüneburg Heath and in Mecklenburg, many new developments must have begun in this tribe which was already known to Tacitus under the name of Lombards (Langobards = long beards). A king emerged from the ranks of the nobility and there are also many references to bondmen. A major change in the tribal structure took place through numerous overlappings with other tribes and through heavy losses in combat which, in turn, brought many prisoners into the tribe. The Lombards even had to adopt many members of other tribes in preparation for future conflicts. Thus it is relatively easy to explain how an initially North Germanic tribe became more of an Elbe Germanic people, the only reminder of its origin being found in some personal names and points of law. The change from the older Vanir religion to a belief in Wodan was also associated with this process of transformation. Apart from archaeological traces, the extended period of residence of the Lombards along the Lower Elbe is also confirmed by many names (Bardowiek, Bardengau). More mysterious are the reasons which led them southwards and the stations on their way, which this tribe took later than most of the other Germanic groups. It seems that most of the tribe set out in the direction of Lower Lusatia in the late 4th century. Following the disintegration of the Hun empire, they were probably in the Bratislava

70 Gold coin of the Byzantine Emperor Justinian I (527–565), (Staatliche Museen, Berlin). The front of this gold solidus (weight approx. 4 g) depicts the ruler in the attire of an emperor, resembling the images of him on mosaics at Ravenna (Imperial orb with cross in the right hand!). The legend reads: D(OMINUS) N(OSTER) JUSTINIANUS P(ATER) P(ATRIAE) AUG(USTUS) (= Our Lord Justinian, the noble (Imperial) Father of the Fatherland).

71 Gold medallion of Theodoric the Great (493–526), diameter approx. 35.5 mm, weight (with rings) 15.32 g (Thermae Museum, Rome). This medallion, which was probably minted in 500 on the occasion of his visit to Rome, shows a frontal view of the king himself, with long hair hanging down. He wears a general's cloak (*paludamentum*) and coat of mail. His right arm is raised, as if in a gesture of benediction, and he carries in his left hand a globe on which there stands a Victory with wreath and palm-branch (the reverse side shows the goddess of victory on a globe alone). The inscription on the front contains a characteristic mistake since it reads REX THEODERICUS PIUS PRINCIS (instead of PRINCEPS) (= King Theodoric, the pious ruler) (or it may be an abbreviation, meaning something like "Princeps Invictus Semper"—the always invincible ruler).

72 Tomb of Theodoric in Ravenna. In its form, the mausoleum of the Ostrogothic king who ruled from 493 to 526 combines Mediterranean and Germanic influences. Built on brick foundations, the tomb is of Istrian limestone, decagonal at the base, circular at the top and crowned by a huge megalithic block with twelve projecting stones. Whereas the architecture recalls the dolmen graves found throughout the Mediterranean region, the decoration—such as the tongs frieze—contains some Germanic elements. The structure was originally surrounded by lattice-work with marble pillars carved in relief.

area, where some sites have been identified. About 507, they defeated the Heruli living in present-day Lower Austria and spread to many areas of Bohemia and Slovakia. A first period of ascendancy is marked by the reign of King Wacho, who safeguarded his sphere of authority by astute treaties of alliance and—like the Ostrogoth Theodoric the Great—through a comprehensive marriage-policy. Diplomatic relations linked the Lombards with the Silingi in Silesia, the Gepidae, Heruli, Thuringians and Franks. They soon came under Byzantine influence as well and were persuaded to become allies by Justinian's envoys who promised annual payments and settlement right (Pannonia). In the long struggle for Italy with the Ostrogoths, Byzantium also used Lombard mercenaries following these agreements.

Finally, hostilities with the Gepidae must have been the main reason for the Lombards moving to Italy although it is true that King Alboin, who formed an alliance with the Avars advancing from the East, was able to throw back the Gepidae in 567, their territory being occupied by the Avars. However, the uncomfortable proximity of the mounted newcomers obviously left the Lombards, who were still fairly weak in numbers, no other choice but to move southwards, which the main body of the tribe—including splinter-groups of the Saxons and other tribes—did without delay. It is also possible that the Lombards were joined by scattered remnants of the Ostrogoths and many Romans since the bureaucracy and fiscality of the Byzantines, who gave new life again to the remnants of the slave-owning structure in Italy, had aroused the hostility of broad sections of the population against Constantinople. Thus the quick successes of the Lombards are to be explained not only by the strike capability of their mounted contingents but rather by an adroit policy of alliance with oppressed sections of the population and with Barbarian minorities dispersed throughout Italy. In 572, Pavia was captured and made the capital of the new empire. The murder of Alboin (572) and the interregnum that soon followed prevented an immediate consolidation of the new state. Due to the specific spheres of influence and power in Italy, this also followed a very different course from those of corresponding events in Spain and France. When the settlement of the Lom-

bards was completed under King Authari (584–590), for the most part on ownerless land and third parts of large estates in Northern Italy (especially the Po Valley, to a lesser extent in Umbria and Northern Tuscany, sparsely in the Lombard duchies of Spoleto and Benevento), the division of Italy into several sovereign spheres was already clearly marked: the Papal sphere, from which the Pontifical State later emerged; the Byzantine sphere, comprising Ravenna, the Romagna, Sicily and parts of Southern Italy; and the Lombard sphere, which had to be content with what was left—a large but ragged area. This division into two or three parts has influenced the history of Italy down to the most recent past.

The incapacity of the Lombards to take possession of the whole of Italy continued to confront them with new problems. It was not often that the southern duchies were closely linked with the kingdom limited to Northern Italy. Enormous efforts by the legislative and executive were needed to protect the mostly ragged frontiers and to accustom both Lombards and Romans, who gradually adjusted to each other—partly *de facto* and partly *de jure*, to the emergent early feudal order. The kings appointed influential administrators to the royal areas in particular and these *gastaldi*, as they were known, competed with the dukes who were striving for independence. Even more important, as the real instruments of the royal machinery of power, were the *gasindi* (servants). Although they were sometimes bondmen, they played a major part in the system of Lombard vassalage. Other retainers were designated as *actor, ministerialis, stolesazo* or *sculdahis* (mayor) which reflects the great Germanic influence in the legal sphere. Thus the old Germanic popular assembly survived among the Lombards in the form of the military assembly. Nevertheless, Neo-Latin influence soon became strong and the final process of fusion was initiated by the gradual conversion of the Lombards to Catholicism. Even kings such as Rothari (636–652), whose edict of 643 has been called "the most outstanding legislative work" (O. Brunner) of this period, could only delay this a little. This book of law was written in Vulgar Latin but included numerous Lombard legal terms. As a kind of synthesis of many Germanic tribal codes of law (connections

73/74 Gold coin of the Merovingian King Childebert III (695–711), (Staatliche Museen, Berlin). The front side of this solidus, which weighs 3.96 g, bears the portrait of the king wearing a diadem and looking to the right, next to it a B and an inscription—partly in horizontal letters—which reads MASSILIA (a reference to where it was minted). On the reverse side, there is a cross on a globe between the letters M A (Massilia) and the inscription HILDEBERTUS RIX (King Childebert).

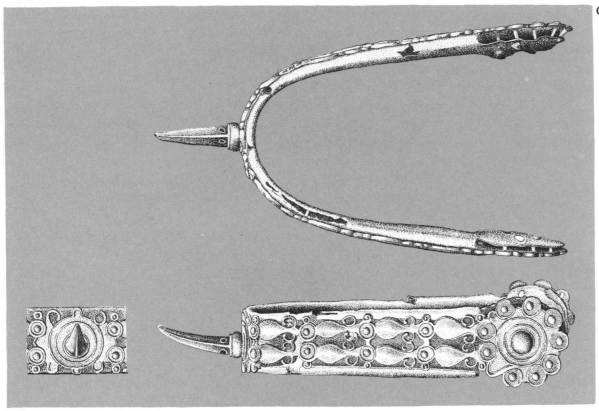

with Saxon and Visigothic law have been identified), it exercised great influence on later codifications and, with the constant addition of supplementary laws (the last by Liutprand), it was replaced only gradually from the end of the 8th century by Frankish royal law. Admittedly, it achieved only limited validity for the Neo-Latin population since the original inhabitants continued to be judged by Roman law.

Of course, in many respects Lombard rule meant a negative turn of events for Italy. With the decline of the towns, which had already suffered much from the Byzantine confrontation with the Ostrogoths, the advanced economy of Italy also experienced a severe setback. The decline in commerce and the crafts led to the re-appearance of a barter economy, a process which was also reflected in the reversion of many towns to rural communities.

On the other hand, the vigour of the Lombards in establishing new settlements, not only in the areas which later became Lombardy, was unmistakable. Archaeologists and place-name researchers have already shed much light on these events, through which the Lombards even emerge, in a certain sense, as the defenders of the tradition of urban settlement in Italy.

This positive role also corresponds to the patronage given by many Lombard kings and noblemen to the arts and culture. This applies to both literature and jurisprudence and naturally to architecture, sculpture and small-scale decorative art. The weapons, pottery and clothing accessories in the Lombard "graveline" burial fields in Northern and Central Italy have shown what was developed from the traditional forms of the Elbe and Danube periods. Of importance here, on the one hand, is the

retention of the plaited band which, in the Danube area, may be an amalgam of Lombard, Slav and Avaric forms. On the other, the plaited band was restyled for animal-style ornamentation, for instance on fibulae. Naturally, the complete Christianization of art in Italy inspired many new ideas and motifs. As will be indicated in the next chapter, too, traditional themes were still used to some extent, as illustrated by the paintings in palaces with scenes from Lombard history or by the design of the Agilulf Plate (probably the front part of a helmet, now in the Bargello in Florence). Despite this, Italian and Byzantine influences were strong and, in particular, dominated court art. This is adequately shown by objects belonging to the Cathedral treasure of the former residence of Monza, particularly the Lombard Crown—an iron circlet within a gold one—or the book cover of Queen Theodelinde which is ornamented with precious stones, pearls and cloisonné and contains eight Antique cameos. The round gold fibulae from the Lombard burial field of Castel Trosino with their many gems and filigree work also reflect Byzantine

influence although some of them have plaited band decoration. These objects, which belong to a type of commodity in general use, illustrate the extent of Byzantine influence and the versatility which resulted precisely in Italy from the mingling of different cultural traditions. It was natural that the traditional influence should be strongest of all in architecture since neither the Goths, nor the Lombards could provide any stimulus here. The most that may have been attempted was perhaps to introduce something of the Germanic tradition of wood-carving in the construction of palaces or churches. However, in the field of sculpture and ornamentation, Germanic influence was more marked.

The Thuringians

This tribe is the last in this somewhat abbreviated list. It emerged by A.D. 400 at the earliest from the old tribe of the Hermunduri but together with groups from the Suebi, Angles and Varni. Even then, it remained in the background of the stage of the Great Migration although it can scarcely be omitted from any attempt to characterize the nature of this movement of peoples, especially when the wealth of contrasts in the overall development of that time is considered. And even for the later development of the German nation the Thuringians were scarcely less important than the Saxons, Franks, Alemans, and Bavarians. The name appears for the first time around 400 and seems to be linked with the second component of Hermunduri, meaning something like "descendants of the Duri". This etymology recalls a long phase in their early history which—as in other tribes—continued to live in sagas about their origins and in heroic epics.

The movement of other tribes and peoples to the South provided the Thuringians, who were gradually changing from their belief in Wodan and the cults of the fertility deities to the Christian faith, with the opportunity in the 5th century to spread out between the Harz Mountains, the Saale and the Bohemian Forest as far as the Danube. They controlled the Upper Pa-

Comb from a grave of the Thuringian empire period

latinate at least for a time and advanced to the Passau area. In the West, their territory bordered on that of the Alemans. This early Thuringian state reached a high-point at the turn of the 5th and 6th centuries, its extensive territory being administered by kings from political centres such as Weimar and perhaps Beesenstedt as well. In addition to craftsmen, local and foreign merchants met here. Intergovernmental relations were handled by legations from the various countries. King Bisin's daughter, Radegunde, became the wife of Wacho, the Lombard king and it is likely that other dynastic links were established in this way. By a marriage with the niece of Theodoric the Great, Amalaberga, whose name indicated that she was a member of the Ostrogothic Amaler dynasty, King Herminafried, a son of Bisin, was ultimately even able to establish close relations with the Germanic hegemonic power of the time. Thus Thuringia, although it was a peripheral state, did have a voice in the process of central political planning which regarded a large block of Great Migration states—especially the realms of the Vandals, Visigoths, Burgundians and Thuringians—as a stabilizing element in the Mediterranean area and beyond and limited the territorial ambitions of the Franks and Byzantines. With the death of Theodoric, this large-scale venture immediately collapsed and since the heirs of the Ostrogothic king had enough difficulty right from the start in safeguarding their base in Italy, they had to leave Burgundy and Thuringia to the mercy of the Franks. After a victorious battle in the area of the Unstrut, the Frankish kings Theuderic and Chlotar conquered the territory of the Thuringians with Saxon help (531). The northern part with the Harz Mountains went to Saxony while the remainder became Frankish—apart from the districts near the Saale which fell into other hands and were settled by the Slavs. The fall of the Thuringian empire was commemorated in the *Nibelungenlied* in the figures of the Landgrave Irnvrit of Düringen and the Margrave Iring of Tenemarken. As regards the legal sphere in particular, there is an echo of this early epoch in Thuringian law which was not recorded until the time of Charlemagne. After the loss of its independence, Thuringia continued to exist—with various centres—as a duchy under Frankish sovereignty. In the struggles with the Sorbs and other Slavs, it achieved a certain degree of independence from the 7th century onwards.

The Thuringian and other Central German sites of the Great Migration period have already been thoroughly investigated. The largest burial fields of the Thuringian empire lie near Weimar, Stössen and Mühlhausen and have already provided many interesting finds. Nevertheless, it can be assumed that much information is still to come, regarding in particular the relationship between locally made weapons, jewellery and commodities and imports which came as tokens of friendship from Ostrogothic Italy and the Frankish and Anglo-Saxon areas. In many graves, local and markedly traditional pottery, for instance turned vessels (Gerbstedt, Leuna) or amber objects, predominate. Gilded silver plate and decorative techniques such as filigree and granulation were in use as early as the 3rd and 4th centuries. The frequent occurrence of intact burials without weapons but with a variety of utensils indicates Gothic influence. The ancient custom of placing a coin in the hand of the corpse must also have come from the East Germans. A few large burial chambers have been discovered with room for a complete store of such utensils and objects. From time to time, the horses they rode were also buried with the dead, a reminder of the ancient cult of Wodan. Glass beakers and bronze dishes took the place of the earlier drinking-horns and geese and chicken on silver platters were placed by the dead as provisions on their way (royal grave at Hasslingen). There are considerable differences in detail—for instance, urn burial or the burial of the intact corpse according to the period. Especially common are the "Thuringian fibulae" with indented fastener-part and golden clasps, ornamented with almandine and ending in eagle-heads (Weimar). For female under-garments, small fibulae of various types were used, mostly made from gilded silver (sometimes set with almandine). During the later period of the Thuringian empire, it was usually the case that weapons were again placed in warrior graves, such as two-edged swords, thrusting-lances, javelins and bows and arrows. Single-edged knives have also been found.

The Emergence
of the Culture
of the Great Migration in Europe

So far our attention has been centred on the collision between Rome—at the end of its era—and the young Barbarian peoples which culminated in new political and social forms. Now is the time to take a look at some of the results of the new age which developed mainly in the West of the former empire. All who concern themselves with the problem will be astonished time and again by the diversity of the structural forms and the cultural and religious manifestations which emerged from this epoch which is usually dismissed as barren and decadent, barbarian and dark. Indeed, there was probably no sphere of life which was characterized by a completely peaceful development, a "classical" spirit or a steadfastly pursued ideal, apart from the important exception of the monks. The ascetic ideal of wordly poverty and the concentration on spiritual aims left a clear imprint on this epoch in particular, as exemplified by Benedict of Nursia, the founder of the monastery of Monte Cassino. It is worth mentioning since monastic art and culture represents—to say the least—a very important element within ecclesiastical culture as a whole, which soon assumed a predominant position. Although the Latins, as the heirs of the Christian and Antique tradition—or of that which they regarded as such, were initially the dominating personalities of the monastic life, many diligent pupils nevertheless soon came forward from the ranks of the Barbarians. Once Arianism had been overcome, the Catholic Church and the monastic institutions experienced a perceptible upswing in almost all the Barbarian states.

Kingship, Church and Society

As already noted, it was above all the dynasties and ruling circles of the Barbarians who made a rapid change to Christianity. Apart from its dogmatic complexity (doctrins of the Trinity, Virgin birth), in its hierarchical structure and the increasingly socio-conservative nature of its teaching the new religion represented an important ally for the central governments of the Barbarians which were initially weak but systematically pursued

the full development of their power. Kings such as Geiseric (428–477) and Clovis (482–511) made use of Arianism or Catholicism to reinforce their authority. Only by this did they succeed in controlling the tribal nobility which was striving for independence or in replacing it by a service aristocracy and in reducing the mass of the free commoners to obedience, these ultimately becoming subjects. The Church certainly played an important part in this early feudal development and there is perhaps no better and certainly no more vivid introduction to it than an episode from Frankish history of 486 as related by Gregory of Tours (II, 27). It starts with the victory over Syagrius and the subsequent plundering of numerous churches by the still pagan Franks: "Thus the Franks had taken away from one church a pitcher of wondrous size and beauty in addition to other religious utensils. The bishop of that church thereupon sent unto the king and requested that at least this pitcher be returned, if not the other holy vessels. When the king heard this, he said to the messenger: 'Follow us to Soissons, where all the booty must be divided. If chance assigns that vessel to me, I will fulfil the request of the bishop.' He then came to Soissons and the whole of the booty was publicly collected together. The king spake: 'Bold warriors, I beg you, apart from my share, that you do not refuse me that vessel'—by which he meant the pitcher mentioned. The wiser ones answered the king: 'All which we see, glorious King, is thine and also we ourselves are subject to thy rule. Now do what thou wilt for none can withstand thy power.' When they had said this, a thoughtless, envious and inconsiderate person cried aloud, drove his battle-axe into the pitcher and shouted: 'Nothing shalt thou have of it but that which the lot truly gives you.' All were ashamed but the king bore the insult with mildness, took the pitcher and gave it to the messenger of the church but secretly he nursed in his breast the abuse. When now a year had passed, he had the whole of the army called together with its weapons to display the splendour of its arms on the field of Mars. And when he had inspected all, he came to him who had pierced the pitcher and spake to him: 'None has such neglected weapons as thou, thy spear, thy sword and thy battle-axe are fit for nothing.' And he seized the other's battle-

Gerovit stone from Wolgast

which took place in almost all the states of the Great Migration. Gregory of Tours lived several generations later than Clovis and, through his history of the Frankish Church, was one of the best-known representatives of the intellectual life of his time. As apparent from the report, he is completely on the side of the king as the central authority responsible for order, justice and decency. He does not say that the state of development of the Franks under Clovis still excluded, *de jure*, a clearly delineated and despotic royal authority. There is only a hint that the king is making a request and in any case the intention here is primarily to underline the mildness and humility which subsequently led to his conversion. The full extent of Gregory's historiographic intentions will not be investigated here since it is not very relevant to the present problem. At any rate, he has more sympathy for the king, still pagan but concerned about Church interests, than for the simple Frankish warrior, out for plunder and insisting on his rights, who appears as an enemy of the Church. What the army took from the Church is returned again by the king—at least symbolically in the shape of the pitcher. From this viewpoint, it does not bother Gregory that Clovis was the real instigator of the injustice done to the Church and that later, as a Christian, he still waged many bloody wars.

An essential feature of the development as a whole is the figure of the opposing warrior who, in the historico-literary system of reference, may best be described as the Frankish Thersites since he bears a remarkable resemblance in his function to the opponent of the prince in the *Iliad* and represents the level of social development of the time, the *status quo ante*. He is one of the peasant-warriors of the Great Migration Period who had the heaviest burden to bear both in the seizure of land and in agricultural production and accordingly insisted on their traditional rights. They often had to exchange their sword for the plough and frequently kept livestock as well. They nevertheless still had a say in the military and popular assemblies and from time to time took important decisions concerning war and peace, for instance, or the election of a new king. Clovis, initially joint ruler and then sole king of the Salians, was himself elected king of the Ripuarians as well by the choice of the people after the murder

axe and threw it to the ground. When the latter bent to pick it up, the king raised his arm and plunged his axe in the other's head, saying: 'So thou did it to the pitcher in Soissons.' When he had died, he allowed the others to return home and caused great fear in them by this deed."

It is not only on account of its vigorousness that this episode is of interest—vividness and frankness were a Germanic tradition in political and legal matters. Exactly as the events are described by Gregory, it reflects a very important development of Sigibert, the Ripuarian king. The episode here shows, however, that the influence of the ordinary warriors in the popular and military assemblies was constantly declining. The aristocracy and the service nobility at the disposal of the aristocracy and the king now played the sole dominating role and the individual warriors could still only express their opinion *de iure* at the most but not *de facto* when the king had the support of the leading circles. Like the king himself, the latter had authority over land and subjects and thus influenced the socio-economic developments of the early feudal system. The king still had to divide his power with this aristocracy—although his authority was gradually becoming unlimited—but not with the mass of freemen, whose status was declining more and more to that of subjects. The actual process took various courses in the individual states. Among the Vandals and Ostrogoths, the royal power developed very rapidly and was not hampered very much by the hereditary or service aristocracy. The monarch achieved a marked ascendancy in all spheres —arrière-ban, jurisdiction, legislation, economics and implementation of the law—and the Vandal king was also supreme in ecclesiastical affairs since the kings of the Hasdingi claimed absolute authority not only over the Arian Church of the Vandals and Alans but also over the Catholic Church. This no-nonsense form of authority, resembling in many ways the approach of the Byzantine rulers, was ended by the rapid conquest of the Vandal and Ostrogothic empires by Justinian's generals Belisarius and Narses. In the Visigothic and Frankish empires, developments took a zigzag course to a certain extent. For the Franks, the royal power was linked with a certain family—the Merovingians—which was later replaced by the Carolingians, who acquired power and influence as seneschals. However, feuds and inheritance divisions weakened the position of the kings who fundamentally were aiming at autocracy, an objective in which they were supported by the Church in return for a certain division of authority. There was often a state of anarchy among the aristocracy, as was particularly evident among the Visigoths, whose king had the unconditional support of the Church, especially at the Imperial Council of Toledo, but could not even gain acceptance of the hereditary principle. While, from the outside,

the office of kingship was endowed with pomp and circumstance by the acquisition of titles such as dominus rex, gloriosus rex or principalis sublimitas, by sacral acts of consecration such as coronation and anointment and even by the formal development of an ideology centred around the sovereign, as is mirrored by legislation and contemporary literature, it was increasingly restricted—especially in the Visigothic state—as far as the actual basis of its power was concerned, i. e., in the socio-economic control of property and people. The constant alienation of the ruling stratum from the king in early feudal society is most clearly expressed by the fact that the aristocrats defended the interests of their followers without placing a heavier burden on them—as far as possible—in the event of war. Betrayal of the legitimate king became a kind of habit, according to the sometimes ironical reports of the historians. Even in 711, many of the Gothic nobles deserted the army of Roderic or crossed over to the Arabs. The latter, it should be remembered, were not only "national" enemies but also ideological adversaries and were able to win the battle of Jerez more easily as a result of this.

The episode quoted also provides a good insight into the social and thus specifically cultural problems of the Frankish empire and other comparable states. It is apparent that the early feudal state, in the course of its rapid development, rode roughshod over all the old rights and customs and created something which was incomprehensible and even hostile when judged from a traditionally Barbarian standpoint. This "something" was the concept of state power. The often manipulated product of Roman state doctrine and ecclesiastical influence, this emerged as something at variance with the Barbarian tradition of popular power which was based on the popular union of the "military democracy". The place of the popular union was taken to an increasingly more apparent extent by a union of subjects in which an hierarchical structure became more and more evident. The later orders of rank (*Heerschildordnungen*), the Church and the service nobility came directly after the king while the free subjects were lower on the scale. According to a maxim of Avitus of Vienne (Gregory of Tours, II, 40), the king was the chief of the people but not the people chief of the king. Thus, any right

75 Silver coin of the Vandal King Gunthamund (484–496), (Staatliche Museen, Berlin). It is 2.08 g in weight and 1.8 cm in diameter. On the front side there is a profile portrait of the king, looking to the right and wearing a diadem. Around this there is the legend D(OMINUS) N(OSTER) REX GUNTHAMUND (I?) (Our Lord King Gunthamund), the whole of which can still be easily read. The reverse sides of these late Vandal coins often depict palms or female figures with ears of corn in their hands and carry the inscription FELIX KARTHAGO (fortunate Carthage), a reference to the wealth of the land.

76 Silver coin of the Vandal King Hilderic (523–530), (Staatliche Museen, Berlin). This coin weighs 1.26 g and is 1.6 cm in diameter. On one side there is a profile portrait of the diadem-crowned king looking to the right, together with the partly effaced inscription D(OMINUS) N(OSTER) HILDIRIX REX (Our Lord King Hilderic).

77 Empress Ariadne (Ivory relief, *c.* 500; height 30.5 cm; width 10.6 cm; Bargello, Florence). The ruler considered to be the Empress Ariadne (married in 466 to the later Emperor Zenon and then, as his widow in 491, to Anastasios I, whom she raised to Imperial rank) is depicted in full court attire. She wears her State robes and crown and carries a sceptre and Imperial orb, surmounted by a cross. The baldachin carried on pillars above her likewise underlines the prestigious character of the relief which probably came from the Byzantine area.

78 Equestrian statue of Charlemagne from the treasure of Metz Cathedral (Louvre, Paris). This bronze statuette from the 9th century was cast in several parts, like other statues of Antiquity, and was originally gilded. It may be interpreted as an ideal representation of the first mediaeval emperor although several individual features are in close agreement with Einhard's description. Moustache, crown of lilies and globe seem to indicate the later years of Charlemagne's reign or even of the Carolingian period (perhaps at the Court school under Charles the Bald). The round head is also characteristic of Charlemagne's portrait on coins.

79 Bronze coin of the Ostrogothic King Theodahad (534–536), (Staatliche Museen, Berlin). Of 9.74 g in weight, it has a diameter of 2.5 cm. It bears a profile of the king looking to the right, with a crown closed at the top and wearing royal attire in Byzantine style, the whole being enclosed within the well-preserved legend D(OMINUS) N(OSTER) THEODAHATUS REX (Our Lord King Theodahad). On the reverse side, there is a winged Victory standing on the prow of a ship and bearing a wreath and palm-branch. It is reasonable to assume that this coin could only have been minted at Rome since Theodahad showed the greatest respect towards the Romans and Byzantines, to whom he considered ceding his territory in return for an annual payment.

80 Bronze coin of the Ostrogothic King Badvila (Totila: 541–552), (Staatliche Museen, Berlin). Weight 2.48 g, diameter 1.5 cm. The legend within a wreath on the reverse side can be easily read: D(OMINUS) N(OSTER) BADVILA REX (Our Lord King Badvila). On the other side of coins of this type, there is sometimes an image of the town-goddess of Ticinum (which had a mint at that time), otherwise a beardless half-length portrait of the king in State robes and wearing a crown closed at the top. There is nothing special about the coins of this ruler, the last king of the Ostrogoths (his successor Teja merely represents the final phase). He opposed Byzantium with a massive programme of reform and energetic preparations for war and, for instance, tried to play off the peace policy of the earlier Emperor Anastasios I against the aggressive intentions of Justinian I.

81 Anonymous bronze coin from the Rome of the Ostrogothic period (Staatliche Museen, Berlin). This heavy bronze coin (follis) weighs 11.23 g and has a diameter of 2.6 cm. On the face, which is in poor condition, however, there is a half-length portrait of Roma, the goddess of the city. Her profile is turned to the right and she wears a helmet, ear pendants and a draped robe. The inscription reads: INVICTA ROMA (unconquered or invincible Rome). The reverse side of coins of this type depicts a winged Victory, an eagle or a female wolf with the twins Romulus and Remus. These coins have an unmistakably retrospective basic character, indicating the specific concern of the Roman Senate.

82 Gold coin of the Merovingian King Theudebert I (534–548), (Staatliche Museen, Berlin). On the face of this gold solidus, which weighs 4.14 g and has a diameter of 2 cm, the king is shown with a helmet (?), armour and shield and bearing an Imperial orb surmounted by a cross in his right hand. The legend reads: D(OMINUS) N(OSTER) THEUDEBERTI P(ATER) P(ATRIAE) AUG (USTUS) (Our Lord Theudebert, the noble Father of the Fatherland). The minting of gold and the use of imperial titles such as the PPAUG was regarded as presumptuous in Byzantium, so Procopius relates.

83 Anonymous bronze coin from Ravenna, dating from the Ostrogothic period (Staatliche Museen, Berlin). Weight 3.31 g, diameter 1.7 cm. The face depicts the head of the richly ornamented goddess of the city, turned to the right and wearing a "mural" crown. The inscription reads: FELIX RAVENNA (fortunate Ravenna). The reverse sides of these coins carry a winged Victory or an eagle with wings spread.

84 Gold coin of the Visigothic King Chindasvinth (642–653), (Staatliche Museen, Berlin). This small gold coin—known as a "triens" (one-third of a solidus)—is 1.9 cm in diameter. On the face, the legend CHINDASVINTUS R(E)X encloses a half-length picture of the king and his son Reccesvind. The clearly marked relief of the surface of the coin is explained by the use of sharp tools.

85 Gold coin of the Visigothic King Wamba (672–680), (Staatliche Museen, Berlin). This triens is 1.47 g in weight and 2 cm in diameter. The right profile of the king is enclosed within an inscription, the deciphering and interpretation of which presents some difficulty. It is probably to be understood as follows: IND. IN. M. E. WAMBA RX (In nomine Dei ... Wamba Rex = in the name of God ... King Wamba). This type of coin was minted in Mérida, a similar one coming from Cordova and Seville.

86 Gold coin of the Lombard King Cunibert (Staatliche Museen, Berlin). This triens weighs 1.34 g and is 2 cm in diameter. It depicts the right profile of Cunibert, wearing a diadem and State robes and with his left (!) arm raised as if he were making a speech. There is the following inscription: DNCUN—INCPER (Dominus noster Cunincpertus = Our Lord Cunibert).

87   The so-called Roman Tower (Römerturm) of Regensburg. In actual fact, this is an early mediaeval tower which was used by Ludwig the German (817–876) as a treasure-tower. It is characterized by massive architecture and a Romanesque upper storey.

88   Cathedra (bishop's throne) from Cividale (Museo Archeologico). This marble chair is in the tradition of an important development which goes back to pagan origins in Rome. In comparison with other bishop's thrones, which were even decorated with precious ivory carvings (Ravenna), this one is relatively modest.

89/90 Einhard Basilica of Steinbach in the Odenwald. The central nave, the apse and the crypt still survive of this monastery church founded about 827 by Einhard, the biographer of Charlemagne. Originally with two side-aisles and three vestibules, this basilica was once a large and splendid architectural ensemble. Particularly noteworthy in the central nave are the brick pillars which—unlike columns— emphasize the function of the walls. The round arch arcades above the simple warriors are also characteristic.

91 Painting from a Late Antique tomb at Silistria. Below the figures depicted on it there is also a Gothic servant (probably a slave) whose hair is arranged in similar fashion to that of the Gothic warriors on the Missorium of Theodosius I. From these and similar observations, it is most likely that the tomb and its paintings date from after the great Gothic invasion (376–378). This hypothesis is also reinforced by stylistic comparisons.

92 Santa Maria Antiqua in Rome. After the temporary reconquest of Italy by the Byzantines, many new churches were dedicated to the Virgin Mary. The Church of Santa Maria Antiqua, built by Pope John VII (705–707) on the slopes of the Palatine Hill, contains a great many frescos by Byzantine artists. These paintings, such as those of the apostles in the presbytery, are examples of the final phase of the influence of Byzantine art on the West. Carolingian culture took much of its inspiration from paintings of this kind.

93 Section of a tunic: horseman and lion. Woollen embroidery on linen (15 by 11 cm, Egypt, 6th/7th century). (Early Christian-Byzantine Collection, Staatliche Museen, Berlin.) Between the borders, some of which are formed of leaves, a horseman in full battle array is visible, complete with helmet, coat of mail, shield (round shield?) and a short sword. The lion above him probably indicates that this is a hunting scene. Plant motifs, scattered over the picture, help to make the whole scene less formal.

94 Mounted Saint. Woollen embroidery on linen (24 by 24 cm); Egypt, from the 5th/6th century. (Staatliche Museen, Berlin. Early Christian-Byzantine Collection.) The rider, who is galloping to the right, is enclosed within a framework of foliage motifs, consisting of a symmetrical arrangement of four flower-baskets and eight animals.

95 The interior of San Appollinare Nuovo in Ravenna. This basilica was built by Theodoric as an Arian palace-church and ornamented by magnificent mosaics. When it was taken over by the Orthodox Church, a "revision" and removal of dubious political or religious motifs took place. Despite this, the pictures of Theodoric's palace (part at upper right) and of the port of Classis dating from the Gothic period have been preserved. Particularly noteworthy are the features of the martyrs who are approaching the throne of Christ from one side and the Virgin Mary, who is depicted adoring the three kings, from the other. Between the windows there stand prophets and patriarchs while above them scenes from the New Testament complete the mosaic ornamentation.

96 Apse mosaic from San Apollinare in Classe, Ravenna. The illustrious triple-nave basilica was built after the Byzantine conquest (549). Columns, capital and masonry reveal Byzantine influence. The apse mosaic, which dates from the time when the church was built, shows St. Apollinaris among twelve lambs as the shepherd of his church while above him Christ appears as a cross between the prophets Moses and Elijah.

to co-determination became meaningless and any kind of resistance unlawful. Admittedly, the king had to comply with demands of an exacting nature in accordance with the norms of the time since the State had to ensure not only law and order but also to protect the Church and the Christian faith in the interests of implementing the divine order of the world. The multiplicity of these duties, which led to further and innumerable tasks in detail, naturally resulted in a constant extension of the royal power. On the other hand, there emerged a permanent opposition to this excessive authority in which caesaropapist tendencies were also apparent from time to time. What cannot be denied, however, are the efforts made by the kings and other mighty personalities of this period to fulfil their political and cultural mission—irrespective of whether they were charged with this by a representative group of their own people, by the Church or by virtue of other legitimations. Like Constantine the Great or Julian the Apostate—to name two quite opposite figures of the late Roman period—the rulers of the Vandals, Goths or Franks also endeavoured to promote achievements of new and lasting importance and, at the same time, to preserve the heritage of the past which was based on good traditions and appeared to guarantee the security and continuity of the course of development. These endeavours were often characterized by very clear thinking. It was considered more expedient to proceed with caution in the interests of peaceful relations with the local population, primarily with the "senatorial nobility" who still held an important position in the various parts of the former Roman Empire, and especially to gain the moral support of the Catholic Church. At the beginning and in addition to the above considerations, the psychologically understandable link with Roman dynasties or at least with time-honoured Imperial institutions also played a role. This was why Theodoric the Great and Clovis were only too pleased to assume the dignity of a Roman general or patricius. This impressed the Latin population and, on the other hand, seemed to ensure a better understanding with Byzantium. Even such a radical innovator as Geiseric, the king of the Vandals, who robbed Rome of the best areas of North Africa and was the first to proclaim the full sovereignty of his state on what was

formerly Roman territory, was guided by sober political facts in immediately seeking a reconciliation with what remained of the Western Roman Empire. While he persecuted—and almost liquidated—the Catholic Church and aristocratic landowners in the area that he ruled, he nevertheless sought to establish a bond of relationship with the Theodosian-Valentinian dynasty through his son Huneric. When Valentinian III was murdered in 455, it was Geiseric, the terror of the Romans, who posed as the avenger of the emperor and thus obtained a pretext for his campaign of pillage against the *urbs aeterna*.

Law and Legislation

This is the appropriate place for a concise and comparative review of the various systems of Germanic law (Barbarian law) which, through the principal fields of penal, adjective and estate law, reflected the major developments of the social structure as a whole. Little is known about the system of jurisprudence in the Vandal empire where, as in the Ostrogothic empire, there was no complete codification of the laws. For the former, a certain amount of information is available in literary sources while for the Ostrogoths there is also the *Variae* of Cassiodorus. As mentioned already, the Burgundians and Visigoths recorded their codes of law at an early date, even though this was under quite different conditions. They were followed by the Franks and later by the Lombards, Bavarians, Friesians, Saxons and Thuringians as well. These various bodies of popular law also retained their validity in all the areas which subsequently formed part of the Frankish empire and, in this manner, influenced the development of mediaeval feudal law.

There is much controversy about the origin and aims of the tribal and popular codes of law—which is what they must be called from at least the time that they were first recorded. For the most part, it was a question of prescriptive law which was expressed to some extent in primitive and religiously based concepts (judicial combat as a divine verdict; "wergild" instead of

97/98 Many centuries have had a hand in the building of the Basilica of Aquileja with its characteristic campanile (bell tower). Underneath this Early Romanesque church, which was consecrated in 1031 and altered during the Gothic period, there are the remainders of churches from the 4th and 5th centuries and, in particular, fine mosaic floors (centred around motifs of water, the mystic catching of fishes and the symbolism of baptism). The crypt is decorated with frescos from the 12th and 13th centuries.

blood feud) or legal axioms deriving from poetry. However, new elements entered the sphere of law from several sides. With the Latin language, Roman legal concepts were also adopted, especially in penal and estate law, and this was likewise the source of the influences which were brought into the popular codes of law by the Monarchy and the Church. In both cases, laws were regarded as being of divine origin, a view which was readily acceptable to the Germanic peoples. However, the interpretations of divine law by the legislators and the mass of the population often varied considerably. Even the first codifications, which were carried out almost at the same time as the creation of the illustrious *Corpus Iuris Civilis* by Justinian and his court jurists (529 ff.), gave rise to long disputes between the supporters of the old prescriptive law and the advocates of a clearly defined body of royal law, between the central authority and particularist aristocratic groups and, not least between the kings and the tribal members who had been downgraded to the status of subjects or serfs, i. e., men such as the "Frankish Thersites". The serfs, who from the start were only legal entities, were excluded from exercising any influence on the law. A contributory factor to this was, of course, the strictly rational thinking of the Roman jurists and authors which was passed on to the new rulers, to whom it appeared convenient when the number of completely free legal persons steadily declined.

Admittedly, the codification of the laws was in many ways an advance. Instead of an often questionable word-of-mouth tradition, law now had the authority of the written word which could be changed but not disregarded. An outright breach of the law—especially by the medium-rank feudal authorities—was now more difficult than before, particularly when the executive power operated in association with the legislative power. To be sure, the figure of the unjust judge appears time and again in the literature of this period (Isidore of Seville), which provides food for thought in many respects. Naturally enough, the executive power was in the hands of the higher or medium-rank service nobility as the better-educated Germanic and Latin section of the population. In most cases, it was apparent that they used the limited freedom of interpretation still permitted by the law in

the interests of their families and social group. The direct influence of central supervisory bodies (royal envoys = missi regis) or the Church could do no more than moderate this abuse since it could not be eliminated even by the new personality principle in the legal system. Nevertheless, the transition from the territorial principle—the dominance of the law within an integrated political area—to the personal principle must still be designated, to a certain extent, as an advance. At least, this represented an attempt to establish a system of law which gave more or more appropriate rights, representing a real benefit for the individual as well. This was expressed by the *Lex Ribuaria* (31,3) in the following words: "... that within the Ripuarian territory, Franks, Burgundians and Alemans or from whatever tribe he may come who has to appear before a court answers in the manner prescribed by the law of the place where they were born." However, this principle, which was formulated in a spirit of compromise, was still limited by its non-recognition of systems of law, such as those of the Slavs or Jews, which applied outside the territory of the Frankish empire. Many verdicts, such as those concerning wergild or penance, were taken according to the law of the injured party. In the 9th century, it then became accepted practice in cases of penal law to follow the law valid in the place where the offence was committed. It was self-evident that the Church should remain subject to Roman law—with the exception of the independent churches acknowledging the authority of the king or other noble patrons.

The codified tribal laws were certainly not exhaustive and in this respect could hardly be compared with Roman law which had been evolved in the course of centuries. Both among the Franks and in the other areas, primary importance was attached to possessive right, criminal law and adjective law and there were considerable differences between the individual areas. The development of Visigothic law, for instance, took a fairly independent course. The difference between the Goths and the Romans, particularly after the conversion to Catholicism in 589, became increasingly more difficult to define. The ban on intermarriage was lifted before 586 and officials were recruited from both Goths and Romans. At a later stage, increasing numbers of Romans

Silver panels of the sacrificial vessel of Gundestrup (North Jutland)

performed military service—illustrating the extent to which the two population groups had adapted to each other. Unlike Frankish law, there was a trend here from the personal principle to the territorial principle. Other special features were the emphasis on the activities of judges and their supervision by the central authority and the Church. Ecclesiastical affairs were decided by the Imperial Council of Toledo, an assembly of Church and worldly dignitaries whose decisions always received the royal placet. The Visigothic law, revised for the last time in 681 as the *Lex Visigothorum renovata*, devoted much attention to Church matters; the fifth book deals exclusively with Church ownership of persons (slaves, freed slaves) and things and helped Church views on law, which were strongly marked by ownership relations and their continuous further development, to become established in society. There was great danger in this, as was recognized and even denounced by men such as Isidore of Sevillé since it mostly happened that the Church, as it became richer and richer, paid less attention to its social obligation to protect the poor and oppressed. The Benedictine influence, which could have helped to bring about a compromise here, was scarcely noticeable in Spain since the Spanish Church as a whole, restricted to narrow, territorial thinking, was not receptive at all to external and even Papal pretensions. Seen from the viewpoint of social history and in the light of the latest investigations (Sánchez-Albornoz), the Spanish Church nevertheless has a special merit: through new forms of land-grants to producers and the bearers of arms (as *beneficium*, *stipendium* or *precarium*), it contributed to a particularly rapid implementation of early feudal forms which were then taken a stage further in France.

The constant fluctuation between the persistence with the urge to sweep away everything from the past cannot be clarified any more easily for the legal system than for the remaining structure of society. It was simply not always a strictly logical process. This might have been because the Barbarian kings and noblemen who suddenly became rulers of large areas and immense numbers of subjects felt that they were of lesser intellectual stature than their own subjects and fluctuated between arrogance

and feelings of inferiority, which gave their policies and cultural endeavours a crude and unfinished appearance and sometimes they even seemed brutal and low-minded. Christianized in all haste—without being able to identify themselves with the dogma—and just as hastily Romanized without understanding Antique concepts or even really comprehending just the formal elements such as the Latin language or the Roman system of jurisprudence, they saw themselves faced with tasks of a gigantic magnitude. The reconstruction of society by overcoming the remainders of the slave-owning society and by the fusion of the Latin and Barbarian elements demanded planning and anticipa-

Clothing of Frankish officials of high rank from the Bible of St. Paul

tion, boldness and moderation; qualities which in one form or another existed in the Antique catalogue of virtues particularly in the ethics of rulers, but were never able to really take effect. Emperors of integrity and sound education such as Marcus Aurelius and Julian had clearly anticipated this debacle and, in their manner, had endeavoured to provide an answer to it but with the Barbarian rulers it was often the case that they were not even really conscious of it. The difficulty of wresting power from a frequently insubordinate nobility and maintaining it mostly consumed their energy prematurely so that social and cultural progress was generally left to itself. Admittedly, men such as Theodoric the Great or—to a limited extent—the Vandal king Thrasamund and the Visigothic rulers Reccared I and Sisebut, through their personal example and restless activity for their states, attained a stature which was generally acknowledged even by their adversaries. However, they were not able to make "civilized Christian states" out of their territories, as many modern researchers like to assert, along the lines of Charlemagne, in particular. Nevertheless, the nucleus of this idea did exist and in the course of generations it developed to an increasing degree. And it cannot be disputed that here and there cultural centres arose with a wide influence, often even over considerable areas. In the Carolingian Renaissance, as it can be termed, this development attained more sharply defined contours and a first climax. Admittedly, the creative cultural work which was carried out here can only be attributed to a certain extent to the encouragement given by the rulers and aristocracy: the aristocratic patrons were normally content to commission works of art or literature or at most to act as initiators. It did not happen very often that kings and nobles themselves emerged as artists or authors (Thrasamund, Sisebut). However, the few surviving examples made a profound impression on their contemporaries and later generations. As was only to be expected, the surviving elements of the senatorial nobility—including men such as Boethius, Cassiodorus, Benedict of Nursia and Venantius Fortunatus—undertook the cultural mission which was beyond the reach of others; they established scientific meeting-places and centres and, as abbots and bishops in accordance with the trend of the time and some-

times as temporal dignitaries as well, attracted younger men with similar views, they founded schools and philosophical-theological centres and in this way also influenced courts and kings. The breadth of their horizons and the variety of their interests secured for these authors an unexpected position among their contemporaries and in later ages, even though they were often, to a greater or lesser extent, on the edge of society and sometimes even outside it.

Literature, Philosophy, Education and Theology

In an almost macabre manner, this applies to Boethius, the son of a noble family and a representative of that style of education and philosophy which was primarily Greek in character and recalls the school of Symmachus. Characteristically, Boethius's wife Rusticiana was also descended from this old senatorial milieu which in the meantime had become converted to an enlightened, pro-educational Christianity. Yet it was precisely this which was the source of tension. Boethius, who knew no narrow limits for his scientific interests and among other things had designed an ingenious water and solar time-keeping device for Theodoric, aroused much displeasure in conservative Catholic circles. His philosophical and theological method, which sought to mediate between Athens and Rome, between Aristotle and the Elders of the Church, was much too rational for many people. And he went beyond the scope of the average understanding of his contemporaries when in his writings he demanded: "Combine as far as you can faith with reason." With this scientific insight, he dared to postulate something which only much later was to influence Scholasticism. Boethius, the first Scholastic, even impressed Thomas Aquinas, who wrote a commentary on Boethius's *Tract on the Trinity*. More noticeable, however, than the tension within the Roman and Catholic camp were the serious differences which emerged between the Romans and the Goths during Theodoric's last years. This is apparent simply from Boethius's promotion to one of the highest positions in the Ostrogothic empire, that of Magister officiorum (approximately equivalent to a court and state minister). Boethius—a philosopher with far-reaching official powers—attempted to eliminate the corruption which was widespread among both Goths and Romans and through this made new enemies, not least among the Barbarians at the court who regarded every Roman as a potential traitor. The mistrust which already existed between Theodoric and the Emperor Justin made the situation worse and when Boethius attempted to extend his protection to the Senator Albinus, who had connections with Byzantium, he was caught up in a trial for high treason. The Senate disassociated itself from its suspect members and Boethius was powerless to do anything except wait in prison for his sentence. It was in this situation that one of the most moving works of the epoch was written— *De Consolatione Philosophiae*. In the first book, Boethius, at first mournful and bitter, considers his desperate position. Intrigues have plunged him into misfortune and prison. He is unjustly accused of high treason. He is incensed that lies and slander have triumphed over righteousness. At this point, Philosophy, a majestic woman whose crown seems to reach as high as heaven, enters his cell. In a series of questions and answers, she gradually enables him to realize the nature of the human condition and to achieve an inner freedom. Is it not inevitable that happiness is transitory? The wheel of fortune turns unceasingly, distributing power, wealth, fame and pleasure at random—things which are constantly sought by men but which they cannot retain. But the virtuous man stands above all the ups and downs of life, is unshaken even in misfortune and knows that his aim is in harmony with the divine order of the world. Reflections about Providence, Destiny, Chance and the free will of Man round off the work. The strange circumstances under which it was written secured it lasting influence. Thus Boethius's "Consolatio" is not simply a work of edification and conversion, as often thought and of which there were many at the time, but rather opens up a new direction, pointing to inner freedom as the form of the human state assigned to divine understanding. At the same time, how-

ever, many of the most important concepts of Plato and Aristotle are fused with the ethics and theory of cognition of Christianity. This is one of the reasons why this work of consolation is still one of the most widely read books of world literature even today. Since it set out to help people in their daily struggle, it was also more frequently read in the Middle Ages than famous but dogmatically much narrower "standard works" such as the "Confessions" of Augustine or the moral works of Gregory the Great or Isidore of Seville. Many translations of the "Consolatio" were made: Alfred the Great translated it into Anglo-Saxon, Notker Labeo into Old High German and Albert of Florence into Italian. Even Dante considered Boethius as the "holy soul who reveals the deceit of the world to him who listens with an open mind".

Boethius was executed in 524 and Cassiodorus may best be regarded as his successor. Appointed Magister officiorum in 523 and later even Prefect of the Praetorian Guard (i.e., chief of the civil administration), he pursued the not unproblematical policy of cultural and ideological compromise between Romans and Barbarians even more energetically than his teacher and predecessor in office. Cassiodorus was indeed able to make himself indispensable to Theodoric and his successors and he was also more clearly on the side of the new rulers than Boethius could have been. This can be inferred from two works with quite different subjects: the *Variae*, a collection—written and composed by Cassiodorus—of 468 letters and documents from the royal chancellery providing a detailed idea not only of the administration but also of the politico-ideological functioning of the Ostrogothic state, and a history of the Goths. This latter work, it is true, survives only in the summarized version made by the Goth Jordanes, who continued the project, but it still permits conclusions as to Cassiodorus's apologetic attitude towards Theodoric and his Italic state. Nevertheless, the fact that Cassiodorus—when he was still in his prime—withdrew entirely from politics in 540 to devote his old age to self-chosen leisure and literature must give rise to speculation. The confusion after the death of Theodoric and the Byzantine campaigns in Italy must have influenced his decision. Initially, he wanted to establish a

Weight from Carthage with the name (or monogram) of Gelimer, the last king of the Vandals

theological seminary at Rome but the troubles of war put an end to this great project. Nevertheless, Cassiodorus persuaded the then Pope, Agapet I (535/536) to establish a library which may be regarded as a kind of predecessor for the universities established during the Middle Ages. Afterwards, this former official set up the Vivarium monastery on land owned by his family in Calabria. Through his own activities there for many years as a teacher and organizer, this became an important educational centre for theological and profane studies. Unlike Benedict of Nursia who called for *ora et labora*, Cassiodorus encouraged his monks to adopt the ideal of a mild asceticism centred on knowledge, following Boethius rather than Augustine or Benedict. In this, he was more inspired by the idea of the wise man living and meditating in a safe refuge, recalling the old concepts of Stoicism, than by the ideal of the Eastern-type ascetic and stylite, totally undemanding but also despising cultural values at the same time. Cassiodorus was certainly influenced by Oriental models as well. These were not the pillar-saints nor the Egyptian ascetics of the desert, however, but the catechist schools of Edessa and Nisibis which were also in the tradition of profane schools. In his important book *Institutiones*, Cassiodorus directs his monks to study the Holy Scriptures but also goes into details of the seven free arts (*artes liberales*) for which he had a high esteem and—unlike Augustine and even Isidore of Seville—did not wish to be withheld from the monks. His respect for intellectual activity went so far that he advised even those monks who could not or would not study

to make copies of books. The physical labour in field and garden, which was an integral part of the Benedictine and other monastic orders and exercised a major influence on the cultural activities of many medieval religious organizations, was therefore of quite minor importance for Cassiodorus: He did not establish a monastery in the narrow sense of the word but rather a centre of learning of an ascetic type at which, through ordered activity in the copying of books and the composition of commentaries, work was done which was as scientifically productive as the conditions prevailing at the time allowed. From his own work, which also included a chronicle of the world (from Adam to the year 519), a commentary of the Psalms and a treatise on orthography, Cassiodorus is characterized more as an encyclopaedic collector and scholar than as an original thinker and writer. With his programme of education which was Christian but still took account of the classical traditions, he occupies a position between Augustine, Boethius and Isidore which, in its originality, cannot be overlooked and in his own time exercised a lasting influence on Romans and Barbarians alike—Jordanes, for instance.

If Boethius and Cassiodorus were primarily respected for their writings and their intellectual influence, Benedict of Nursia —of whom mention must also be made in this connection—was chiefly known for his practical work which, however, knew neither chronological nor regional limits. Like Boethius, Benedict was a member of the aristocracy and belonged to the famous family of the Anicii. This is remarkable, above all, because of his

Germanic (Vandal?) horseman from a mosaic found near Carthage

prescriptions which later developed into the Benedictine rules followed for the first time at Monte Cassino. There is some doubt as to the exact year in which the famous monastery at Monte Cassino, the mother-house of the Benedictine Order, was founded. Perhaps solely for the sake of a parallel, its founding was associated with the closing of the ancient Platonic Academy of Athens by Emperor Justinian (529). At any rate, Benedict—whose sister Scholastika set up a Benedictine convent for women at the same time—continued his work at the monastery until his death (543). Despite destruction on several occasions, this famous establishment has remained the centre of the Order up to the present day. The origins and the nature of the Benedictines—like those of monks in general—are the subject of lively controversy. Strict links with the Holy Scriptures—the ascetic interpretation of their principles is a basic part of the actual rules—are self-evident. The three principal undertakings demanded by Benedictus—the tie with the monastery (*stabilitas loci*), complete change in outlook through the chastity and the renunciation of property (*conversio morum*) and unconditional obedience—convey at first sight the picture of a rigorous ascetic community, totally isolated from the outside world. It is clear that some of the roots of the Benedictine monastic life came close to flight from worldly society and represented a cultural and economic restriction to the monastery itself. This reflects the influence of Oriental monasteries and anchorites, Benedict's own life and socio-economic uncertainty in this late phase of the Great Migrations. Benedict's *ora et labora* (pray and work) was associated with a clear and irrevocable obligation whose quasi military character is unmistakable. As a monk, one was in the service of Christ (in the militia Christi), in whose place the abbot exercised the military command over the whole group, the *schola servitii*. In view of the conditions at the time, which naturally forced numerous uprooted people as well to enter the monasteries and convents, this rigorous strictness was scarcely avoidable. In actual practice, it is likely that the requirements were often less severe since Benedict, in the details of the rules, is careful not to insist on impossible demands which formed part of the rules of later orders. For him and his fellow-militants, the main thing was a

consistently ascetic way of life since, although members of the Late Antique nobility—and not long afterwards their Barbarian counterparts, too—rose to leading positions in the Church, they mostly avoided an all too ascetic and frugal life. The most important stages of his life—unfortunately much embroidered with legends—are set out in the biography written by Gregory the Great and in a few other sources. Born about 480, he first devoted himself to the usual studies at Rome but soon—allegedly at the age of fourteen—he felt himself called to be a hermit. About 510, he was chosen for the first time as the abbot of a cave monastery. He subsequently established small monasteries in the Anio Valley and probably elaborated for them a set of

99 Germanic helmet of Stössen from the first half of the 6th century (Landesmuseum für Vorgeschichte, Halle). The gilded helmet consists of six segment-frames with a thin centre-reinforcement which are connected together by a small circular plate. The iron intermediate plates (between the segment-frames) have mostly disintegrated. They were held together by a broad strip of sheet-iron on which there is a gilded bronze band bearing punched ornamentation. The cheek-flaps are fixed to this. There are triangular punched decorations on the

segment frames and there is a cross between the Greek letters alpha and omega. Vines and birds on the bronze band likewise reveal Christian influence. (For the pressed sheet the same matrices were used as for the helmet found at Planig so that both helmets probably came from the same workshop.)

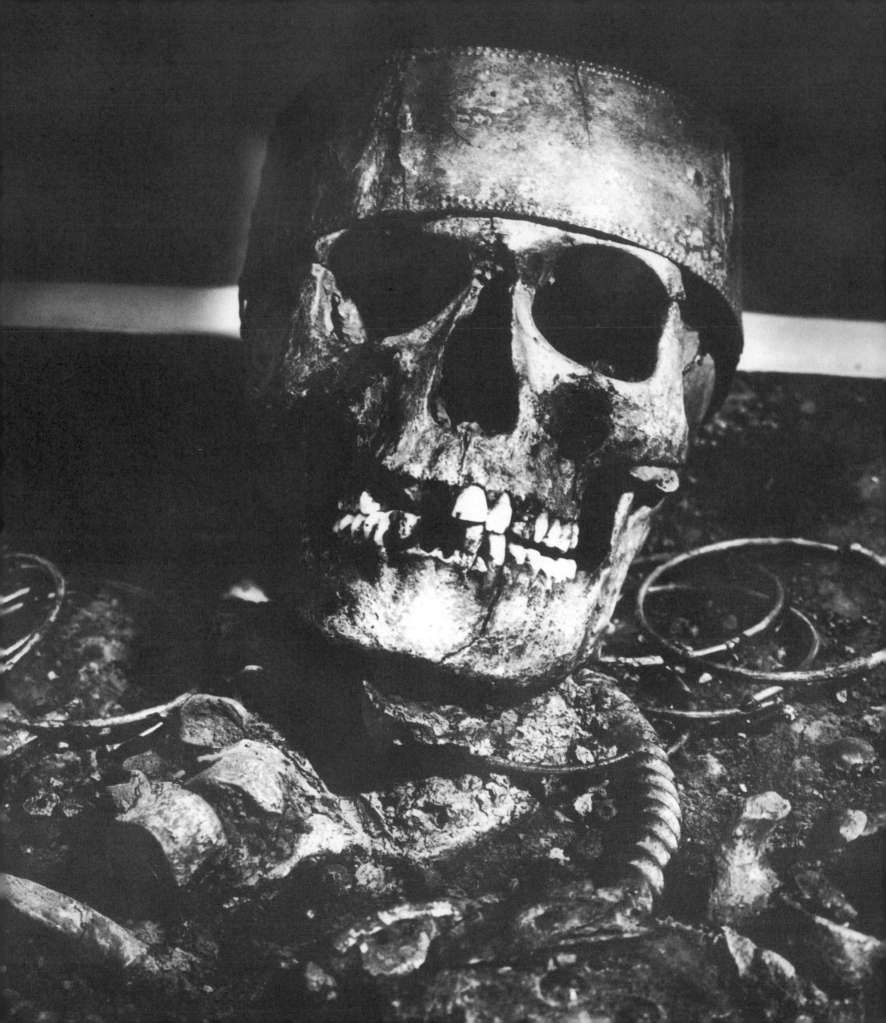

100 Princely grave from the necropolis of Donja Dolina (Northern Bosnia). The rings laid over the skull and the other fine objects in the grave show that this was a person of high rank. Agreement has not yet been reached on the date of this grave.

101 Frankish (Merovingian) finds (Landesmuseum Wiesbaden), consisting of a bangle, a curved fibula and two fittings with animal-style decoration.

102/103 Tombstone from Niederdollendorf, 12 km south of Bonn (Rheinisches Landesmuseum, Bonn). Limestone; bas-relief. Height 43 cm; from the 7th century. The face of the tombstone shows the dead warrior with a broad sax in his left hand and combing his hair with the right. Above him there is the serpent of death. The reverse side shows a figure in a nimbus with a lance and a plait band, in all likelihood a Germanic impression of Christ. The geometrical style is also noteworthy.

Following two pages:

104/105 Altar of Pemmo (Ratchis), Cividale, Cathedral (Museo Cristiano). According to the consecration inscription on it, the altar was the gift of Duke Pemmo (died *c.* 737) and King Ratchis (744–749). One side-panel (Ill. 104) depicts the Adoration of the three Magi while the other (Ill. 105) shows the Visitation of the Virgin Mary. The double plait band at the outer edge is a sign of Germanic influence.

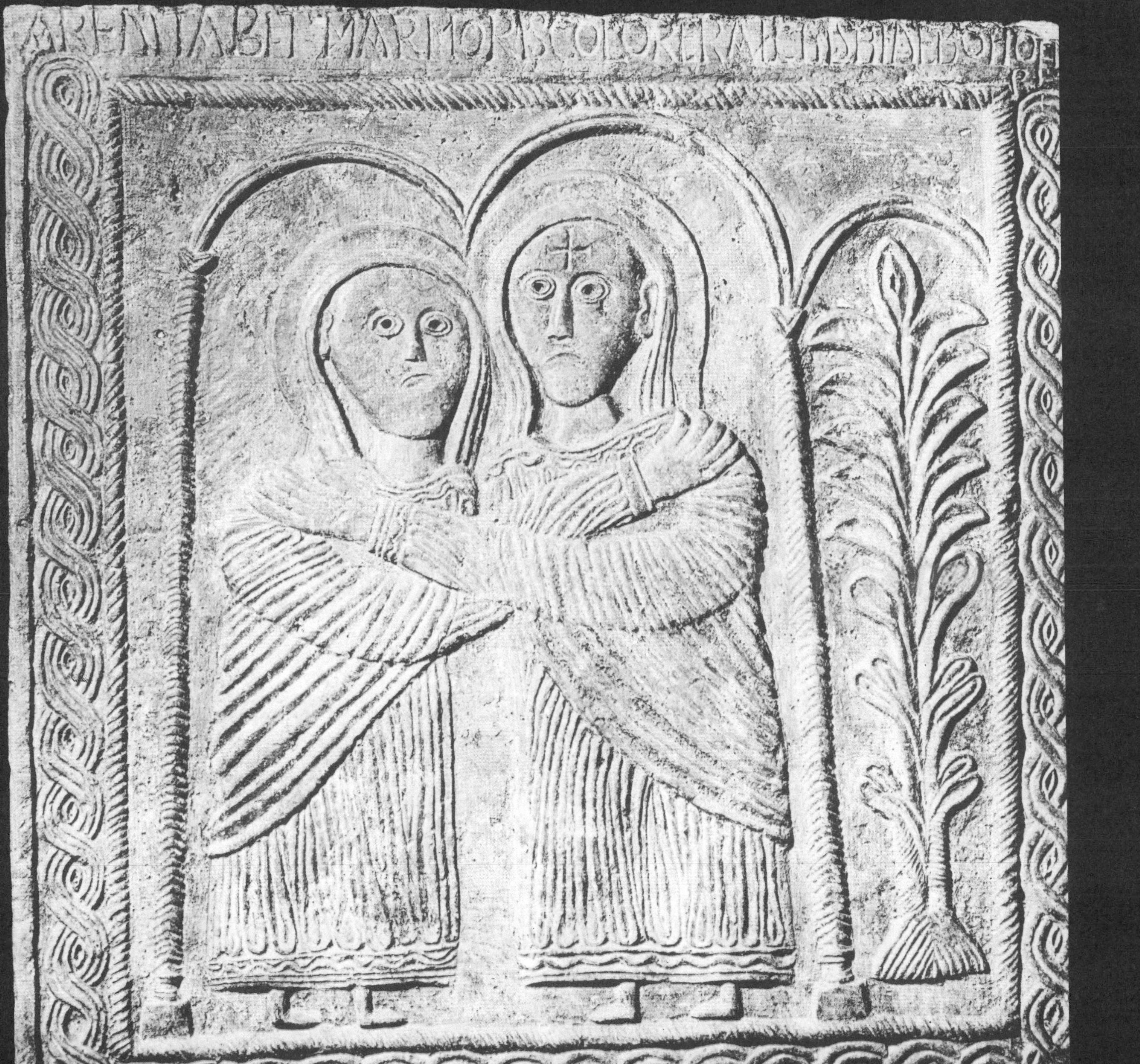

106 Frankish (?) tombstone from Moselkern (Rheinisches Landesmuseum, Bonn). An interesting feature of this tombstone with its many perforations is the large number of cross symbols on it.

107 The Horseman's Stone of Hornhausen from the 7th century (Landesmuseum für Vorgeschichte, Halle). This 78 cm high sandstone monument depicts the sharply outlined figure of a horseman with lance and round shield above an intertwined serpent with two heads. Similar pictorial stones, which can be interpreted as pagan or Christian, are found mainly in Sweden.

108 Tombstone of a priest from Gondorf (Rheinisches Landesmuseum, Bonn). Limestone; bas-relief. This 8th century tombstone
depicts a priest (Christ?) with two doves on his shoulders. The interpretation of the creatures in the corners (griffins?) is the subject of
controversy.

109 Frankish (?) tombstone from Leutesdorf (Rheinisches Landesmuseum, Bonn).

110/111/112/113 The Roman "limes" stronghold of Iatrus near Krivina in Northern Bulgaria dates back to the early 4th century. Excavations have been carried out here by the Central Institute for Ancient History and Archaeology of the Academy of Sciences of the GDR in association with the Bulgarian Academy of Sciences. Illustrations: The bath with heating installation (*praefurnium*) in the foreground (Ill. 110; second half of 4th century). The opening at the right was used as an air and smoke outlet. The (Roman) triple-comb with circular point-decoration is made of bone (Ill. 111; second half of the 4th century). The hinged bronze fibula of Roman origin is notable for its glass flux inlay (Ill. 113; end of the 2nd century). The golden ear-ring with polyhedral ornament is of East Germanic origin (Ill. 112; second half of the 5th century). These small objets d'art are now all in the Museum of Russe (People's Republic of Bulgaria).

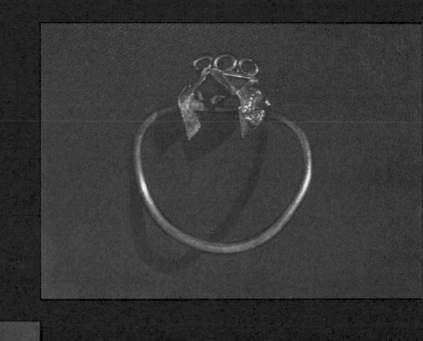

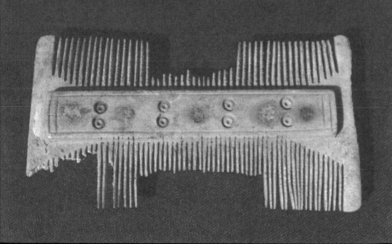

114 Iron-smelting furnace of Gera-Tinz (Museum für Ur- und Frühgeschichte, Weimar). This is a characteristic iron-smelting furnace, as used from early times until well into the Middle Ages. In furnaces such as these, charcoal was used to heat iron ore to temperatures of 700 to 800 °C in the shaft and 1100 to 1300 °C in the lower part of the furnace. The weight of the iron obtained was only 17 to 20% of the ore used and that of the malleable iron some 7 to 10%.

115 Pottery kiln from Pleszów, Nowa Huta (Cracow). This kiln of the Igołomia type (Igołomia = northeast from Cracow) is characteristic of those used for making ceramic ware during the Roman period when production was often on a large scale. In this area there were about 50 double-chamber pottery kilns, in one of which there was still a complete batch of fired ceramic ware.

116/117 Iron-making site at Słupia Stara, near Opatow (People's Republic of Poland). The size of the site demonstrates the importance of iron production and the necessity to erect several furnaces—plus hearths, charcoal pits and small houses or huts—at the same time.

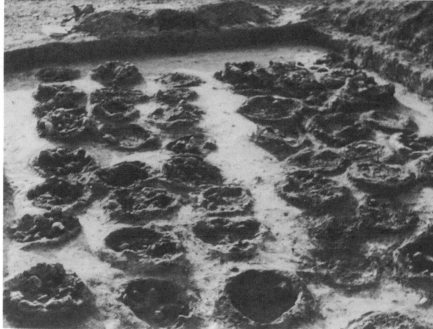

118 Curved fibula from Laucha, Nebra district, from the 6th century (Landesmuseum für Vorgeschichte, Halle). This gilded silver fibula is richly decorated with almandine inlays. It is of the cast type of curved fibula with rectangular, double-edged head-plate, baroque base and animal heads with open jaws.

119/120 Visigothic belt-buckles from Palazuelos, Estables (Guadalajara) and Calatayud (Museo Arqueológico Nacional, Madrid), probably dating from the 7th century. The pierced plate (Ill. 119)—a fine example of stippling technique—depicts a man fighting a griffin. Ill. 120 shows two heraldic lions in the centre of an animal plait design; particularly worth noting here is the human head on the tongue of the buckle (possibly a modification of the motif of Daniel in the lions' den?).

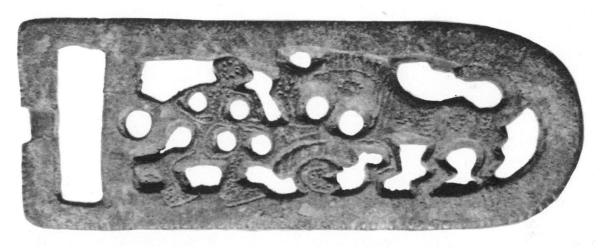

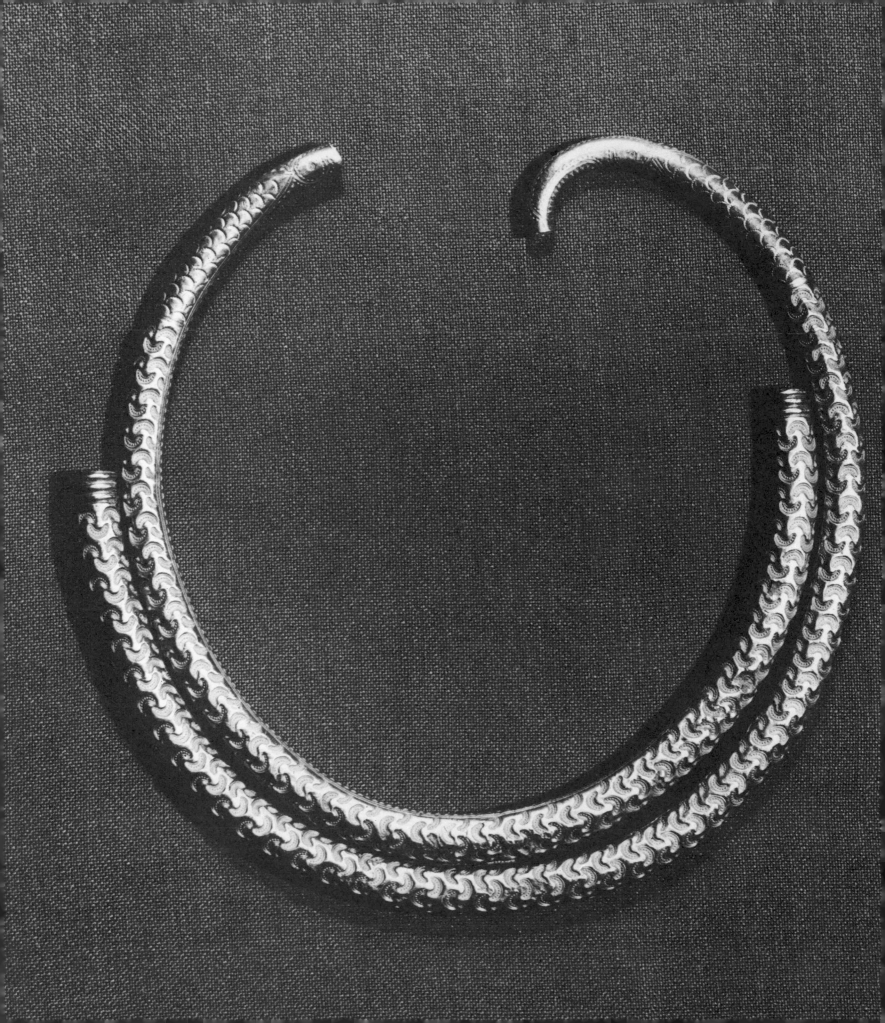

121 Gold circlet with stamped ornamentation (formerly: Neu-Mexiko, Saatzig district/People's Republic of Poland).

122 This gilded bronze belt-buckle with simple ornamentation was found at Castel near Valence d'Agen (district of Tarn-et-Garonne) and is of Visigothic origin. Without doubt, it belongs to the Tolosanian empire (418–507). Now in the possession of the Bibliothèque Nationale, Paris.

123 Two bird-fibulae, gold with red and blue inlays from the burial field of Schwabmünchen.

124–127 Frankish (?) eagle-fibulae (Römisch-Germanisches Museum, Cologne). Judging by the style and execution, the eagle fibulae are probably Gothic work. They are characterized by a great variety of design and are often of gold with almandine inlays.

128 This ornamental bracteate of gold was found in Pliezhausen (Württemberg). It is more likely that the armed horseman is a hunter than a warrior (Altertümersammlung, Stuttgart).

129 Merovingian find (Schnütgenmuseum, Cologne). The horseman forming a single entity with his mount certainly reflects Oriental influence. Perhaps the Antique and Oriental concept of hybrid creatures—half-beast, half-man—also played a part in this.

harmonious monastic life, consisting principally of prayer and manual work but not excluding other activities. In accordance with the ideas of Augustine, who regarded the work of monks as being primarily concerned with theological and educational duties, Benedict permitted training and educational activities right from the beginning and suitable monks gave instruction to the *pueri oblati* brought to the monastery. However, from the time of Cassiodorus at least, the Benedictines were also encouraged to engage in actual scientific work and important achievements were subsequently associated with men such as Gregory the Great, Boniface, Alcuin and Benedict of Aniane.

Two other effects of the early Benedictines cannot be overlooked. In accordance with the basic principle of their Order, they cultivated ownerless land, abandoned estates or plots which were bequeathed to the monastery. Through their collective labour, the monks and their helpers, mostly serfs, achieved results which were superior to the average attainments of the early feudal mode of production. The often notable crops were utilized in an economical manner and were distributed in accordance with social considerations. Since the poor and those incapable of earning a living also shared in the social product of the monastery, the monks always found enough helpers (seasonal workers) and soon large areas of the monastic estates were also rented to tenant-farmers. The positive aspects of this development cannot be ignored but, naturally, they cannot be seen in isolation. The fact that the Benedictine and the other early medieval monasteries as a whole often became big landowners must of course be associated with the development of the early feudal structure of power, a particularly vivid illustration of which were the private monasteries and private churches, for instance. The monasteries and their abbots often became very dependent on the kings or other temporal lords in the course of this but they themselves, of course, also exercised considerable juridical and economic pressure on their own serfs and freemen. This also applied when the State demanded contributions from the independent monasteries which largely had to be provided by their tenants or serfs. This meant compulsory labour, taxes and military service, without which an early feudal centralized

power could not survive. This very interesting development, of which there is evidence even before the time of Charles Martel and his victory over the Arabs, cannot be examined in detail here. The relationship with the Benedictines and the other Orders founded during this epoch justifies the reference to them at this spot although the processes in the history of law associated with it really belong to a general analysis of the legislation of this period.

The universal historical significance of the three men mentioned is beyond dispute. They are only overshadowed by the Spaniard, Isidore of Seville (*c.* 560 to 636), who was not only the last European of the Early Fathers but also one of the most important teachers of the Middle Ages. His significance in the history of human education and in the branch of knowledge of encyclopaedism so important today can scarcely be exaggerated.

Little is known of Isidore's life. A member of an educated family of fugitives originating from the region of Cartagena which had found refuge from Byzantine oppression in Visigothic territory, Isidore received a sound education at an early age. Guided by his brother Leander, who was his predecessor as bishop of Seville, Isidore devoted most of his attention to theological and philosophical problems at least until his rank as a Church dignitary allowed him time for other intellectual interests as well. The outstanding event in his ecclesiastical career was undoubtedly the conversion of the Visigoths to Catholicism (589) which was also of paramount historical importance. This point in time marks the beginning of close collaboration between State and Church in Spain, the strengthening of the royal power and, at the same time, the exercise of Church influence on the State through the Toledo Imperial Councils. The fact that Isidore chaired the fourth of these councils (633) shows just how keenly he felt himself to be the apologist of this new development which, in the political and socio-economic sense, was already a kind of early feudalism. This aspect alone makes his situation completely different to the destiny of the three men mentioned before. Whereas these were in opposition to the ruling society or at least felt themselves called to seek an unyielding confrontation with it, Isidore largely identified himself with the aims of Visigothic

Cult figures from the Fisher Isle near Neubrandenburg

Spain in which he saw—as is clear from his "History of the Goths"—a type of state-structure with a future. When Isidore exposes the shortcomings of this society—which he did on frequent occasions—he nevertheless makes proposals for the elimination of breaches of the law, social grievances and so on, these being matters which were painful to him as a moral theologian but did not appear to him to affect the basic foundations of the structure as a whole. With Isidore, there is scarcely any trace of the pessimism of Boethius or Cassiodorus. Negative experiences from his youth, such as the expulsion of the family from Byzantine territory or the persecution of the Catholic Church by Leowigild, the last Aryan king of the Visigoths, are not reflected in his works or are at least put on a secondary level. Nevertheless, he did draw a conclusion from all this since he demanded the strict supervision and persecution of heretics, which included the members of the Mosaic creed.

The theological achievement of Isidore consists less, however, in his anti-heretical writings than in his well-founded moral theology which examines the social grievances of his time and, in particular, champions the interests of the poor. This is something which has only recently been appreciated. Even though the commitment also has its roots in the traditions of the Early Christians and in the works of Augustine and Gregory the Great, it nevertheless has a considerable original element. Naturally enough, Isidore does not succeed in avoiding every contradiction since on the one hand he defends the emergent early feudal structure and, on the other, condemns the social shortcomings associated with it. As regards the question of the conditions of serfdom, which can be included under the old collective term of slavery, he even persists in an outdated point of view since he justifies this institution and displays a sceptical attitude towards the widespread tendency to free the serfs. Otherwise his "Theology for the poor" contains many positive elements, just like his "Monastic rules" or his profane scientific works which were of epoch-making importance, especially his *Etymologiae*. Although Isidore's scientific work, when seen as a whole, includes little that was really original and creative, in the breadth of its subjects and especially in its objectives it is nevertheless of pioneering importance. Although he was mainly a compiler, Isidore outshines even Boethius and Cassiodorus who were certainly superior to him in scientific stature. This is due to the moral earnestness and pedagogic fervour which gave him the strength to overcome all the narrowness and intolerance of the dogma of the age in his restless quest for more knowledge and understanding. In his "Synonyma" which, as a conversation between poverty-stricken Man and his faculty of Reason, recalls the pattern of Boethius's "Consolatio", he expresses the problem in something like the following words (II, 65): "There is nothing better than Wisdom, nothing sweeter than Intelligence, nothing more attractive than Knowledge, nothing worse than Folly … nothing more hateful than Ignorance, the mother of Error and the Source of all vices." Such demands, by themselves, would have gone unheard, of course, if Isidore had not energetically tackled the problem analyzed here in various works, especially in the 20 books which have survived of his encyclopaedic *Etymologiae*. This compilation, in the elaboration of which Isidore was assisted by many helpers and which after his death continued under the supervision of Bishop Braulio of Saragossa, represents from an etymological viewpoint the sum of the entire body of knowledge of this time. Isidore does not draw a distinction between the words but often gives a brief and vivid word/object history, showing how the original meaning of a word has changed down to the "present"—mostly through intermediate stages. In this manner and via the Greek or Latin origins, he frequently arrives at the current Vulgar Latin or Barbarian (mostly Germanic) word/object relations, thus throwing light on the most diverse social circumstances of the emergent feudal society with its strange mixture of Late Roman and Germanic elements. The most important aspect of this is that the *Etymologiae* include really all the branches of knowledge—down to the actual practical spheres. For traditional reasons, the first books naturally deal with the seven liberal arts, i.e., grammar, rhetoric, dialectics, arithmetic, geometry, music and astronomy. Book four is concerned with medicine. The first part of the fifth book is devoted to law and legislation and the second to chronology and the reckoning of time. Books six to eight examine theological and ecclesiastical questions. The ninth book is concerned with a particularly wide range of subjects, including languages, peoples, empires and civil and military structures and relations. While the subject order is normally placed first, the tenth book contains a large number of short etymologies listed in alphabetical order. The eleventh book discusses the biology of Man (examining also abnormalities and fabulous creatures, e.g., half-human and half-animal), while the twelfth deals with zoology. The thirteenth and fourteenth books are devoted to geography, whereas states, cities, buildings and communication structures are the subject of the fifteenth. The remaining books complete the sum of the knowledge of the time and deal with the following subjects: rocks, earths and metals (16), agriculture and horticulture (17), the art of war, combative and circus games (18), ship-construction, clothing and building (19), and finally nutrition and domestic utensils (20). As even this review shows, here is a real mine of information for any reader with any interest at all in the older periods of civilization.

What do these authors show, what is evident from Isidore of Seville in particular? Although the answer as a whole contains more positive than negative aspects, it has to be stated, to begin with, that the Great Migration represented a step backward in the cultural development of mankind, above all in intellectual culture. It is not only the language that shows evidence of the penetration of Vulgar and "Barbaric" elements and is loosened up to such an extent that its lexical, grammatical and syntactic structure provides the basis for a series of new and initially popular dialects and languages from which the Romance languages evolved. This starting point, which was more negative than otherwise, gradually led to a stage which quite definitely represented something new and positive. The relaxation in the training in logic, which was likewise associated with the linguistic deterioration and within the decline and even ultimate disappearance of the normal school and education system, also ended in rustic and "Barbaric" stages which in many places lasted for centuries—especially in those regions in which urban developments and the economy with developed commodity-money relations had died out. The range of regional variations was very

wide and it is only possible to give an outline of this here. Thus positive after-effects of Late Antique instruction, training by grammarians and rhetoricians, were still to be found in the 5th and 6th centuries in Italy, Southern Gaul, North Africa and Southern Spain. Barbarians appeared occasionally in the role of patrons or pupils but not yet as teachers. Their integration in the system of education or what remained of it, which had survived mainly in the monastic schools, was a long drawn-out process. Exceptions such as the enlightened kings Thrasamund and Sisebut—to whom Isidore dedicated his *De natura rerum*—only proved the rule. Admittedly, this situation was reversed when the Barbarian rulers needed large numbers of educated persons for administrative and juridical duties so that sometimes they even recruited freedmen and slaves from neighbouring areas for this purpose. As can be imagined, they also occasionally installed poets at their courts—Ennodius was patronized by Theodoric the Great and Venantius Fortunatus won the admiration of the Frankish aristocracy, including Queen Radegunde—and encouraged the literary endeavours of tolerant bishops. Once some of the states of the Great Migration had become well-established and no longer needed all their resources to withstand Roman attempts to turn back the clock (at the earliest only after the death of Justinian I), a greater interest in culture and art developed there, too. Understandably, it was almost always rational considerations that prevailed in the process of selection: Roman jurists were used in the administration and in the codification and completion of the body of legislation, physicians of the old school were sought for service at the courts, and architects of Roman origin built the numerous sacral edifices and the relatively few profane structures which were endowed or founded by the Barbarian kings. To avoid exaggerated improvization, these rulers were ultimately obliged to encourage the development of education on a fairly limited scale since, without it, the specialization in these professions and similar ones would have been unthinkable. Episcopal and monastic schools assumed a dominating position, although there were regional variations. After the complete closure of secular educational establishments and the disappearance of educated laymen, the entire educational

system—including the upbringing of princes—passed into the hands of monks and clerics. This phenomenon naturally became typical of the entire mediaeval period and exercised a considerable influence on the educational process, the selection of study-material and pedagogic methods. The onesidedness of this system of education is undisputed. Despite its narrowness, it was characterized by notable achievements in many spheres already mentioned, especially since the concentration on certain subjects—theology, specific philological and philosophical questions, religious art—sometimes permitted such a profound approach that even within the dogmatic limits it was able to produce unique and even genial works. Evidence of intellectual and literary culture is provided not only by Cassiodorus or Isidore but also by Gregory of Tours or—to name only a few of the later writers—Bede, Boniface, Alcuin and Hrabanus Maurus. Far more striking, however, are the often anonymous works of artists and craftsmen which have survived and which are examined in the following section.

The Arts: Architecture, Sculpture and Metalworking

Almost anyone who explores the artistic scene of this transitional epoch will certainly first of all try to identify its specific architectural features. Antique and Barbarian traditions in architecture could have led to a synthesis, or one might seek signs of an evident continuation of Antique ideas or of Barbarian influence. It is the almost unanimous opinion of modern research that the influence of the conquering Barbarians was extremely slight and rare. In wooden architecture—as illustrated by the Scandinavian stave churches, for instance—there is naturally a fairly continuous Northern mode of construction evident. In stone sculpture and architecture, however, the predominance of Antique concepts and their continued development is quite clear. Early mediaeval Spanish churches are nowadays seldom regarded as examples of Visigothic culture but are simply dated in the

Visigothic period. It is only in the decoration that Germanic influence is often apparent here as in the animal style—whose origin and spread has also recently been questioned—or in geometrical abstract ornamentation such as the famous tongs frieze of Theodoric's tomb at Ravenna. Reference may be made here once more to the Barbarian styling of utensils, and particularly of weapons. Since the Germanic tribes remained warlike for hundreds of years or at least represented the most important element in the military feudal hierarchy (above all as the service nobility of the *leudes, buccellarii, satellites, spatharii,* etc.), Germanic influence on weapons and military equipment was much more marked, even in details, than on other objects of everyday life. This is clearly demonstrated in the illustrated section. It is true, of course, that architecture—as in the Roman Late Antique period—was also characterized by strategic features in many areas which were in a particularly exposed position from the military point of view. This naturally applied to ecclesiastical architecture as well so that in many places structures were built which can be regarded as early fortified churches. Military structures of functional severity existed side-by-side with buildings of notable sumptuousness, an idea of which can be obtained from the description of the fortified estate of Nicetius, the Bishop of Trier and a former monk, by Venantius Fortunatus (Carm. 12, 21–42): "A rampart with thirty towers encircles the hill where a building stands on what was once a wooded spot; the walls extend from the crest of the hill far down into the valley of the Moselle, the waters of which form the boundary of the estate on this side. On the rock there stands a splendid palace, rising up like a second hill over the first. Its walls enclose a vast area and the building itself is almost a fortress. Marble columns support the noble edifice, from the top of which, on summer days, the boats can be seen which glide across the river. The spacious palace has three levels and, looking down from above, it seems as if the structure covers the fields around. The tower, which dominates the slope of the approach, houses the chapel dedicated to the saints and the arms of the warriors. There is also a ballista situated there with a two-fold missile which sows death and recoils from itself. Water is brought there in conduits which follow the convolutions of the hill. It drives a mill which grinds the corn for the people dwelling there. On the once barren slopes, Nicetius has planted sweet grapes and green vines now cover the rock on which bracken formerly grew. Orchards flourish here and there and fill the air with the scent of countless blossoms." The poet's detailed description recalls in many respects the country houses or palaces of late Antiquity which are known to us to some extent from mosaics or contemporary descriptions and in which there was a similar proximity of profane and ecclesiastical buildings performing military, domestic, economic or religious functions. However, the dimensions of the estate of Nicetius may well be exaggerated; the art of construction and architectural composition seem to have achieved an ideal synthesis and an optimal effect here so that the residential and prestige functions and the utility and defence potential are guaranteed in equal measure.

There have seldom been complexes of this magnitude; very large resources were needed for their construction plus a multitude of dependent persons—tillers of the soil, building workers and other artisans and soldiers—which were by no means always at the disposal of the average nobleman. This is why small churches and more modest villas and palaces frequently had to suffice. Even the palace of Theodoric in Ravenna—and his tomb—were of fairly restrained dimensions. It was, of course, magnificently styled and furnished which led to Charlemagne stripping it of numerous mosaics and columns which he dispatched to Aachen.

The palaces of the Frankish and Visigothic rulers were—at best—of a similar pattern. Those of the Vandal kings, who—like the Vandal nobility—were regarded as particularly rich, were probably the most prestigious. Their owners had rapidly developed a taste for high living and built luxurious country residences with fountains and thermal baths, as reported by Procopius (*Wars of the Vandals*, II, 6). The specific conditions in North Africa, following its liberation from Roman exploitation, permitted many an escapade which would have been out of the question elsewhere. The Burgundian Palace in Geneva, for instance, presents in a confined space only a superficial remodelling of Antique

Section of a North Germanic house with turf-walls:
1 mud-floor, 2 paved fireplace with loam plaster, 3 loam plaster,
4 turf-wall, 5 grass-layer, 6 tussock-layer, 7 hay-layer, 8 turf-layer

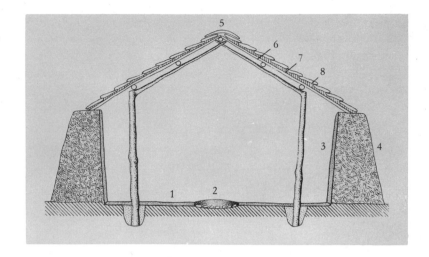

buildings enclosing a small courtyard. In those places where sacral buildings were constructed of wood, it was not possible in any case to achieve much in the way of sumptuousness, or the result was an uncivilized medley of wooden and stone structures (for example thermae), such as the residence of Attila.

To begin with, simplicity was also pre-eminent in church architecture. Admittedly, even in the Arian churches of the Ostrogoths, attempts were made to transfer the outstanding features of the ancient art of wood-carving to stone capitals, and in the Catholic basilicas there are early signs of a more exacting or more sophisticated taste both in the architecture and in sculptured and ornamental furnishings. Naturally enough, the principal idea behind the constant enlargement or improvement of these buildings was to honour the founder or the martyr associated with the building and also the fact that many churches became the place of burial for a princely dynasty. In most cases, two or four side-aisles flanked the central hall, light entering from the clerestory, the window zone soaring high above the roofs of the side-aisles. The transept was later interposed between the nave and the apse while a vestibule (narthex) and a column-lined courtyard (atrium) were added to the end of the nave. However, local variations were numerous and mostly began in a modest way. Even such a famous church as St. Martin's at Tours was not

very large, according to Gregory. When the same historian remarks that it had one hundred and twenty columns, fifty-two windows and eight doors, this probably means that it had superposed rows of columns along the side-walls, of which there are also other examples (Germigny-des-Prés, Saint-Laurent in Grenoble). The vigorous demand for columns and capitals led to the emergence in Aquitaine and elsewhere of marble carvers who were an important group among the craftsmen of this epoch. Their workshops supplied finished parts such as capitals and sarcophagi over long distances so that it was only the basic structure of many buildings which was erected by the local craftsmen; the more elaborate decoration was brought from far away or—as spoils of war—taken from Antique edifices. Not to be forgotten either are the travelling sculptors, inlay-workers, painters and, of course, metalworkers who put the finishing touches to the larger structures and were responsible for much of their artistic merit.

The impression is confirmed time and again that it was continuity and slow improvement which dominated ecclesiastical and other architecture of this period—even with the conscious or unconscious incorporation of Barbarian elements. Naturally enough, Eastern and especially Byzantine or Syrian influences made an impact, particularly in Italy, and even reached as far

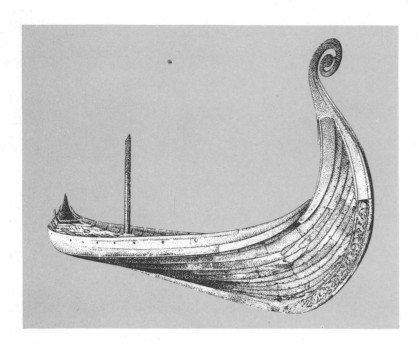

Longship from Oseberg

as Spain through the temporary occupation of the South (Baetica) by Byzantium. Three well-known churches here date back to the 7th century: San Juan Bautista in Baños de Cerrato (661), San Pedro de la Nave in Zamora province and Santa Maria in Quintanilla de las Viñas in Burgos province. Jean Hubert, an outstanding authority on the subject, had this to say about them (p. 83 ff.): "The church of Quintanilla de las Viñas has not been completely preserved in its original state; the principal nave is mediaeval. Nevertheless, the external view of the choir and the transept makes an unforgettable impression on every visitor since the fine masonry is decorated with a very delicately worked relief-frieze arranged in two rows. The perfection of this structure, which is directly in the tradition of the columned halls of Late Antiquity, equals the perfection of Syrian churches or Byzantine buildings of the 6th century. These three Spanish churches are only small but they have magnificent proportions. The ground plan, in which there is no apse, is made up of the skilled combination of straight lines. A kind of interior cellular articulation is intended to lighten the vaulting of individual parts of

the building. As in Antique structures, the windows do not have a diagonal reveal and the columns are simply placed in front of the walls—not a single one forms part of the masonry. On the other hand, other traits are new and they are especially striking since they appear as the early antecedents of the architecture and sculpted work of the Romanesque period. In the church of Quintanilla de las Viñas, in particular, the ornamentation and the scenic representations sculpted in stone play an important role. A rectangular panel shows the figure of Christ, set in a really naive manner between two angels, and another the personification of the sun. Like those of San Pedro de la Nave, the capitals of this church support high abacus panels. It is even more astonishing that two of the basket-type capitals of San Pedro de la Nave are decorated with Old Testament scenes—the sacrifice of Abraham and Daniel in the lions' den. The figures stand out from the flat background and give the impression of a fresco which has been transferred in bas-relief to the stone surface. Only slight traces can now be seen of the painted colours which once covered the whole of these sculpted groups. The execution

of the human figures is less exquisite than that of the foliage scrolls which ornament the arch supports or the upper wall zone." Hubert then emphasizes the perfection of the masonry of the walls and vaulting and underlines the influence of this still Antique Spanish architecture up to the time of the Moorish conquest and, incidentally, even in Southern France as well.

Simple but imposing is also Santa Maria de Naranco, originally a royal hall or a two-storey royal palace, which was rebuilt by Ramiros I (842–850) and, with an altar dedicated to St. Mary, was completely converted into a church in the 12th century. The barrel vaulting rests on arches which are supported by columns resembling carved wood. At its narrow sides, the upper hall has magnificent galleries and inside, over an interesting medallion, there are two duelling swordsmen. The original worldly character of the structure is clearly indicated by such ornamentation. In Italy, the church of Santa Maria foris portas at Castelseprio, one of the few sacral structures of the 7th century still surviving there, has a similar "classic" simplicity in its lines. The building consists of a rectangular altar room at the centre of three apses and a vestibule. In 1944, in the east apsis of the church, paintings of scenes from the life of Christ were discovered, arranged in three zones one above the other. Displaying Byzantine influence, they represent some of the best examples of sacral painting known from this period when eastern ideas mingled with native and Lombard elements.

It is likely that here we have evidence of influence by one of the tribes of the Great Migration in the sphere of fresco painting. As already indicated, influences of this kind are otherwise mostly limited to metalworking (arms, ornaments) and to some fields of sculpture. Backed up by ancient traditions and stimulated by the advanced techniques of production instruments of the Mediterranean areas, the Germanic tribes produced outstanding work in toreutics but tended to lag behind in the sculpting of stone and marble. In some cases, centuries passed before this situation changed. Lombard sculptures are most easily recognized in the Church of Santa Maria in Valle in Cividale. Stucco reliefs at the entrance, showing six female saints, and especially a lunette with vegetable ornamentation and palmettes and plaits point in the

Bronze ornamental discs from the Frankish area

same artistic direction as the tomb of Theodoric with its tongs frieze. Particularly characteristic of the Lombardo-Italic art of the time is the Agilulf Plate, now in the Bargello in Florence. The gilded copper plate depicts the king, who ruled from 591 to 616, on his throne, his right hand raised as if he were speaking and surrounded on both sides by warriors with Germanic helmets, round shields and lances and by Victories and dignitaries with royal regalia. This, the earliest known portrait of a Germanic king on his throne, is particularly precious by virtue of the inscription it bears: "VICTORIA D (OMINO) N (OSTRO) AGILUL (FO) REGI" ("Victory to our lord King Agilulf"). This supports the remarks made above concerning the character of kingship at this time and of the pyramids of early feudal society. The feudal need for prestige and representation is also reflected, of course, in the architecture of the period but more markedly in art on a smaller scale which—like the fairly common votive crowns—documents political and religious interests at the same time. This is particularly apparent in the votive crown of King Reccesvind which is now in Madrid but probably came from a church. Together with about a dozen other crowns, it is part of the treasure of Fuente de Guarrazar near Toledo. The golden ring contains precious stone inserts, some of which are in cellular settings. Fixed to the crown are letters of gold bearing precious stones in cellular mountings and proclaiming "RECCESVINTHUS REX OFFERET" (King Reccesvinth offers it). A small cross within the crown is an example of pure Byzantine technique. Exquisite court art of this and similar kinds was found in all the later states of the Great Migration. Christian motifs or at least Christian decoration is never missing. With the sacral objects, often gifts donated by nobles and rulers, it is self-evident. In the figurative presentation and in their profusion of colours, each of the great variety of reliquaries, patens, chandeliers, chalices, altar crosses or ciboria seems more splendid than the next. It is usually Christ Himself who is depicted, sometimes with Mary or with apostles and angels. The Germanic plait band ornamentation is also frequently found on sacral objects of this kind, for instance on reliquaries from communal houses.

In the ornamentation of everyday objects, however, the Christian element is not so prominent whereas the Germanic tradition is more in evidence. The burial gifts placed in the grave of the Frankish Queen Arnegundis (c. 525–570) and found in a limestone sarcophagus in the Basilica of St. Denis reveal but little use of the cross motif in decoration although the set of articles there—belt-trappings, pins and gold-disc fibulae with almandine inlays—would have provided plenty of opportunities for this. It was rather the familiar techniques, admittedly at a more sophisticated level, and the traditional motifs which predominated. Thus the animal-style plait band was still favoured, especially on fibulae and belt fittings. There is much evidence of a tendency to abstract and geometrical stylization. This is often found with the decorative discs which were fixed to the loose ends of women's belts or on shield centres.

Eagles and other creatures alternate with mounted figures armed with lances. There is even a Lombard representation, in sheet-gold, of a mounted saint with a lance surrounded by an animal-style plait band. It is probably to be attributed to the rough, warlike way of life of this transitional period that on the reverse side of the warrior gravestone of Niederdollendorf there is obviously even a picture of Christ with a lance and plait band ornamentation, assuming that this unclothed figure with a radiant nimbus and open heart does not in fact symbolize some sort of pre-Christian idea of reincarnation. What is certain, however, is that many early Christian motifs were restylized and used for purely ornamental purposes. This is also true of the Burgundian and Visigothic area. The same applies to ancient Oriental symbols such as animals at the tree or fountain of life.

The manufacture of arms during the main period of the Great Migration also advanced, without doubt. The primary purpose of the improvements made was of course to achieve a better combat capability but the weapons of the ruling class in particular are characterized by artistic elements, as, for instance, on their chain- and plate-armour, segment-frame helmets and swords. The hilts of their long swords (*spatha* when single-edged, *semispatha* when double-edged) and of the single-edged short sword (*sax*) are often ornamented with gold and almandine in cellular mountings, and even the blades, with their silver mount-

Chaucian well from Stickenbüttel near Cuxhaven (reconstruction)

ings and rich decorations, served more than a purely practical purpose. Animal designs and even warriors in wolf masks or other motifs are probably an indication of magical concepts and apotropaic intentions. Traditional or mixed motifs certainly retained their influence even in the Christian period. And there is no doubt that idiosyncracies of this kind were no more vigorously combated by the Church initially than other pagan customs, such as those associated with burial. This is illustrated by the fact that the Franks continued to bury gifts with their dead in the grave-line cemeteries, as they are sometimes known, until the eighth century and later. It was only then that the Church succeeded in claiming the traditional burial treasure as "soul treasure" for which the requiems for the dead represented the equivalent. The chief weapons of the Franks, who increasingly took the lead in development, were the sword and particularly the spear. Used both as a javelin and as a lance, the spear was often the sole weapon of attack and was sometimes even regarded as a symbol of kingship. (On his signet-ring, Childeric is shown with cuirass and spear.) When the king handed one of his relations his spear, he simultaneously handed over his sovereign power as well. Accordingly the tips of both the ordinary spear and the *ango*—the barbed spear—were very carefully made. These tips were attached to the shaft by iron nails which were sheathed in bronze or silver sheet and shaped as decorative pegs. Circular ornaments and engraved lines are not uncommon. The *franziska* may be regarded as a specifically Frankish weapon and was primarily used as a throwing axe. When it disappeared in the 8th century, its place was taken by the double-edged battle-axe, the *hiltebarte*. As regards the shield, a reference to this has already been made in connection with shield centres, which merit historical interest from the artistic viewpoint. To begin with, armour and helmet were not part of the standard Germanic combat-kit; the expense involved limited their use to the nobility and their henchmen. From the various shapes of helmet, there gradually developed the typical Germanic helmet which—in parallel with the improvements in weapons—offered considerable protection. The pictorial examples show that there was ample opportunity for splendid decoration along the edges and on the segments and cheek-flaps. Thus the bronze helmet of Morken (*c.* 600) even has a flap of iron chain-mail protecting the nape, which was not a feature of the earlier helmet of Stössen (*c.* 500), and in addition to the delicate chased work on the plates of the headband has three human masks set between lion-like monsters. Vine tendrils, which are part of Christian iconography, provide the frame for this.

The versatility of artistic expression is thus astonishing, even on utility objects. Perhaps this might be regarded in a certain sense as a counterweight to ecclesiastical art, as a self-assertion of the profane sector in relation to the Church. Worldly or pagan motifs, which even penetrated the sphere of religious architecture, are often a counterpart to Biblical motifs. In the North—in Scandinavia and Britain—which was on the perimeter of these developments, there is particularly clear evidence of the gradual development of the pagan and worldy outlook from fairly primitive to more artistic forms which often have little that is Christian about them. But in Central and Southern Europe, too, the original substrate broke through time and again until a fusion of Antique, Christian and Barbarian forms was ultimately achieved. This process continued for far longer than the period under review here.

Society and Civilization
after the Great Migration

THE EPOCH AND ITS PHASES, AS EXAMINED above, were characterized by a multiplicity of stresses and contradictions. Although these are already apparent when analyzed from the viewpoint of social history in a fairly narrow sense, they assume an even greater prominence when a look is taken at contemporary literature and other sources from the cultural sphere of the time.

Without distorting the actual facts, it is often difficult to arrive at a logical and correct interpretation or to put events in their right historical perspective. This is demonstrated, for instance, by the evaluation of the legal sources which are particularly clear in their objectives but often scarcely permit any modern historical interpretation. This is even true of that sphere of life and branch of production which at that time dominated all others—agriculture. At any rate, enormous difficulties are encountered in obtaining a clear picture of the agrarian structure of the emergent feudal system, even for such an important area as that of the Gallo-Frankish sphere in which—admittedly under the stimulus of Visigothic Spain—the first definite manifestation of feudal modes of production appeared. The *Lex Salica*, a major legal source, does indeed permit a certain insight into the structure of the tribe, the family in its more comprehensive form and the rural community, it also provides indications of the emergence of the private ownership of land (*allod*) and points towards the division of society into service nobility, freemen, serfs (*liten*) and slaves. Nevertheless, the perseverance of many generations of researchers was needed to identify reliable evidence of the actual conditions and even now it is difficult to separate the revolutionary process of the 5th century from that of the 6th or 7th.

Some of the basic trends are clear enough. As in Late Antiquity and to a more marked extent than among the Germanic tribes of the Great Migration period, the scene was dominated by agriculture. The main activity was the growing of corn which was done by ploughing according to the two-field and later the three-field cycle. Ploughs with iron plough-shares were pulled by oxen. Other implements, such as the harrow, were also used, of course, but the advanced techniques of late Roman times, which even included a reaping machine, were forgotten again. In addition to the tillage of the soil, the decline in warlike activities was marked by an expansion of horticulture, which was of importance for the production of vegetables. The larger the courts and the organization of the Church became, the greater was the demand for wine. The trades of the vintner and cupbearer were familiar occupations, even though they were often performed by serfs. Animal husbandry, which had been carried on widely by almost all the Germanic tribes since time immemorial, increasingly gained in importance. Horses, cattle, pigs, sheep, goats and various kinds of poultry were kept in the farmyards, meadows and woods. The initially common utilization of the land, the woods and meadows, led to the settlers of a village having a herdsman, at least on a joint basis.

At that time, agrarian production was normally centred in the villages which were inhabited by free Frankish peasants, the settlers, with their slaves and serfs. In the areas which were still inhabited by Latin populations, a different social structure must be assumed and it is from these districts that the word "villa" was taken, as is found in the sources. In most cases this no longer referred to the residence of the local landowner but to a village- or hamlet-like settlement consisting essentially of farms. The old word for village (*vicus*) still continued to be used, however. It is apparent that there were soon not only hamlets and villages but also residences and fortifications, many of which subsequently became castles. This is shown by the appearance of terms such as *castellum* (Latin "small military camp" and later "castle"), *curtis* ("royal estate"; "landed property; village") or *burgus* (Germ.-Latin "castle", also "frontier fortification") which all played a typical part in the formation of place names. The first part of a place-name frequently indicates the person who was the founder or the representative of the tribe that settled there.

Njeussychin offers an attractive explanation of how an originally self-contained village settlement, consisting of a community of settlers possessing equal rights, could gradually become a differentiated settlement in which a single individual could achieve a dominating position by power and wealth and be

130 Lorsch, Carolingian Gatehouse. This simple building (*c.* 775) is one of the finest examples of Carolingian architecture in Germany. Antique elements, deriving from the triumphal arch, are combined and interspersed with a new architectural concept expressed in the alternately red and white surface and in the linking of gate and chapel —there is a chapel to St. Michael in the upper storey.

131 The marble sarcophagus with the "Adoration of the Magi"—a theme found in many variations at this time—is in the chapel on the south side of the famous Basilica of S. Vitale in Ravenna which was consecrated by Archbishop Maximian in 547.

132 Votive crown of the Visigothic King Reccesvind (653–672) (Museo Arqueológico Nacional, Madrid). This example of Visigothic work, which nevertheless reveals Byzantine influence, is of gold and contains precious stones, some of which are in cellular mountings. The individual letters—formed of gold with precious stones in cellular mountings—are to be interpreted as RECCESVINTHUS REX OFFERET (King Reccesvind offers this), making it very likely that the crown originated from the famous Visigothic legislator. It is part of a hoard of treasure found at Fuente de Guarrazar near Toledo in 1850.

133/134 Santa Maria de Naranco, 2 km northwest of Oviedo (Spain). Originally the royal hall of Ramiros I (842–850), this structure is in the tradition of Spanish architecture during the Visigothic period. The barrel-vaulted, two-storey building was reached by a twin flights of steps. The loggias in the hall are a reminder of the original profane purpose of the building which was converted into a church between 905 and 1065.

135/136 St. Michael's Church in Fulda was built about 820 by the Abbot Eigil as an obsequial church. The rotunda, which was in the tradition of the early Christian churches (and contained a tumulus with a model of the Holy Sepulchre in Jerusalem) was remodelled in the 11th century. Apart from four column-capitals in the upper storey, all that is left of the original building is the crypt with its circular barrel-vaulting supported by a low centre-column with a capital imitating Ionic style.

137/138 Santa Cristina de Lena, Asturia (Spain). The interior of this little church, which was begun in the 9th century, if not before, is characterized by rich articulation with blind-storeys supported on columns of various designs. The raised altar area is separated from the main hall by arches carried on columns. The ornamentation is notable for chip-carvings and tracery panels which are certainly evidence of Germanic influence and exercised an influence on the pre-Romanesque architecture.

139/140 San Pedro de la Nave (Zamora province). Like Santa María in Quintanilla, this church dates from the 7th century and there are similarities in the architecture and masonry technique employed. However, the ground-plan is in the shape of a cross. The fine stone capitals are richly decorated with figure ornamentation (Daniel in the lions' den, the sacrifice of Abraham, etc.). As in Antique architecture, the columns are placed before the walls.

141 Bell-tower of San Apollinare in Classe, Ravenna. An early example of the free-standing campanile, which later became widespread in Italy.

the landowner of the peasants who had become dependent on him. He postulated that royal henchmen (*antrustiones*), in possession of an appropriate letter of authority from their lord and against whom it was not possible to protest, were sent to these settlements. Any protest was penalized with an impossible fine —200 solidi—to prevent the village population from making use of an otherwise customary right, which stated that newcomers could be removed again from the village community within a year. This supposes a procedure which has much in common with the episode of the "Frankish Thersites" described by Gregory of Tours. On that occasion it was a question of implementing the royal claim to war-booty, i.e. in the military sphere, whereas here it was the socio-economic foundation which was attacked. The purpose of the royal challenge— which as a rule was rapidly followed by legislation—is clear enough: it was a question of the implementation of the new royal law, in the face of which the older tribal law, which reflected the interests of the communities of the free population, had to yield. To this extent, the decree of the *Lex Salica* (XIV, 4) in question here is particularly revealing since, with the rights and possibilities of the royal henchmen to penetrate a self-contained community of settlers, it naturally increased the power of the central authority itself.

The unscrupulous manner in which the men in possession of the king's confidence—who as members of the service nobility could also hold the highest offices of state—sought to attain the standing of a "feudal lord" is related by Gregory of Tours (IV, 46) in another episode which is likewise of very great interest in respect of the general history of culture and education. This is what he wrote: "However, since I wish to tell of the fate of Andarchius, I consider it useful to first say something of his origin and homeland. He was said to have been a slave of Felix, a man of senatorial family. Selected for personal attendance on his master, he pursued literary studies together with him and in this manner acquired an excellent education. For he was entirely at home in the works of Virgil, in the books of the Theodosian Law and in the art of reckoning. But this knowledge made him arrogant, he began to look down on his master and placed him-

self under the protection (*patrocinium*) of the Duke Lupus when this latter came to Marseilles at the command of King Sigibert. When Lupus returned from there, he took him in his following but recommended him on this occasion to King Sigibert and gave him into his service. The latter sent him to various places and entrusted him with public offices. He was henceforth regarded as a respected man and when he came to Clermont he made friends with a citizen of this city by the name of Ursus. He then

Long-swords and thrusting swords (spatha and sax)

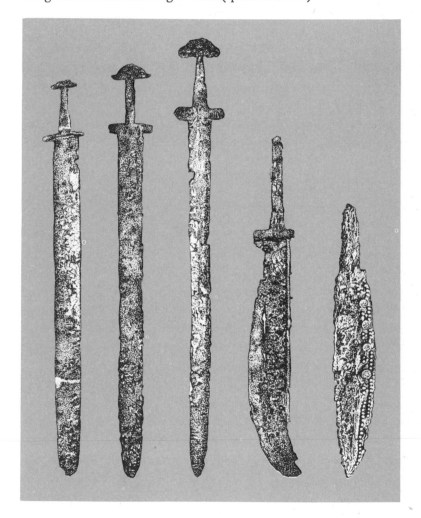

142/143 Santa Maria in Quintanilla de las Viñas (Burgos). Of this basilical monastery church, which probably dates from the 7th century, only the 10-m wide transept and the square altar-area survive; the central nave was built during the Middle Ages. Particularly impressive are the ground-plan with the intentional union of straight lines stressed by the outstanding masonry, the sculptured figures and the three-dimensional execution of the ornamental frieze depicting Christ between two angels (cf. text p. 202).

wished to marry the daughter of this man and since he was cunning he secretly placed, so it is said, his armour in a book-chest, in which otherwise documents were kept and said to the wife of Ursus: 'In this chest which I give to you I have put more than 16,000 pieces of gold. They are yours if you succeed in arranging for your daughter to be betrothed to me.' "

The intrigue of Andarchius was successful to the extent that Ursus was put in the wrong and condemned to pay damages when he refused to give his daughter to the royal henchman. Gregory concludes the episode in these words: "Ursus, however, went to the district of Vélay. When his property was transferred to Andarchius, this latter also came to Vélay. He entered the house of Ursus and commanded that a meal should be prepared for him and water heated for a bath. When, however, the slaves of the house would not obey the harsh man, he struck some with clubs, others with rods, hitting some on the head so that they bled. The servants were now afraid, the meal was prepared, he took a hot bath, intoxicated himself with wine and stretched out on his bed. There were only seven slaves in his retinue, however. When these, overcome by fatigue and wine, had fallen into a deep sleep, the servants of the house assembled and locked the doors, which were made from boards. After they had taken the keys, they broke up the sheaves of corn, which still stood in stacks, and placed them around the house and over it so that it was completely covered. Fires were then lighted at several places and it was only when the beams of the house burnt up and collapsed on the unfortunates inside that these woke up and began to shout. But nobody paid attention to them and the fire consumed them together with the entire house. Ursus, full of fear, went into the Church of St. Julianus but, after he had made gifts to the king, received back the whole of his property."

This episode vividly illustrates the process of development at that time within the agricultural sphere, the struggle between the forces of the central authority, to which the wicked Andarchius belonged, and the other landowners. Naturally, it is a particular variation which is described here, namely the confrontation between a royal agent (antrustio?—the position held by Andarchius is not clearly stated in the source) and a wealthy urban inhabitant, who was probably of Latin origin. Should it be thought that this example is not very characteristic, it must be said that the agrarian structure probably included just as many landowners of an older type as Frankish service nobility and settlers and that confrontations of the kind described were scarcely less important than the basic type outlined above in the development of feudalism.

Characteristic for the story of Andarchius, which for all that was taken from real life, is the rapid rise of the slave which was favoured by several factors: 1) by his education which, admittedly, was obviously coupled with the unscrupulousness of the careerist, 2) by his change from less influential to more powerful patroni and finally to the king, and 3) by the influence or natural authority which he—probably still formally a slave up to this time—acquired with freemen (rich citizens such as Ursus).

This is an interesting and—up to a certain degree—also a typical component in the emergence of early feudalism. It is not just a question of the economic power of the individual which—as demonstrated by the case of Ursus—could rapidly change. Of greater importance was the social position, particularly close relations with and within the ruling stratum which gave even a slave opportunities which exceeded his wildest dreams. This is illustrated by Andarchius who, at least at the time when he entered the royal service, must still have been a slave. Just as in the slave-owning society of Antiquity, the acquisition of wealth and social standing must normally have gone hand in hand. Just as many a slave of the Roman emperors had previously done, it also proved possible for a royal slave of the Great Migration period to gain great power and influence and himself to have slaves, freedmen and other dependants at his disposal. Since there was now no clearly defined producer class nor any other coherent class—the individual strata were only gradually reforming as classes—, it may have been that the influence of men such as Andarchius exceeded all reasonable bounds. As the example of the seneschals of the Merovingians clearly demonstrates, they sometimes even used the power of the king exclusively to their own advantage and in this way really did rule in place of the supreme "liege-lord".

In the final analysis and in the long run, the development of power on this scale was of course only possible when the persons concerned had a large enough share (preferably increasing) of land as the means of production. It was only as the owners—or at least possessors—of farms, villas and suchlike on an appropriate scale that they had a sufficient socio-economic base since serfs and other dependants plus livestock and other instruments of production were practically an integral part of this. Without this base, it was difficult for a vassal of importance or a big land-owner to survive in this period of early feudalism. To be sure, these landowners needed less of the surplus product than the latifundia proprietors of Late Antiquity. In comparison with that period, life had become easier—this is apparent when architecture and other products of the craftsman-artist are considered. As a consequence of this, there was also a reduction in the intensity of exploitation. Without doubt, this is of great significance for the transition from a slave-owning society to the feudal order. There was frequently no great clash of interests between the settlers and the big landowners and it often happened that there was not even a detectable disharmony between the serfs and the poor freemen on the one hand and the wealthy landowners on the other. When slaves took the part of their former master against a new one installed by the king, the inference is clear. At any rate, one of the explanations for such good relations is probably to be sought in the reduced exploitation which resulted from the penetration of the unprejudiced and unpretentious tribes of the Great Migration. The central administration of the new states also claimed much less of the social product than the Late Roman and Byzantine administration with its rigid and tax-minded machinery had done. Taxation was accordingly reduced and could be paid in kind or in money as appropriate. Thus a certain class-harmony appeared for a time which, particularly in the final phase of early feudalism, was only destroyed by the waging of wars on a fairly large scale. This resulted in attempts to intensify exploitation once more—to a large extent in purely liege-law and feudalistic forms. The class-struggle then broke out again with the peasants (bondsmen) who—in various legal forms—were dependent on the Crown, the aristocracy and the Church on the one side and the liege-lords on the other. The latter possessed large or medium-sized estates and sought to raise the ground-rent by economic and other means of constraint.

The change in the socio-economic structure and the military happenings of the Great Migration itself led at least from the end of the 4th century onwards to a decline in town life and in large areas of the West to an almost complete disappearance of urban civilization. Antique civilization and all that which can be designated as urbanism had been intimately associated with the town as such in the centuries dominated by Greece and Rome. Even the classic Greek authors had regarded the polis as the focal point of cultural activities and, indeed, of all social life—immortalized by Aristotle in his designation of man as a "zoon politikon". In the period of Late Antiquity however, and until well into the Middle Ages, quite different cultural centres emerged. As mentioned already, these were the monasteries and convents and the outwardly often very modest residences of the kings which offered places of refuge for the arts and sciences. Numerous examples have already indicated what a vigorous interest was taken in culture and how many beautiful works, testifying to the sense of art and the technical and scientific achievements in the cultural sphere of this epoch, have come down to us. The picture which can now be drawn of this time is not at all complete, too much has been lost by chance or deliberately and systematically destroyed. Even the historians of this period, such as Orosius, Cassiodorus, Procopius or Isidore of Seville directly and indirectly state that the cultural inventory was mainly threatened from two sides: by the Barbarians who initially often plundered and destroyed in a senseless fashion and by antagonistic religious factions, which in their dogmatic fanaticism frequently fought each other until the very last breath. For the sake of simplification, it could certainly be asserted that the culture of Late Antiquity actually owes its death-blow to these two groups. It was not only the Vandals (the origin of the exaggerated catch-word "vandalism" which was not coined until 1794) who devastated the provincial Roman populations and especially the towns with unsurpassed ferocity. What then remained of public buildings such as theatres, gymnasia, religious buildings and so on continued to be utilized in the most diverse ways. Many of them, like the surviving theatres or amphitheatres, still fulfilled their original purpose, whereas others were converted to stables, or gradually became derelict. It is understandable that the storms of the Great Migration often brought about repeated changes in populations with greatly varying habits and ways of life. Archaeological investigations have frequently identified a number of changes in the function of public and private buildings and defensive fortifications. It was not unusual for a castle to become the home of a small group of settlers or the refuge of an ascetic religious community, and public buildings with solid foundations were often incorporated in the reduced perimeter wall of a Byzantine city, as is known from post-Vandal North Africa in particular. These variations, of which many more examples could be quoted, clearly show that the Great Migration caused people to lose a good deal of their living space, of their social product and, in many cases, of their cultural heritage as well. They had to come to terms with life on a more modest scale and at best could only very gradually make good the losses they had suffered. It was also a question of a systematic and skilful organization of labour without which—in view of the primitive means of production of the time—great technical, cultural and intellectual achievements could scarcely be contemplated. The erection of many palaces, churches and even small towns shows that this period was able to equal the standard of Antique civilization and, in details, to even surpass it. Nevertheless, there were exceptions which can be proved from the technical aspect in particular. There was no further development of the art of building; indeed, it stagnated for a long time, a fact which even isolated architectural innovations cannot hide. The same is true of sculpture and painting. Even improvements in arms (the ear-piece helmet, the franziska and various leather protections for the neck and the shoulders covered with iron) were of an isolated character only, unless the Byzantine East (Greek fire) or the Islamic sphere is included.

That intellectual culture declined at least as much as technical and artistic culture is obvious. It has already been seen that the entire school and education system of Antiquity—which was regarded as especially noteworthy despite the harsh restrictions which resulted from the privilege of education—ceased to function any longer. It was only in a few places, primarily in churches and monasteries and in a few residences, that a certain continuity of education was ensured. In the linguistic and factual sense the process of "Barbarization" had progressed to such an extent, however, that real teaching—on the basis of the seven liberal arts and the various disciplines—was scarcely possible. In this respect, a bridge was gradually established again by monastery schools, and sketchy textbooks and encyclopaedias normally appeared in place of great libraries which had fallen victim to destruction. Instruction was usually dominated by purely practical motives since, as a rule, it was enough if the pupils who completed the course of study were capable of performing a limited professional task, in an administrative capacity, for instance, or as a judge or in the clergy. Those with higher ambitions most easily achieved them by demonstrating their ability for years on end as the pupils of a respected master, as the representatives of high-ranking clerics or royal officials and acquiring as wide a range of abilities as possible—also by educational or missionary journeys. Only then did they have a chance of overcoming narrow-minded doubts and dogmatic antagonism towards education which prevailed in the West at least from the time of Augustine and to which numerous important works of Classical and post-Classical literature had fallen victim. The strict religious "censorship" practised at that time both by the Roman bishops and by numerous authorities in the individual territories, was not merely directed against newly published works—from all spheres of knowledge and life—but rather sought and destroyed, time and again, all the surviving remnants of Jewish and heretic literature. If the material used, normally parchment, was too valuable, the heretic or pagan text was removed so that the material could be used again. It was in this manner, for instance, that a work of Cicero was eradicated in the monastery of Bobbio so that the resolutions of the Council of Chalcedon could be recorded on the parchment sheets thus made available. All this shows that the Church did not fear to take even drastic measures in the intellectual confrontation—a phenomenon which is paral-

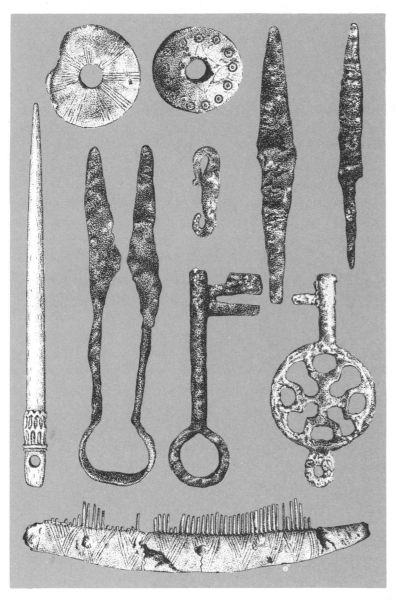

Domestic objects from Haithabu

lelled by the rapid process of change within the Church itself from the 4th century onwards which changed it from a persecuted to a persecuting organization. However, the claim of sovereignty of the Orthodox Church, which soon became a claim to sole representation in the intellectual sphere particularly, exacted the sacrifice of numerous valuable objects which were neutral in their interpretation and would certainly now be regarded as a precious cultural heritage under any circumstances. This reminds one of the burning of books and the destruction of paintings in modern times. To be sure, men like Augustine, Cassiodorus and Isidore kept a sense of perspective in their repression and elimination of Ancient works. It is true that they prevented the circle of the faithful, especially the monks and young people, from having access to literature which was regarded as suspect or to theatrical performances considered pernicious on account of their lascivious nature, but they did not call for a radical campaign of destruction. As a consequence, much ancient literature was preserved in monastic libraries and in other isolated places which is of inestimable value for its directness and naiveté, its intellectual profundity or its realistic description of the conditions of the time. Incidentally, this also applies not least to the works of theological authors themselves. In their endeavours to refute pagan and heretical ideas, they often engage in lengthy controversies and analyses and thus reflect, in particularly lucid manner, precisely that which they consider to be dangerous. And, above all, they also provide a direct insight into their own period with its often contradictory movements. This is because they were not only theologians and historical philosophers of a Christian type but also the chronists of their age which they see as the logical consequence of earlier periods and the continuation of pagan Antiquity with its four universal empires. These are numerous variations of this new conception of history which was already saturated with feudal features but had only two objectives. These were on the one hand the Christian completion of history in the last age of the world which was to precede the return of Christ (whose incarnation was now starting to be used everywhere as the basis for date indications) and the justification of the direct present or of the political powers in whose territory the chronist in question lived (Jordanes, Isidore of Seville, Bede). In the writing of their chronicles, the individual authors also expressed certain regional or personal ideas, of course. They primarily wrote for the kings or influential persons, to whom their works were dedicated or by whom they had been commissioned and for whom they sought to present—together with other information worth knowing—the picture of an ideal ruler—*Fürstenspiegel* ("Princes' Mirrors"). Against the background of the social contradictions and tensions which characterized this transitional period, too, this must be viewed as an attempt to master the past and the present and to bring about a thoroughly Christian society. The ethics of power set the pattern, logically enough, for the ethics of other professional classes, since thought on this subject again became gradually characterized by an hierarchical approach. It was natural that the "God-given order" should have been handed down from the top and that care was taken not to deviate in any way at all from the scheme of things once this had been decided. Thus the structure, arrangement and presentation of the *Fürstenspiegel* were thoroughly conventional and this applied to the *Vitae* of rulers and saints, too. Their primary aim was to interpret the virtues of the rulers and cardinals concerned from the Christian standpoint but otherwise in the way that Xenophon of Athens had done for his Greek readers in his *Cyropaedia*. As a result, they created new branches of mediaeval literature. Hagiographic and other literature of a similar nature exercised both a positive and a negative influence on this period and left a permanent mark on it. Like the Christian craftsmen-artists, these writers set out to permeate the whole of society by using their own methods and looking at it from a specific viewpoint. This undertaking met with opposition but initially, however, this was expressed only in a veiled manner, especially in form and detail. Antique or Barbarian elements came to the fore time and again and made this period of the Middle Ages more varied and brighter. Nevertheless, for the characterization of developments at this time, it must be stressed that there were practically no official counterweights to Christian literature and ecclesiastical art—i.e., profane poetry, history, specialist literature and secular architecture, sculpture and painting. Furthermore, it is to be noted that practically no word anywhere has been recorded as coming from the lower social classes and the broad masses of the people. It must be disputed that literature had any direct effect.

Arabs, Berbers,
Avars, Slavs and Normans

MIGRATIONS OF ENTIRE PEOPLES OCCURRED time and again in connection with changes which took place at the dawn of history when high civilizations emerged and "primitive" tribes came into conflict with more advanced peoples. The Mediterranean area in particular, with its fertile river basins and its subtropical and seemingly paradisal climate, was the objective of such migrations but at the same time it was also a melting pot in which the migratory peoples intermarried with those already settled there to their mutual advantage. Many elements of this mingling—and not just the linguistic and cultural ones—endured for centuries. It was not by chance that they influenced the ethnogeny not only of the older groups (Franks, Anglo-Saxons, Avars, Bulgarians, Slavs) but also of emergent nations —Western Franks (French), Italians, Spaniards, etc. For the Great Migration discussed here, this naturally applies on a much greater scale than for the previous movements of tribes and peoples. This lasting effect is best explained by the magnitude of the human groupings involved in this process, by the long duration of this cycle of migrations and by the size of the territories affected.

At least the outlines of this problem will become apparent when the "end" of the Great Migration is examined. Immediately on the death of Mohammed (632), an Arab migration was initiated, spreading in a not particularly systematic but far-flung process towards the North, East and West. The Arabs advanced as far as the Caucasus and Indus in one direction and up to the Pyrenees and even into the valley of the Loire (battles of Tours and Poitiers in 732) in the other. It is not only the political and military significance of this migration which is well-known today. What is more important—as long since realized—is that it had a great influence on the economy and society of Western Europe—far beyond the actual territories conquered—and, at least indirectly, made a contribution to the consolidation of the European type of feudalism since without the use of the liege-lord system on a large scale it would have been almost impossible to throw back the mounted Arab armies in France and Spain. Nowadays, it is generally accepted that Islam forced the Catholic Church and theologians to face up to a confrontation and that it

also played an intermediary role in the introduction of the Oriental and Greek cultural heritage to the West. Nevertheless, the North African and Berber element is still underestimated, due to the expansion of Islam, although it had already achieved a markedly independent status even in the Late Roman and Vandal periods.

In the 6th and 7th centuries, parts of Southern and Central Europe were invaded by yet more tribes which caused a stir in the most diverse ways. Of these, the most notable were the Proto-Bulgars, the Avars and the Slav tribes. The Proto-Bulgars, part of the Turkish family, advanced from the North into the Balkan mountains around 680. Together with Slav tribes and in constant struggle with Byzantium, they founded the First Bulgarian Empire (681–1018, capital at Pliska). One hundred years previously, the nomadic Turco-Tataric tribe of the Avars had established its first state in the Carpathian basin and, after the withdrawal of Lombard and other Germanic groups, gradually tried to include Hungarian territory within its sphere. The expansion of the Avars, which can be traced in the main—like that of many Slav tribes—from the archaeological evidence left behind by their settlements, was, however, held up to begin with. Some of the Western Slav tribes were organized in a strong alliance in 623 or thereabouts by the Frankish merchant Samo with their centre in Bohemia or Southern Moravia. The eastern boundary is disputed or it may have been vague but after a victory over the Frankish King Dagobert I (631) the influence of this short-lived state extended as far as Passau and Central Germany. In the course of this expansion westwards, there is no doubt that assistance was given to the expansion of other Slav groups which at this time moved into territories extending as far as the Lower Elbe, the Saale and the Upper Main (Obodrites, Liutians, Sorbs). These tribes had all achieved the form of a military democracy, which was the last stage of pre-class society. In connection with the general development of the productive forces, the process of social differentiation began to spread through all the Western Slavs and some of the Southern Slavs. Large estates were acquired by the tribal aristocracy who made increasing use of serfs. There was a decline in the influence of the popular as-

144 This find is from Guterstein (Baden) and is perhaps of North Germanic origin. It is the silver upper part of a scabbard and depicts a deity in the shape of an animal (Museum für Vor- und Frühgeschichte, Berlin).

Preceding two pages:

145 Large gold fibula from the period of the Great Migration (Old-saksamling, Oslo). This fibula dates from the 4th or 5th century and, apart from precious inlays, is also characterized by representations of human heads at the side and lower end.

146 Hilt, Vallstenarum (Gotland), (Historical Museum, Stockholm). The gilded bronze hilt (length 12.5 cm) is characterized by gold cellular work with garnet inlays and dates from c. 600.

147 Upper part of a pictorial stone from Gotland (Historical Museum, Stockholm) dating from the 9th or 10th century. The composition, recalling the ancient animal style, is probably intended to depict a part of the after-life bridge leading to Valhalla.

148 Runic stone (pictorial stone) from Lund (Museum). It is possible that the horseman represents Thor, who apparently holds a hammer in his right hand, or another deity of the Nordic Pantheon.

149 Pictorial stone from Gotland (Historical Museum, Stockholm), *c.* 700. The stones, decorated with images in bas-relief, were frequently erected in Sweden and on the island of Gotland in the 5th, 8th and 11th centuries in burial fields or at the side of tracks. In many respects they recall the horsemen stones (cf. Hornhausen No. 107). In the first period, geometrical decorations alternate with pictures of individual people and animals but in the second period vivid series of pictures from sagas or from the lives of dead heroes are frequently found. Ornamentation in East Swedish runic style is characteristic of the third period. At the top the stone here obviously depicts Odin on his stallion Sleipnir being welcomed by Frigga with the horn of mead. Above this there was probably a valkyrie, leading a dead warrior to Valhalla. The depiction of a ship is at least a realistic indication of the historical events of the time.

150 Shield-centre from Ultuna (Uppland) from the 7th century, (Historical Museum, Stockholm). It is of iron with tinned facings of bronze foil; on top an animal vertebra made of gilt bronze.

semblies and they were frequently replaced by assemblies of the nobility. This cleared the way not only for the formation of fairly large tribal associations but also for the development of state structures which—like the state of Samos or the Moravian empire of the 9th century—were made up of a number of tribal associations. The nobility began to lay claim to the land of the peasants to an increasing extent and then often to make them dependent on them, during this process of feudalization, in town-like settlements of craftsmen and merchants. Up till about the end of the 8th century, the Slavs and the Teutons were hindered in the consolidation and expansion of their territories by the Avars. Until the time of Charlemagne, the power and influence of the Avarian khanate remained considerable since the Avarian mounted nomads exploited or plundered the neighbouring areas which had mostly been settled by farming communities. In 796, however, an agreement between the Franks and the Southern Slavs led to a multi-front war against the Hungarian bases of the Avars. With the fall of their principal fortress, the Avars lost their dominating position. Their territory passed under Frankish and Slav rule and, with the culture of the new rulers, soon Christian influences came to Hungary.

At the end of this epoch and still during the lifetime of Charlemagne, a new wave of invasions came from Scandinavia with the Vikings (Normans, Varangians in Russia) who spread southwards and in the course of generations not only reached almost every part of Europe but even ventured to Asia Minor, Greenland and the Northeast of America. The history of this expansion is outside the scope of the present subject but is of value and worth mentioning for the sake of delimitation and comparison. *Beowulf*, the famous Old English epic, which contains not only Germanic but Antique and Christian elements as well, provides an insight into the world of the early Vikings. They combined old traditions with new characteristics. With untamed savagery, they attacked not only all the conveniently located coasts but even inland cities (Paris) which could be reached with their speedy longships. The plundering expeditions of fairly small mariner contingents and followings, which sailed off for adventure under the sign of Odin or Thor, were subsequently followed by larger ethnic groups which settled entire islands and territories (Faroes, Iceland, Greenland, the Baltic lands) and founded or occupied early feudal states (Normandy, England, Southern Italy-Sicily). These movements, which were often linked with social tensions, naturally led to a more rapid emergence of regional and central feudal powers in Denmark, Norway and Sweden as well, these becoming established, mostly with the assistance of the Church from the 10th century onwards. With the ability to speedily adjust to more advanced civilizations, the Vikings were epoch-makers not only as ruthless conquerors but also as explorers, traders and legislators. Without the enzyme of this new conqueror-stratum, European feudalism would have developed less quickly. The cultural gradient and the cultural exchange between East and West was likewise influenced to a large extent by the Norman contacts with the Byzantine and the Arab world.

Schematic representation
of the stronghold of Behren-
Lübchin, Teterow district

Fortified refuge (reconstruction)

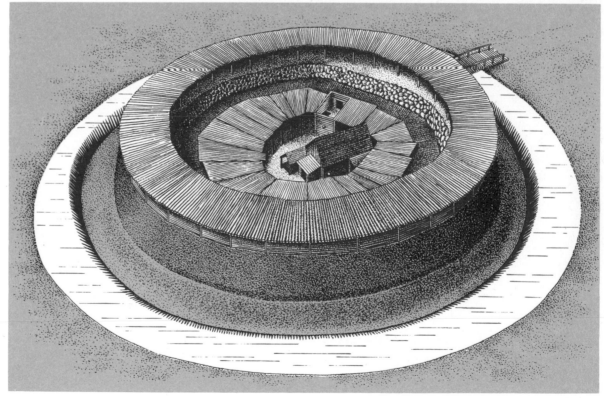

Chronological Table

	General History	Culture, Science, Literature	Art and Technology	Philosophy and Religion
up to A.D. 300		Pappos of Alexandria describes the simple mechanical devices (lever, pulley, arbor-wheel, wedge, screw) and discovers the basic mathematical principle of cross-ratios Beginning of Germanic heroic poetry (Jungsiegfried, Wieland)	Roman amphitheatre in Verona	
300–325	Formation of large Germanic tribes completed (Alemans, Franks, Saxons, Thuringians)	Julius Firmicus Maternus uses the term "Scientia chimae" for chemistry (Egyptian influence)	Diocletian has palace built in Spalato (Split) to where he moves in 305	Porphyrios of Syria (d. 304), pupil of Plotinus, whose doctrine he records; opposes Christianity
301	Maximum price decrees of Diocletian (unsuccessful)		Vivid catacomb frescos in Rome	Translation of the Bible into Coptic
305	Diocletian and his co-regent Maximianus abdicate		Important mosaic floors of the Roman palace of Piazza Armerina (Sicily)	Gregorian Church established in Armenia
306	Constantine I (the Great), son of Constantius, proclaimed regent of the West in York; up to 323 Licinius co-regent in the East		Christian Antiquity adopts the winged Eros figures (= angels)	
312	Victory of Constantine over Maxentius at Ponte Molle in Rome	c. 311 Decimus Magnus Ausonius, "last Roman poet", born (d. 393)	Basilica of St. John Lateran, first Greek church in Rome	Emperor Constantine issues Edict of Milan for the Christians (313)
324	War between Constantine and Licinius	325 Reform of Roman coinage (solidus)		325 Council of Nicaea (adoption of the doctrine of Athanasius, condemnation of doctrine of Arius)
325–337	Constantine sole ruler	330 Jamblichos develops doctrine of Plotinus		
330	Proclamation of Constantinople as capital. Imperial reform	330 District register of the City of Rome lists 28 public libraries		

	General History	Culture, Science, Literature	Art and Technology	Philosophy and Religion
337–340	Rule by three emperors: Constantine II (the West), Constantius II (the East), Constans (central region)			
340	Persian War of Constantius			
340–350	Rule by two emperors: Constantius II (the East), Constans (the West)			341 Pagan sacrifices forbidden, temples closed Wulfila begins translation of the Bible into Gothic Ascendancy of monastic life, emanating from Egypt
350–361	Constantius II sole ruler	after 350 Change from the book-roll to the codex form (still in use!)	c. 350 Roman basilica in Trier	
357	Constantius's triumph over the Persians celebrated in Rome; Julian's victory over the Alemans		c. 350 Ostrogoths adopt South Russian-Pontic cultural elements (cloisonné work, advanced animal style)	
358	Settlement of Franks in North Brabant		c. 350 Halo appears in pictures of Christ	
360	Julian proclaimed "Augustus" at Paris			
361–363	Julian sole ruler			361 Pagan reaction in the person of Julian
363	Persian War and death of Julian			362 Edict against the Christians
364–375	Valentinian I (the West) and Valens (up to 378 in the East); fighting along the Rhine; building of the last limes	c. 370 Ausonius: Bissula songs to an Aleman maiden captured in war	Water-powered stonesaw in the Eifel Mountains	c. 370 St. Basil the Great founds Basilias, benevolent institution (also hospices) 372 Death of Athanasius (doctrine of Athanasianism)
367	Gratian raised to the rank of "Augustus			372–c. 400 Martin, Bishop of Tours
368–369	Fighting in Britain			

	General History	Culture, Science, Literature	Art and Technology	Philosophy and Religion
375	Death of Valentinian I during the war against the Quadi	c. 375 Colossus of Barletta S. Maria Maggiore in Rome (mosaics)		373–397 Ambrose, Bishop of Milan (participation in political affairs; martyr cult; hymns)
375	"Great Migration" begins with the advance of Huns westwards	Prosperity of Trier as Roman residence		
376	Visigoths under Fritigern cross Danube			
378	Defeat and death of Valens in the battle of Adrianople; victory over the Alemans by Gratian	after 378 "History of Rome" by Ammianus Marcellinus		
378–383	Gratian			381 Council of Constantinople; State Church on Nicaean principles
379–395	Theodosius the Great	390 Christians destroy Serapeion Library in Alexandria		390 Penance of Theodosius for Thessalonica massacre
383–392	Valentinian II (in the West, influenced by Germanic generals)	393 Theodosius the Great ends Olympic Games		391 Christianity becomes State religion
387	Division of Armenia between Rome and Persia			
392	Flavius Eugenius installed as anti-emperor by the Frankish general Arbogast			
394	Victory of Theodosius at the Frigidus			
395	Death of Theodosius, division of the empire: in the West Honorius (to 423), Arcadius (to 408) in the East	397 Nonnos: "Dionysiaka"		395 St. Augustine Bishop of Hippo Regius (writings against heretics; Confessions; The City of God: historical theology)
395–410	Visigoths under Alaric	398 Macrobius Theodosius: "Saturnalia"	after 400 Ravenna developed as capital of the Western empire (mosaics)	398 Saint John Chrysostom, Patriarch of Constantinople (famous preacher and moral theologian)

	General History	Culture, Science, Literature	Art and Technology	Philosophy and Religion
408	Overthrow and execution of the general Stilicho			
410	Capture of Rome by Alaric, who dies at Cosenza	411 Sulpicius Severus: "Vita S. Martini"		
		413–426 St. Augustine: "The City of God"		
from 418	Tolosanian empire of the Visigoths; attempts to establish states by the Vandals and Suebi in Spain	418–419 Orosius writes history of the world "against the pagans"		
425–455	Valentinian III emperor of Western Rome (under regency of his mother Galla Placidia and General Aetius)	425 University of Constantinople founded		425 Syrian translation of the Bible (Peshitta) 425 The moral theologian John Cassianus founds monasteries in Marseilles
429	Conquest of North Africa by the Vandals under Geiseric (Vandal empire from 439 to 534)		432 Moses mosaic in S. Maria Maggiore	430 St. Patrick brings Christianity to Ireland
437	On Roman instructions, Huns destroy Burgundian empire centred around Worms	438 "Codex Theodosianus" (Emperor Theodosius II)		431 Third Council of Ephesos against the Patriarch Nestorius (Nestorian sect up to 13th century)
443	Burgundians establish empire in Savoy and around Lyons	after 440 Salvian of Massilia: "Of the World Government of God" (ascetic and pro-Barbarian tendency)		440–461 Pope Leo I the Great 445 Leo I obtains recognition of the Papal primacy by Valentinian III
448	East Roman-Byzantine empire tributary to Attila			
449	Britain occupied by Angles, Saxons and Jutes			449 "Robber synod" of Ephesos recognizes that the human and divine in the person of Christ constitutes only one nature
c. 450	Advance of Slavs as far as Elbe and Saale rivers			

General History	Culture, Science, Literature	Art and Technology	Philosophy and Religion
451 Roman army under Aetius with Visigothic assistance defeats Huns under Attila (battle of Châlons)			451 Fourth ecumenical Council of Chalcedon (human and divine nature of Christ unmixed and indivisible)
452 Huns invade Italy			
453 Disintegration of Hun empire on death of Attila			
455 Vandals under Geiseric capture Rome; Vandals supreme in Mediterranean area (thalassocracy)			
457 Childeric king of the Salian Franks (Tournai)			
466 Euric king of the Visigoths			
471 Theodoric the Great king of the Ostrogoths (to 526)	c. 475 "Codex Euricianus" (Visigothic law)		
476 Romulus Augustulus, emperor of Western Rome, overthrown by Odoacer (Patricius); end of Roman Empire in the West	c. 476 Under Proclos non-Christian philosophy flourishes for the last time in Athens		
481 Clovis king of the Salians and later of all the Franks	c. 481 The historian Zosimus regards Christianity as responsible for the disintegration of the empire	481 Finds from the tomb of Childeric I show Gothic influence on Frankish art (gold, geometrically decorated ornaments and weapons)	483 Dispute over dogma between Rome and Byzantium (to 519)
486 Clovis defeats Syagrius and eliminates remainders of the Western Roman Empire; Paris capital of Frankish empire in 508			
489 Theodoric the Great defeats Odoacer at Verona	c. 490 Dracontius of Carthage: "De laudibus Dei"	490 Theodoric the Great presents the king of the Burgundians with a water clock	492—496 Pope Gelasius I places episcopal power on an equal footing with temporal power (doctrine of the two swords)

General History	Culture, Science, Literature	Art and Technology	Philosophy and Religion
493 Theodoric the Great founds Ostrogothic empire in Italy, conquers Sicily (hitherto in Vandal hands) and takes Malta in 494			
496 Clovis subjugates Alemans			498/499 Clovis baptized by Remigius at Rheims
c. 500 Arthur, king of the Celtic Britons, resists Saxons: development of legends (Arthur and the Knights of the Round Table, model of chivalry)	c. 500 Writing of the Babylonian (Aramaic) Talmud	c. 500 First layout of the Vatican palace	498 Nestorians found church in Persia (Patriarchate of Ctesiphon)
c. 500 The Bavarians move into present-day Bavaria from Bohemia	c. 500 Burgundian law codified by Gundobad

c. 500 Heyday of the alchemists' school in Alexandria (quest for the philosophers' stone) | c. 500 Mosaic art flourished in Byzantium and Ravenna (Ravenna: Mausoleum of Galla Placidia, San Apollinare Nuovo)

c. 500 Theory of music (Boethius) and composition of hymns (Romanos from Syria) | |
c. 500 The Czechs settle in Bohemia			
505 The Lombards destroy the Herulaean empire between the Theiss and the Danube		c. 500 Goose-quills come into use as writing instruments	
507 Clovis completes Frankish empire by the conquest of Visigothic territory		c. 507 Wooden coffins and other wooden equipment in use among the Alemans	
507–711 Visigothic empire of Toledo			519 Byzantine Church accepts Roman dogma
511 Death of Clovis, division of empire between his four sons (residences: Soissons, Metz, Paris, Orléans)	524 Anicius Torquatus Severinus Boethius executed (adviser of Theodoric; translator of Aristotle; "Consolation of Philosophy"		521 Death of Ennodius (advocated primacy of Pope, for whom the title of honour "papa" is reserved)
526 Death of Theodoric the Great; immortalized in saga as "Dietrich of Bern". Disintegration of the Ostrogothic coalition of states of the Great Migration		c. 525 Baptistery of the Arians in Ravenna (central structure with mosaics)

c. 526 Tomb of Theodoric in Ravenna | 525 With his Easter tables, Dionysius Exiguus introduces the Christian system of chronology |

	General History	Culture, Science, Literature	Art and Technology	Philosophy and Religion
527	Justinian I, emperor of Eastern Rome (Byzantium), influenced by his wife Theodora; ambition to restore unity of empire by wars		c. 527 Description of paddle-wheel boat with whim gin	c. 525 The Greek merchant Cosmas Indicopleustes reaches the African and Indian coasts ("Christian knowledge of localities", Earth described as a four-cornered disc)
529	Regensburg capital of the Duchy of Bavaria	c. 529 With the founding of the Benedictine Order, establishment of first European monastery schools		527 Death of Fulgentius of Ruspe; important disciple of St. Augustine and pioneer in the struggle against Vandal Arianism
531	Franks (and Saxons) conquer Thuringian empire			
532	Belisarius suppresses uprising of blue and green party in Constantinople (Nika insurrection)		c. 532 Justinian rebuilds the severely destroyed Constantinople (25 churches, including Hagia Sophia)	529 Benedict of Nursia founds monastery of Monte Cassino (Benedictine rule)
533–534	Vandal empire destroyed by Justinian's general Belisarius (King Gelimer)			
534	Frankish kings subjugate Burgundian empire (attempt expansion into Switzerland and then into Northern Italy)	534 "Corpus Iuris Civilis" published		
535	War begun by Belisarius against the Ostrogothic empire (ended in 553 by Narses)			
536	Frankish empire wins Provence from Ostrogoths	c. 537 Cassiodorus (Senator) publishes "Variae" (also a history of the Goths and Christian educational works)	c. 540 Depiction of the emperor in mosaics at Ravenna. Justinian: white, belted undergarment, embellished with gold, purple cloak with four-cornered inset, pearl diadem, pointed shoes; Theodora: long, light-coloured robe with precious stones along the hem, embroidered purple cloak, pearl diadem with pendants, pointed shoes	537 Pope Vigilius undecided in a dispute over doctrine with Byzantium
540	Byzantium loses Syrian Antioch to Persia			

	General History	Culture, Science, Literature	Art and Technology	Philosophy and Religion
541–552	Totila king of Ostrogoths, reconquest of Italy and internal reforms	c. 542 Gildas the Wise (of Roman descent?) begins independent historiography of Britain	546 Floating mills used for the first time during siege of Rome by Goths	546 "Three Chapters' Dispute" between Pope Vigilius and Justinian
		551 "History of the Goths" by Jordanes (Lower Italy)		
552	Totila slain in struggle against Narses	c. 550 Aristocratic culture in Sassanid empire: hunting, polo, string-music, chess, cosmetics, dancing	c. 550 Breeding of silkworms comes to Europe via Byzantium (553 State monopoly in Byzantium)	
553	Teja, the last king of the Ostrogoths, killed in decisive battle near the Vesuvius			
554	Narses, first exarch of the East Roman province of Italy (Ravenna)		c. 550 Zero and the negative numbers become known in India (Indian mathematics influence Persians and later Arabs and Europeans)	
559	Belisarius drives back Huns from Constantinople	c. 560 Procopius, companion of Belisarius, writes about the wars of the time (also history of building and secret history with scathing criticism of Justinian and Theodora)		
561	Frankish empire, united under Chlothar I (son of Clovis), divided into Austrasia, Neustria and Burgundy; struggles of the "Noble Parties"			
565	Death of Justinian I			
567	Lombards (with Avars) destroy Gepidae empire			
568	Lombards under Alboin found empire in Italy (Pavia)			
c. 570	Avars establish empire in Hungary/Lower Austria	c. 575 Alexander of Tralles writes a medical therapeutic collective work in Rome		
		c. 580 Legislation of Leowigild in Visigothic empire (lifting of the ban on marriage between Goths and Romans)		

	General History	Culture, Science, Literature	Art and Technology	Philosophy and Religion
to 586	Destruction of the empire of the Suebi by Visigoths under Leowigild who also throws back Byzantines in Southern Spain and founds cities		586 Etshmiadsin Evangeliar (Byzantine illustrated manuscript in Armenian monastery)	
589	Visigoths converted to Catholicism (Reccared I)	594 Gregory of Tours writes "Gesta Francorum" (beginning of the recording of history in Frankish empire)	c. 590 St. Gereon's church in Cologne	589 Third Council of Toledo under Leander, the brother of Isidore of Seville
c. 600	Czechs and Slovaks (under Avarian supremacy) settle in Bohemia and Moravia	c. 600 Venantius Fortunatus, Bishop of Poitiers: histories of the saints and temporal poems (journeys along the Rhine and Moselle)	c. 600 Advance of the goldsmith's art during Merovingian period: engraving, damascening, cloisonné work; frequent pictorial motif: man between two animals (Daniel in the lions' den)	c. 600 Canterbury first bishopric of England
c. 600	Serbs move into present-day territory	c. 600 second (High German) consonant shift		c. 600 Religious tolerance in Sassanid empire: Zoroastrianism, Nestorian Christianity and Judaism
		c. 600 Pope Gregory I (the Great) calls for pictures as substitute for Bible for the illiterate, develops doctrine of purgatory, encourages cult of saints and reliquaries, writes "Dialogues" and "Handbook of the duties of the clergy"	c. 600 In Egypt climax of Coptic art: Egyptian, Hellenistic, Byzantine and Arab influence	c. 600 Pope Gregory founds choir school, has church vocal music collected in "Antiphonar"
			c. 600 "Lombard" helmets of Germanic type (consisting of a number of metal panels)	
		after 600 Isidore of Seville writes not only works on moral theology and natural science but also the "Etymologiae", a comprehensive encyclopaedia (d. 636)	after 600 In Central Europe two-field system of cultivation instead of multi-year crop/grass cycle	
607	Venice for the first time a state under a doge			607 Celebration of all martyrs in the Catholic Church
610–641	Heraclius I Byzantine emperor (628 victorious peace with Persians)			610 Mohammed appears as the Prophet
				615 Death of Columba; as Irish missionary founded monasteries in Burgundy and Lombardy

General History	Culture, Science, Literature	Art and Technology	Philosophy and Religion
616 Death of Lombard King Agilulf; introduced Christianity; his concept of rule is illustrated by the Agilulf Plate			
618 In Neustria, Austrasia and Burgundy, seneschal as leading official of royal court			
622 Hegira of Mohammed	622 Hegira of Mohammed becomes basis for the Islamic system of reckoning time (based on simple lunar year)		
623 Slav state of the Frankish merchant Samo (to 656)			625 Dagobert I founds Abbey of St. Denis
629–638 Dagobert I king of the entire Frankish empire; rules independently as last Merovingian			625 Strasbourg becomes bishopric
630 Mohammed captures Mecca	c. 630 A Christian priest from Rome travels to Peking		630 Mecca a place of pilgrimage for Moslems; all the tribes of the Arabian peninsula accept the doctrine of Mohammed
632 Abu Bekr, Mohammed's father-in-law, first caliph			
634 Omar I, second caliph, conquers Syria, Egypt and Persia	after 640 Arabic becomes the dominating language of the Orient (expansion)	644 Swedish helmet ornamentation with Odin on eight-legged horse with shield, spear, two ravens and serpent	
	644 Rothari, king of the Lombards (636–652) codifies Lombard law	c. 645 Gold treasure of the Anglo-Saxon King Ethelbert (ship burial of Sutton Hoo)	
	c. 650 Unlike the Byzantines with their heavy clothing, the Frankish warriors wear short trousers, smock, cloak, sandal-like shoes with straps up to the knees and are armed with helmet, belt, sword, battle-axe and spear		c. 650 Evangelist Bishop Emmeram founds monastery in Regensburg

General History	Culture, Science, Literature	Art and Technology	Philosophy and Religion
	654 Reccesvind, king of the Visigoths, completes codification of the law ("Liber iudiciorum")		
672 Unsuccessful siege of Constantinople by Arabs up to 678	672 The Venerable Bede born; Old English monk and historian	672 Defenders of Constantinople use "Greek fire" (mixture of sulphur, rock salt, resin, crude oil, quicklime, etc.)	673 Birth of Boniface, "Apostle of the Germans" (martyrdom 754)
679 Founding of the East Bulgarian empire			681 As Archbishop of Canterbury, Theodore of Tarsus organizes Catholic Church in England
687 Carolingians obtain hereditary right to the rank of seneschal for the whole Frankish empire			
697 Carthage destroyed by Arabs			692 Synod of Trulla puts Bishop of Constantinople on equal footing with Bishop of Rome
8th century Carolingians extend empire to include Thuringians, Alemans, Swabians, Bavarians and later the Lombard empire, Saxony, Carinthia and the Spanish Marches	8th century spread of the monastery schools in Frankish empire (religion, Latin, arithmetic, some natural sciences)	8th century Use of waterwheels for powering mills spreads throughout Europe	8th century building of mosques (often triple-nave basilicas; cupola structures)
8th century Arabs complete conquest of North Africa and after destruction of Visigothic empire (711 ff.) advance as far as France (repulsed at Tours and Poitiers in 732)		8th century Stone churches replace wooden structures in England	
	716 Codification of the tribal law of the Alemans	705 Stone rotunda church built on Marienberg near Würzburg (still in existence)	718 Boniface brings Christianity to Thuringia, Hesse, Bavaria, and Friesland and founds monasteries and bishoprics
	720 Birth of Paulus Diaconus, Lombard historiar	736 Boniface bans consumption of horsemeat (horse sacrifices!)	
	c. 750 "Hildebrandlied" (Monastery of Fulda)	*c.* 750 Hops cultivated as spice for beer in Bavaria	763 Monastery of Lorsch established (gatehouse still in existence)

Literature

Sources

AMBROSIUS: *Corpus Scriptorum Ecclesiasticorum Latinorum (CSEL)*, vols. 32, 62, 64.

AMMIANUS MARCELLINUS: *Römische Geschichte*, Latin and German, edited by W. Seyfarth, 4 Parts, Berlin, 1968–1971.

APOLLINARIS SIDONIUS: *Opera*, edited by Ch. Lütjohann, Berlin, 1887 (MGH AA, vol. 8); edited by P. Mohr, Leipzig, 1895.

AUGUSTINUS: *CSEL*, vols. 25, 28, 33, 34, 36, 40, 41, 42, 43, 44, 51, 52, 53, 57, 58, 60, 63.

AUGUSTINUS: *Zweiundzwanzig Bücher über den Gottesstaat*, German transl. by A. Schröder, 2 vols., Kempten and Munich, 1914 (Bibliothek der Kirchenväter = BKV vol. 16).

AUSONIUS: *Opera*, edited by H. Schenkl, Berlin, 1883 (MGH AA, vol. 5, 2).

AUXENTIUS: "Vita Ulfilae", in: H. Giesecke, *Die Ostgermanen und der Arianismus*, Leipzig, 1939.

BENEDICT OF NURSIA: *S. Benedetto, La Regola*, edited by D. Anselmo Lentini, Latin-Italian, Montecassino, 1947; *Die Regel*, German transl. by C. Kößler, Graz, 1931.

BOETHIUS: *Trost der Philosophie*, German transl. by K. Büchner, Leipzig n. d.

CASSIODORUS: *Variae*, edited by Th. Mommsen, Berlin, 1894, (MGH AA 12).

Chronica minora saec. IV, V, VI, VII = Monumenta Germaniae historica. Auctores antiquissimi (MGH AA), vols. IX and X, edited by Th. Mommsen, Berlin, 1892 ff.

Codex Iustinianus: edited by P. Krüger, Berlin, 1929.

Codex Theodosianus: edited by Th. Mommsen and P. M. Meyer, Berlin, 1905.

Edda: 1st vol. "Heldendichtung", transl. by F. Genzmer, with introduction and notes by A. Heusler, Jena, 1928; 2nd vol. "Götterdichtung und Spruchdichtung", transl. by F. Genzmer, with introduction and notes by A. Heusler, Jena, 1932.

ENNODIUS: *Opera*, edited by W. Hartel, Vienna, 1882 (CSEL, vol. 6); edited by F. Vogel, Berlin, 1885 (MGH AA, vol. 7).

EUGIPPIUS: *Das Leben des Heiligen Severin*, Latin and German, edited by R. Noll, Berlin, 1963.

Fontes ad historiam regni Francorum aevi Karolini illustrandam: revised by R. Rau, Berlin, 1956–1960 (Ausgewählte Quellen zur deutschen Geschichte des Mittelalters, vol. 5, Parts 1–3).

GREGORY THE GREAT: *Dialogi*, edited by U. Moricca, Rome, 1924; Moralia in Job, J. P. Migne, Patrologiae cursus completus. Series Latina (MPL), vol. 7.

GREGORY OF TOURS: *Zehn Bücher Geschichten*, on the basis of German transl. by W. Giesebrecht, revised by R. Buchner, Berlin, 1956 (Ausgewählte Quellen zur deutschen Geschichte des Mittelalters, vols. 1, 3).

HIERONYMUS: *CSEL*, vols. 54–56, 59.

ISIDORE OF SEVILLE: *Isidors Geschichte der Goten, Vandalen, Sueven, nebst Auszügen aus der Kirchengeschichte des Beda Venerabilis*, transl. by D. Coste, Leipzig, ³1909 (Die Geschichtsschreiber der deutschen Vorzeit, vol. 10);
Opera, MPL, vols. 81–83;
Origines (Etymologiae), edited by W. M. Lindsay, Oxford, 1911.

IOHANNES CASSIANUS: *Opera*, edited by M. Petschenig, 2 vols., Prague–Vienna–Leipzig, 1886–88 (CSEL, vols. 13 and 17).

IORDANES: *Romana et Getica*, edited by Th. Mommsen, Berlin, 1882 (MGH AA, vol. 5, 1).

IULIANUS: *Epistulae, Leges, Poemata, Fragmenta, Varia*, edited by J. Bidez and F. Cumont, Paris, 1922;
Œuvres complètes, vol. I, 1, edited by J. Bidez, Paris, 1932.

The Koran: German transl. from the Arabic by M. Henning, introduction by E. Werner and K. Rudolph, Leipzig, 1968.

Leben des Heiligen Bonifatius von Willibald, der Heiligen Lioba von Rudolf von Fulda, des Abtes Sturmi von Eigil, transl. by M. Tangl, Leipzig, ³1920 (Die Geschichtsschreiber der deutschen Vorzeit, vol. 13).

Notitia dignitatum: edited by O. Seeck, Berlin, 1876.

OPTATUS OF MILEVE: *Libri VII* (Contra Parmenianum Donatistam), edited by C. Ziwsa, Vienna, 1893 (CSEL, vol. 26).

OROSIUS: *Historia adversum paganos*, edited by C. Zangemeister, Vienna, 1882 (CSEL, vol. 5).

Passiones Vitaeque Sanctorum Aevi Merovingici, edited by B. Krusch, Hannover–Leipzig, 1902 (MGH SRM, vol. 6).

Paulus Diakonus und die übrigen Geschichtsschreiber der Langobarden, transl. by O. Abel, Leipzig, ³1939 (Die Geschichtsschreiber der deutschen Vorzeit, vol. 15).

PROCOPIUS: *Opera omnia*, on the basis of the edition by J. Haury, edited by G. Wirth, Leipzig, 1962–64;
Vandalenkrieg, Gotenkrieg, transl. by D. Coste, Leipzig, ³1913, ³1922 (Die Geschichtsschreiber der deutschen Vorzeit, vols. 15 and 6).

SALVIAN OF MASSILIA: *De Gubernatione Dei*, edited by C. Halm (MGH AA, vol. 1, 1), Berlin, 1877;
German transl. by A. Mayer, Kempten–Munich, 1933 (BKV², vol. 11).

Scriptores Historiae Augustae: On the basis of the edition by E. Hohl, edited by Ch. Samberger and W. Seyfarth, 2 vols., Leipzig, 1965 ff.

SULPICIUS SEVERUS: *Opera*, edited by C. Halm (CSEL, vol. 1), Vienna, 1866;
Schriften über den Hl. Martinus, German transl. by P. Pius Bihlmeyer, Kempten–Munich, 1914 (BKV², vol. 20).

SYMMACHUS: *Opera*, edited by O. Seeck, Berlin, 1883 (MGH AA, vol. 6, 1).

Laws

BEYERLE, F.: *Die Gesetze der Burgunden*, Weimar, 1938 (Germanenrechte, vol. 10).

BEYERLE, F.: *Die Gesetze der Langobarden*, Weimar, 1947.

CONRAT, M.: *Breviarium Alaricianum. Römisches Recht im fränkischen Reich*, Leipzig, 1903 (reprint Aalen, 1963).

Die Gesetze der Angelsachsen: edited by F. Liebermann, 3 vols., Halle, 1903/16.

ECKHARDT, K. A.: *Lex Salica: Recensio Pippina. Die Gesetze des Karolingerreiches 714–911*, vol. I, Weimar, 1953 (Germanenrechte, Texte und Übersetzungen, vol. 2).

Edictum Theoderici regis: edited by F. Bluhme, Hanover, 1875/89 (MGH LL 5).

Leges Burgundionum: edited by L. R. von Salis, Hanover, 1892 (MGH LL 1, 2,1).

Leges Visigothorum: edited by K. Zeumer, Hanover–Leipzig, 1902 (MGH LL 1,1).

Literature

Abriss der Geschichte antiker Randkulturen: revised by P. Lambrechts et. al., edited by W.-D. v. Barloewen, Munich, 1961.

ALTANER, B.: *Patrologie*, edited by A. Stuiber, Freiburg, ⁶1960.

ALTHEIM, F.: *Niedergang der Alten Welt*, 2 vols., Frankfort on the Main, 1952.

BACH, H. and S. DUSEK: *Slawen in Thüringen*, Weimar, 1971.

BACKES, M. and R. DÖLLING: *Die Geburt Europas*, Baden-Baden, 1969.

BAETKE, W.: *Die Religion der Germanen in Quellenzeugnissen*, Frankfort on the Main, [2]1938;
Das Heilige im Germanischen, Tübingen, 1942.

BIELER, L.: *Irland — Wegbereiter des Mittelalters*, Olten–Lausanne–Freiburg, 1961.

BODMER, J.-P.: *Der Krieger der Merowingerzeit und seine Welt*, Zurich, 1957.

BOSL, K.: *Frühformen der Gesellschaft im mittelalterlichen Europa*. Beiträge zu einer Strukturanalyse der mittelalterlichen Welt, Munich–Vienna, 1964;
Franken um 800. Strukturanalyse einer fränkischen Königsprovinz, Munich, [2]1969.

CAPELLE, W.: *Das alte Germanien. Die Nachrichten der griechischen und römischen Schriftsteller*, Jena, 1929.

CLAUDE, D.: *Adel, Kirche und Königtum im Westgotenreich*, Sigmaringen, 1971;
Geschichte der Westgoten, Stuttgart, 1970.

CONRAD, H.: *Deutsche Rechtsgeschichte*, vol. 1, Karlsruhe, 1954.

COURCELLE, P.: *Histoire littéraire des grandes invasions germaniques*, Paris, [3]1964.

COURTOIS, CHR.: *Les Vandales et l'Afrique*, Paris, 1955.

DANNENBAUER, H.: *Die Entstehung Europas. Von der Spätantike zum Mittelalter*, 2 vols., Stuttgart, 1959–1962.

DEMPF, A.: *Sacrum Imperium*, 2nd reprint, Darmstadt, 1954.

DEVOTO, G.: *Geschichte der Sprache Roms*, German transl. by I. Opelt, Heidelberg, 1968.

DIESNER, H.-J.: *Der Untergang der römischen Herrschaft in Nordafrika*, Weimar, 1964;
Kirche und Staat im spätrömischen Reich, Berlin, [2]1964;
Das Vandalenreich. Aufstieg und Untergang, Leipzig–Stuttgart, 1966;
Kriege des Altertums, Berlin, 1971 ([2]1974);
Isidor von Sevilla und seine Zeit, Berlin, 1973.
Isidor von Sevilla und das westgotische Spanien, Berlin, 1977 (Trier, 1978).

DILIGENSKIJ, G. G.: *Severnaja Afrika v IV—V vekach*, Moscow, 1961.

DOPSCH, A.: *Die Wirtschaftsentwicklung der Karolingerzeit*, Part I,2. Weimar, [3]1962.

DÖRRIES, H.: *Konstantin der Große*, Stuttgart, 1958.

FÉVRIER, P.-A.: *Art de l'Algérie antique*, Paris, 1971.

FIEBIGER, O. and L. SCHMIDT: *Inschriftensammlung zur Geschichte der Ostgermanen* (Denkschriften der Akademie der Wissenschaften in Wien, Phil.-hist. Kl. 60,3; 70,3; 72,2).

FONTAINE, J.: *Isidore de Séville et la culture classique dans l'Espagne wisigothique*, 2 vols., Paris, 1959.

FORRER, R.: *Keltische Numismatik der Rhein- und Donaulande*, 2 vols., Graz 1968 f.

FREND, W. H. C.: *The Donatist Church*, Oxford, 1952;
The Rise of the Monophysite Movement, Cambridge, 1972.

GAMILLSCHEG, E.: *Romania Germanica*, 3 vols., Berlin–Leipzig, 1934–1936.

GAUTIER, E. F.: *Geiserich*, German transl. by J. Lechler, Frankfort on the Main, 1934.

GEFFCKEN, J.: *Der Ausgang des griechisch-römischen Heidentums*, Heidelberg, 1920.

HAENDLER, G.: *Geschichte des Frühmittelalters und der Germanenmission*, Göttingen, 1961 (Die Kirche in ihrer Geschichte, vol. 2, part E).

HAHN, I.: *Das bäuerliche Patrocinium in Ost und West* (Klio vol. 50, 1968, pp. 261–276).

HAUCK, A.: *Kirchengeschichte Deutschlands*, 5 vols., Leipzig, [7]1956.

HAUSSIG, H. W.: *Kulturgeschichte von Byzanz*, Stuttgart, 1959.

HEWKES, S. CH. and G. C. DUNNING: *Krieger und Siedler in Britannien während des 4. und 5. Jahrhunderts* (43.–44. Bericht der Römisch-germanischen Kommission 1962–1963, Berlin, 1964, pp. 155–231).

HERRMANN, J.: *Zwischen Hradschin und Vineta*. Frühe Kulturen der Westslawen, Leipzig–Jena–Berlin, 1971.

HEUSLER, A.: *Lied und Epos in germanischer Sagendichtung*, Darmstadt, [2]1960.

JAHN, M.: "Die Wandalen", in: Reinerth, H., *Vorgeschichte der deutschen Stämme*, l. c., vol. 3, pp. 943–1032.

KLEIN, R. (Editor): *Das frühe Christentum im römischen Staat* (Wege der Forschung, vol. 267), Darmstadt, 1971.

KLINCK, R.: *Die lateinische Etymologie des Mittelalters*, Munich, 1970.

KOCH, U.: *Die Grabfunde der Merowingerzeit aus dem Donautal um Regensburg*, Berlin, 1968.

KRAFT, H., *Kirchenväterlexikon*, Munich, 1966.

KRANZ, G.: *Europas christliche Literatur von 500 bis 1500*, Munich–Paderborn–Vienna, 1968.

KÜHNERT, F.: *Allgemeinbildung und Fachbildung in der Antike*, Berlin, 1961.

LÁSZLO, G.: *Steppenvölker und Germanen*, Budapest–Vienna, 1971.

LEIPOLDT, J.: *Der soziale Gedanke in der altchristlichen Kirche*, Leipzig, 1952.

LIETZMANN, H.: *Geschichte der alten Kirche*, ²vols. 2–4, Berlin, 1953.

MANITIUS, M.: *Geschichte der lateinischen Literatur des Mittelalters*, 1st part, Munich, 1911 (= Handbuch der klassischen Altertumswissenschaft, vol. 9, 2nd section, 1st part).

MARROU, H. I.: *Saint Augustin et la fin de la culture antique*, Paris, 1958.

MASCHKIN, N. A.: *Römische Geschichte* (German), Berlin, 1953.

MESLIN, M.: *Les Ariens d'Occident (335–430)*, Paris, 1967.

MILDENBERGER, G.: *Die thüringischen Brandgräber der spätrömischen Zeit*, Cologne–Vienna, 1970.

MISCH, G.: *Geschichte der Autobiographie*, 2nd vol., 1st part, Frankfort on the Main, 1955.

MITTEIS, H.: *Der Staat des hohen Mittelalters*, Weimar, ⁴1953; *Lehnrecht und Staatsgewalt*, Darmstadt, ²1958.

NJEUSSYCHIN, A. I.: *Die Entstehung der abhängigen Bauernschaft als Klasse der frühfeudalen Gesellschaft in Westeuropa vom 6. bis 8. Jahrhundert*, German edition by B. Töpfer, Berlin, 1961.

NORDEN, E.: *Alt-Germanien. Völker- und namengeschichtliche Untersuchungen*, Darmstadt, ²1962.

PÁRDUCZ, M.: *Die ethnischen Probleme der Hunnenzeit in Ungarn*, Budapest, 1963.

PIRENNE, H.: *Geburt des Abendlandes*, Amsterdam, ²1941.

PRINZ, F.: *Frühes Mönchtum im Frankenreich. Kultur und Gesellschaft in Gallien, den Rheinlanden und Bayern am Beispiel der monastischen Entwicklung (4.–8. Jahrhundert)*, Munich–Vienna, 1965.

RASIN, J. A.: *Geschichte der Kriegskunst*, vol. 1, German transl. by A. Specht, Berlin, 1959.

Realencyclopädie der classischen Altertumswissenschaft (Pauly–Wissowa–Kroll): edited by K. Ziegler, Stuttgart, 1894ff.

Reallexikon für Antike und Christentum: edited by Th. Klauser, Stuttgart, 1950ff.

Reallexikon der germanischen Altertumskunde: edited by J. Hoops, 4 vols., Strasbourg, 1911–1919.

REINERTH, H. (Editor): *Vorgeschichte der deutschen Stämme*, 3 vols., Leipzig–Berlin, 1940.
(Caution is advised when consulting this work)

RICHÉ, P.: *Education et culture dans l'Occident barbare*, Paris, 1962.

ROSTOVTZEFF, M.: *Gesellschaft und Wirtschaft im römischen Kaiserreich*, German transl. by L. Wickert, 2 vols., Leipzig, 1929.

SÁNCHEZ-ALBORNOZ, CL.: *En torno a los orígenes del feudalismo*, 3 vols., Mendoza, 1942; *El 'stipendium' hispanogodo y los orígenes del beneficio prefeudal*, Buenos Aires, 1947; *Estudios Visigodos*, Rome, 1971.

SCHÄFERDIEK, K.: *Die Kirche in den Reichen der Westgoten und Suewen bis zur Errichtung der westgotischen katholischen Staatskirche*, Berlin, 1967.

SCHLETTE, F.: *Germanen zwischen Thorsberg und Ravenna*, Leipzig–Jena–Berlin, 1972.

SCHMIDT, K. D.: *Die Bekehrung der Ostgermanen zum Christentum*, Göttingen, 1939.

SCHMIDT, L.: *Geschichte der deutschen Stämme bis zum Ausgang der Völkerwanderung*. 1. Die Ostgermanen, revised 2nd edition, Munich, 1941; 2. Die Westgermanen, 2nd completely revised edition, Munich, 1938.

SCHNEIDER, C.: *Geistesgeschichte des antiken Christentums*, 2 vols., Munich, 1954.

SCHUG-WILLE, CHR.: *Byzanz und seine Welt*, Baden-Baden, 1969.

SCHWARZ, E.: *Germanische Stammeskunde*, Heidelberg, 1956.

SEECK, O.: *Geschichte des Untergangs der antiken Welt*, 6 vols., Stuttgart, ²⁻⁴1920f. (6th vol. 1920).

SIMONS, G.: *Die Geburt Europas* (= Zeitalter der Menschheit. Eine Weltkulturgeschichte), Time-Life International (Nederland) N. V.

STAJERMAN, E. M.: *Die Krise der Sklavenhalterordnung im Westen des römischen Reiches*, transl. and edited by W. Seyfarth, Berlin, 1964.

STEIN, E.: *Geschichte des spätrömischen Reiches*, vol. 1, Vienna, 1928; *Histoire du Bas-Empire*, vol. 2, edited by J.-R. Palanque, Paris–Brussels–Amsterdam, 1949.

STRAUB, J.: *Vom Herrscherideal in der Spätantike*, Stuttgart, 1939.

STROHEKER, K. F.: *Germanentum und Spätantike*, Zurich–Stuttgart, 1965.

THOMPSON, E. A.: *The Goths in Spain*, Oxford, 1969.

TRIER, B.: *Das Haus im Nordwesten der Germania Libera*, Münster, 1969.

WERNER, J.: *Beiträge zur Archäologie des Attila-Reiches*, Munich, 1956 (Abhandlungen der Bayerischen Akademie der Wissenschaften, Phil.-hist. Kl., New Series, H. 38 B).

WESTERMANN, W. L.: *The Slave Systems of Greek and Roman Antiquity*, Philadelphia, 1955.

ZÖLLNER, E.: *Geschichte der Franken bis zur Mitte des 6. Jahrhunderts*, Munich, 1970.

Other works of reference

ALTHEIM, F.: *Attila und die Hunnen*, Baden-Baden, 1951.

BÖHNER, K.: *Die fränkischen Altertümer des Trierer Landes*, 2 vols., Berlin, 1958.

BRÜHL, C.: *Fodrum, Gistum, Servitium regis*, vol. 1, Cologne, 1968.

DOPPELFELD, O. and R. PIRLING: *Fränkische Fürsten im Rheinland*, Düsseldorf, 1966.

FILIP, J.: *Enzyklopädisches Handbuch zur Ur- und Frühgeschichte Europas*, 2 vols., Prague, 1966.

GRAUS, F.: *Volk, Herrscher und Heiliger im Reich der Merowinger*, Prague, 1965.

HACHMANN, R.: *Die Germanen*, Munich–Geneva–Paris, 1971.

HUBERT, J., J. PORCHER and W. F. VOLBACH: *Frühzeit des Mittelalters*, Munich, 1968.

MÜLLER, W. (Editor): *Zur Geschichte der Alemannen* (Wege der Forschung, vol. 100), Darmstadt, 1975.

RADDATZ, K.: *Die Bewaffnung der Germanen in der jüngeren römischen Kaiserzeit*, Göttingen, 1967;
Der Thorsberger Moorfund, Gürtelteile und Körperschmuck, Neumünster, 1957.

SCARDIGLI, P.: *Die Goten, Sprache und Kultur*, from the Italian by B. Vollmann, Munich, 1973.

SCHULZ, W.: *Leuna*. Ein germanischer Bestattungsplatz der spätrömischen Kaiserzeit, Berlin, 1953.

STERNBERGER, M.: *Die Schatzfunde Gotlands der Wikingerzeit*, Stuttgart, 1958.

Studien zu den Militärgrenzen Roms: Cologne–Graz, 1967 (Beihefte der Bonner Jahrbücher, vol. 19).

WERNER, J.: *Waage und Geld in der Merowingerzeit*, Munich, 1954;
Das alamannische Fürstengrab von Wittislingen, Munich, 1956;
Das Aufkommen von Bild und Schrift in Nordeuropa, Munich, 1966.

Photographic Acknowledgements

Berlin, Academy of Sciences of the GDR:
110, 111, 112, 113

Berlin, Institut für Denkmalpflege:
47, 54, 55, 58, 59, 60, 61, 62, 63, 65, 66, 67, 68, 102, 121, 122, 123, 124, 125, 126, 127, 128, 144

Berlin, Staatliche Museen:
70, 73, 74, 75, 76, 79, 80, 81, 82, 83, 84, 85, 86

Bonn, Studio Service:
34

Budapest, Corvina Archivum:
31, 32, 33, 49, 50, 56, 57

Cologne, Römisch-Germanisches Museum:
17, 45, 53

Cologne, Wilhelm Nyssen:
90, 132, 135, 136, 139, 140, 142, 143

Cracow, Muzeum Archeologiczne:
115, 116, 117

Florence, Alinari:
26, 27, 30, 44

Frankfort on the Main, Harald Busch:
36, 37, 38, 51, 52, 101, 103, 106, 108, 109, 129

Halle, Landesmuseum, Foto L. Bieler:
99, 107, 118

Leipzig-Markkleeberg, Wolfgang G. Schröter:
93, 94

Leipzig, publishers' archives:
133, 134, 137, 138

London, British Museum:
64, 69

Madrid, Museo Arqueológico Nacional:
40, 41, 119, 120

Munich, Claus Hansmann:
1, 4, 35, 39, 42, 43, 48, 78, 88, 100, 104, 105, 145, 146, 147, 148, 149, 150

Rome, Deutsches Archäologisches Institut:
5, 14, 16, 77

Rome, Foto Anderson:
3, 19, 22, 92, 95, 96

Rome, Fototeca Unione:
2, 15

Sofia, Zentralfoto:
10, 11, 23, 24, 91

Sonthofen/Allgäu, Lala Aufsberg:
6, 7, 25, 29, 71, 72, 87, 89, 97, 98, 130, 131, 141

Stuttgart, Helga Schmidt-Glassner:
8, 9

Trier, Landesmuseum:
12, 13, 18, 20, 21, 28

Uppsala, University Library:
46

Weimar, Museum für Ur- und Frühgeschichte Thüringens:
114

DATE DUE
